Advance Praise for *Undercover Jihadi*

"This is an amazing story of Mubin Shaikh who had the courage to work undercover to stop what could have become a series of disastrous bombings and assassination attempts both in Canada and in the United States. With her wealth of knowledge of the terrorist mindset, Anne Speckhard tells his story and that of the Toronto 18 masterfully and dramatically."
—**Peter Bergen,** author of *Manhunt: The Ten-Year Search for bin Laden from 9/11 to Abbottabad*

"Anne Speckhard and Mubin Shaikh have teamed up to tell us one of the most riveting stories of the year. *Undercover Jihadi* shows how real kids— first and second-generation immigrants—living in a Western country, get on the deadly terrorist trajectory and what can be done to get them off of it. Mubin Shaikh is one of the few people in the world to have actually been undercover in a homegrown terrorist cell and Anne Speckhard tells his story flawlessly. A must read!" —**Rita Cosby**, Emmy-Winning TV/Radio Host and Best Selling Author of *Quiet Hero: Secrets From My Father's Past*

"Fascinating, frightening, enlightening ... Anne Speckhard's ability to dissect the human mind is only equal to her genius in understanding the human heart. *Undercover Jihadi* is a must-read." —**Halli Casser-Jayne,** host of The Halli Casser-Jayne Show, Talk Radio for Fine Minds

"Finally a book that opens a window into the minds of terrorists. A must read for anyone who tries to understand them!" —**Marc Sageman**, author of *Understanding Terror Networks and Leaderless Jihad*

"Mubin Shaikh's story reads like a thriller, with twists and turns at every step. But it's a true story, and that's what makes it so important. It gives compelling insights into the process through which young Western Muslims embrace extremism—a subject that, despite hundreds of reports and studies, we are still struggling to understand. It also shows, in fascinating detail, the workings of counter-terrorism agencies. All in all, this is a must read, a page-turner, and a great source of insight and lessons for students of terrorism and counter-terrorism." —**Professor Peter Neumann**, International Centre for the Study of Radicalisation, King's College London

"This is a magnificent description of how terrorist activity attracted and then alienated a son of Muslim immigrants to Canada, Mubin Shaikh. Anne Speckhard, who wrote the biography is a psychologist who has produced some excellent terrorist studies and possesses a literary gift that makes this intriguing book almost impossible to put down. Among the many lessons to be learned is the importance of encouraging Muslims who truly understand Islam to explain to jihadists how they have been distorting the religion they believe they are fighting for. The book is a necessary text for all university courses on terrorism. Students will never stop thinking and talking about it." —**David C. Rapoport,** Professor Emeritus, UCLA, Founder and Editor *Terrorism and Political Violence,* Author of *Four Waves of Terrorism: An Essay in Generations*

"A fascinating window into the mind and soul of a young Muslim caught in the cross fires of conflicting values and engaged in a desperate struggle to do the right thing. A must read for anyone interested in how extremism could happen in the seemingly least likely circumstances…"
—**Arie W. Kruglanski,** Distinguished University Professor, University of Maryland, College Park

"*Undercover Jihadi* illuminates why some Western Muslims are drawn to jihad as Anne Speckhard insightfully tells Mubin Shaikh's compelling story. Torn between Western and Muslim identities, Mubin oscillates between freewheeling Western exploration and hedonism and strict Muslim rectitude and duty. Extremes in one direction lead to compensating extremes in the other, in a search for identity and integrity. A committed Islamist militant, Mubin is shaken by the September 11 attacks and resolves to study in Syria, where he experiences firsthand the tyranny of Assad's police state and gains a new appreciation for Canada's freedoms and tolerance. He is instructed by an Islamic scholar, who takes him through the entire Koran, exposing the shallowness of jihadi religious arguments. Mubin returns to Canada a changed man and soon is working undercover for the Canadian authorities to determine if Islamist extremists pose a threat. Active in multiple investigations, he infiltrates a terrorist cell—the Toronto 18—that plans to attack nuclear facilities, capture Parliament, and behead the Prime Minister. He skillfully wins their trust—although some suspect he is a spy —becoming their military trainer. *Undercover Jihadi* is both a genuine spy thriller and a powerful personal testimony of one man's journey to the edge of jihadi violence and back." —**Todd Leventhal,** (personal views/not government endorsement) Center for Strategic Counterterrorism Communications, United States Department of State

"This is the story of how a courageously honest Canadian man found himself attracted to the lure of militant Salafi-jihadism, and how he came to work with the Royal Canadian Mounted Police (RCMP) rather than a terrorist group in Syria. Now that the trials of the "Toronto 18" are over, Mubin Shaikh is able to tell the details of his undercover work. This is a riveting tale, in large part because of the way it is told. It is a gripping read, bracingly honest, and terribly important." —**Jessica Stern,** Lecturer at Harvard University and author of *Terror in the Name of God* and *Denial: A Memoir of Terror*

"*Undercover Jihadi* provides a unique and very personal account of an individual who was radicalized into the mindset of a terrorist and who ultimately helped to prevent major terrorist acts in Canada. Mubin Shaikh and Anne Speckhard's very readable book will be of interest to the academic specialist and those in the public who wish to understand the human dimensions of terrorist motivation, organization and strategy. In addition the book should be assigned reading for any terrorism course." —**Stephen Sloan,** Professor

Emeritus, University of Oklahoma

"This is a must read book for counter-terrorism policy makers and practitioners who rarely get the opportunity read such an insightful insider account as this. With her usual skill, Speckhard helps us to learn important lessons from Mubin's remarkable experience." —**Robert Lambert**, Ph.D., Lecturer, Handa Centre for the Study of Terrorism and Political Violence, School of International Relations, University of St. Andrews, UK

"A compelling story with an inside view of terrorism." —**Farhana Qazi,** Foreign Policy Analyst & Public Speaker, 21st Century Leader Award, National Committee on American Foreign Policy, NY Humanitarian Award, Southwestern University, Texas

"Mubin Shaikh's story will have you riveted. Reading *Undercover Jihadi* is better than watching an episode of *Sleeper Cell*." —**Mia Bloom, Ph.D.** author of *Dying to Kill: The Allure of Suicide Terrorism* and *Bombshell: The Many Faces of Women Terrorists*

"Anne Speckhard's biography of Mubin Shaikh is a remarkable story of a North American counter-terrorism operative on a dangerous mission! Having worked with Speckhard in Baghdad at the height of violence in Iraq, I can attest to her determination to investigate and write on topics that can help us to better understand ideologically driven violence." —**Rohan Gunaratna**, Professor Security Studies, Head, International Centre for Political Violence and Terrorism Research, Singapore. Author of *Inside al Qaeda: Global Network of Terror,* Columbia University Press

"*Undercover Jihadi* is surprisingly gripping for a biography and very well written. The Toronto 18 plot is an important chapter in the history of Canadian terrorism. It brought the threat of terrorism into the consciousness of the average Canadian who may have previously thought that it could not happen in Canada. This was the first plot to illustrate Canada's vulnerability to group terrorism and underscore for the public, that Canada is not immune to this threat. The information in this book is well presented and provides new insights—credible and not readily known information about this important period and event. New details both about the Toronto 18, as well as Mubin Shaikh, who infiltrated the group, are revealed. These details will grab your attention and make the book difficult to put down. I highly recommend *Undercover Jihadi*." —**D. Elaine Pressman, Ph.D.**, Senior Research Fellow, NPSIA, Carleton University, Ottawa

"This is a compelling account of a courageous man's effort to help Canadian authorities prevent what could have been a truly horrible terrorist attack. It often reads like a fast-paced spy thriller but also offers unique insights into the modern security challenge of homegrown jihadist terrorism." —**Professor James Forest**, Director of Security Studies, University of Massachusetts, Lowell

"A truly unique and compelling story about how conflicts of religious and social identity can make the appeal of jihadism – which offers clarity, prestige, and importance – almost irresistible. Rather than participate in violence however, Mubin Shaikh sought a deeper understanding of the religious context that was being manipulated to justify and obligate his participation in terrorism. Through a rather unprecedented level of access and candid detail we learn first-hand how Mubin ultimately ended up working directly with the Canadian government to counter the terrorist threat as others in his inner circles continued on the path toward violence. Anne Speckhard and Mubin Shaikh have created a must-read." —**Anthony F. Lemieux**, Ph.D., Associate Professor of Communication, Transcultural Conflict & Violence Program (2CI), Georgia State University

"Anne Speckhard has once again provided a clarity of thought made possible through earned experience and contributed significantly to the body of knowledge. She is a true pracademic—a practitioner with academic credentials and credibility. Convincing a target or adversary that you are someone you are not is both an art and a skill, uncommon to most. Mubin Shaikh demonstrated he has mastered both at considerable personal risk." —**Dr. Kathleen Kiernan**, Naval PostGraduate School, Adjunct Professor

"Dr. Anne Speckhard has written another policy relevant work about terrorism. In this biography of Mubin Shaikh, she elucidates his journey from extremist militant views after studying Islam in Syria to becoming a counterterrorism operative. This book is essential reading for counterterrorism officials interested in learning first-hand about deradicalization."
—**Max Abrahms,** Assistant Professor of Political Science, Northeastern University and member of the Council on Foreign Relations

"If anyone understands the mind of terrorists and is qualified to write on this subject, it is definitely Anne Speckhard. As the author of an earlier publication, *Talking to Terrorists,* she has the knack of getting right into the subject matter immediately in minute detail without losing the reader's interest. The book reads like a gripping novel, while maintaining focus on the main topic. Her style is interesting without being flowery and it is clear that she has done her research thoroughly. The book is a must for both professionals and laymen." —**Joe Charlaff,** Israeli freelance journalist, writing about homeland security and counter terrorism for American and British journals

"This is the remarkable story of a young Canadian, born of Indian Muslim parents, who evolves from his role as obedient son to that of aspiring violent extremist and then, as a reformed jihadi, successfully infiltrates an extremist plot as a government agent. Those of us interested in understanding the roots of radical Islam and the trajectory of so-called "homegrown terrorists", are fortunate to have such a down-to-earth and highly readable personal account from just such a person, Mubin Shaikh. Why do native-born Canadians or Americans, who have their whole lives ahead of them in such rich lands of opportunity, become alienated and radicalize? Mubin's story gives us rich insights into this very complex and important question. It peels away some of the mystery."—**Ambassador John Negroponte**, Yale University, Lecturer and Research Fellow; former U.S. Deputy Secretary of State; former and the first, U.S. Director of National Intelligence; former Ambassador to the United Nations and to Iraq

"Anne Speckhard's latest foray into the world of counterterrorism provides unique insights into an often criticized, yet highly effective investigative tool, which has proven essential over time. Chronicling effective use of the undercover technique, Dr. Speckhard outlines valuable lessons to be learned for both law enforcement, and the for the community whom they are sworn 'to protect and to serve.'"—**Michael E. Rolince**, FBI Special Agent in Charge (Ret.) Counterterrorism Division, Washington D.C. Field Office

Undercover Jihadi

Inside the Toronto 18
Al Qaeda Inspired, Homegrown
Terrorism in the West

Anne Speckhard, Ph.D. & Mubin Shaikh, Ph.D. (cand.)

First published 2014
by Advances Press, LLC
McLean, VA

Book Design by Advances Press
Editing by Jilly Prather, www.JillyPrather.com
Copy Editing by Vanessa Veazie
Cover Design by Jessica Speckhard, www.SpeckhardSavc.com
Front cover photo courtesy of Rocco Stragapete

Every effort has been made to contact and acknowledge copyright owners,
but the author and publisher would be pleased to have any errors or omis-
sions brought to their attention so that corrections may be published at a
later printing.

Library of Congress Control Number: 2014945488

ISBN 978-1-935866-59-6 – Undercover Jihadi – Hardcover
ISBN 978-1-935866-60-2 – Undercover Jihadi – Paperback
ISBN 978-1-935866-61-9 – Undercover Jihadi – e-pub

Dedication

To all those who serve the cause of peace and justice, without the luxury of limelight. And to our families who put up with all our counter-terrorism activities.

Table of Contents

Foreword

By Jessica Stern

This is the story of how a courageously honest Canadian man found himself attracted to the lure of militant Salafi-jihadism, and how he came to work with the Royal Canadian Mounted Police (RCMP) rather than a terrorist group in Syria. Like many Western recruits to jihad, Mubin lived between two worlds – the socially and religiously conservative world of his immigrant parents and the permissive society of his neighbors and friends. As a child, he was the good boy his parents wanted him to be, learning to recite the Koran by heart, although he did not understand the words. But he grew into a young man who had sex with girls he barely knew, drank liquor, and took illegal drugs. In an attempt to find his way back to Islam, he joined an Islamic movement, Tablighi Jamaat. The goal of Tablighi Jamaat is to strengthen the faith of believers. While traveling with the Tablighi, he met some Salafi jihadists, on their way to fight in Afghanistan. They appeared to be the kind of men Mubin dreamed of becoming – prayerful but fierce warriors on the path of Allah. They knew how to recite the Koran. They had big guns. They had cool outfits. They carried ammo belts and looked intensely masculine. And they were ready to fight the enemy, whomever that might be. They gave Mubin a chance to shoot their AK-47s, and soon he was hooked. Suddenly, proselytizing on behalf of Tablighi Jamaat – who view jihad as an internal battle within the self—seemed quite tame. He desperately wanted to join the jihadists. They seemed to offer a way out of confusion—a clear identity, and a way to restore his honor. Eventually, Mubin found his way to Syria, where he fell in with some pretty dangerous men.

Why do individuals, living in the cushy West, join fanatical terrorist organizations to fight what they claim to see as a holy war? There is no single pathway, no common socioeconomic background, not even a common religious upbringing among Westerners attracted to jihad. A surprisingly high number of the Westerners joining militant Islamist groups are converts or, if Muslim, ignorant about Islam, as Mubin admits that he was, despite being able to recite the Koran by rote.

What many of these terrorists have in common, at least according to my own interviews, is the desire to forge a new identity and to find a source of dignity. Many are drawn by the lure of avenging wrongs visited on the weak by the strong. But they are also seeking adventure and a more glamorous life, jihadis have admitted to me. Many have experienced alienation and marginalization, and have had bad or humiliating encounters with the police.

At first, Mubin's story sounds a lot like these other stories we've heard about young men who become seduced by jihadi chic. But Mubin's story ends in a surprising way. He learned to read and understand the whole Koran, not just the parts that promote violent jihad, and as a result, he changed his views. He walks the reader through this process. And even more atypical, Mubin tells us things about himself that few people want to reveal to others. He had a particular reason for needing to find a way to restore his honor. He was sexually abused as a child. His mother could not bear to believe that her relatives were preying on her children. She urged Mubin to forget the sexual abuse, and tried to forget it herself, leaving Mubin even more alone with the hazy memory of sexual predation, and the blank periods, the dissociation, that followed the trauma. He tried to swallow his shame, but it began to leak out in the form of rage, and a strong desire to forge a new identity. How often does this kind of humiliation propel young men into violence?

Just as clergy sexual abuse was long an open secret in the West, it remains one in South Asia. I have felt, in my own interviews of terrorists, that there was an element of sexual humiliation, but it was rarely more than an intuition, and I have never explored this issue. Also troubling is the rape of boys by warlords, the Afghan National Army, or the police in Afghanistan. Such abuses are commonplace on Thursdays, also known as "man-loving day," because Friday prayers are considered to absolve sinners of all wrongdoing. Could such sexual traumas be a form of humiliation that contributes, at least in some cases, to the rage and outpouring of anger in acts of contemporary Islamist terrorism? We may never know, but Mubin's story does make the reader hope that scholars will eventually be able to learn more.

Mubin Shaikh was lucky in many ways. A highly educated Syrian Islamic scholar was able to show him that the passages he was citing from the Koran, which seemed to support individual militant jihad, were based on a selective and narrow reading. He would soon realize that his mentors – the extremist Salafis who had taught him to embrace jihad in the sense of war, were quoting passages of the Koran out of context. They were cherry-picking passages that seemed to promote violence, as is common for religious terrorists of all faiths. The scholar taught him to read the whole text. Murder to exact revenge was forbidden. Muslims must never lower themselves to the level of an enemy who commits atrocities, but should abide by the rules of war, the sheikh explained. Mubin realized, he tells us, that he had been looking for something to validate the anger that he felt, from all those years of feeling alienated, not good enough, and like a person who had been contaminated. "I wonder how many others who actually commit terrorist acts are just like me—angry kids who picked up a book of scripture and turned it into a book of violence and aggression?" he asked himself. Mubin decided he would dedicate his life to helping others avoid the mistakes he had made. Thus, the work he did with the police, and also, this book.

Terrorism spreads, in part, through bad ideas. The most dangerous and seductive bad idea spreading around the globe today is a distorted and destructive interpretation of Islam, which asserts that killing innocents is a way to worship God. Part of the solution must come from within Islam and from Islamic scholars, who can refute this ideology with arguments based on theology and ethics. But bad ideas are only part of the problem. Terrorists prey on vulnerable populations—people who feel humiliated and victimized or who find their identities by joining extremist movements. Our arsenal against this terrorism must begin with improving trust in law enforcement. The intelligence we need is going to come from neighbors, friends, and parents, who are often desperate to stop their children from risking their lives for a bad idea. It is going to require that communities come together to fight the appeal of terrorist gangs. It's going to require that brave individuals, including Muslims like Mubin, come forward to work with the police and the government to stop the violence.

This is the story of Mubin Shaikh's jihad, which was of a very different sort from the one he had earlier been attracted to. He went under cover to infiltrate a Canadian terrorist group. He attended training camps with the would-be jihadists, who, as part of their training, watched so many films of beheadings that decapitation began to seem routine. He risked his life to uncover the details of their plots, which included beheading the Canadian Prime Minister, storming Parliament with guns, and detonating bombs throughout downtown Toronto. They hoped to expand to include targets in the United States. Mubin Shaikh's jihad was to stand up for his Muslim faith, which told him that murdering noncombatants is forbidden. He risked his life to protect the lives of many innocents.

Now that the trials of the "Toronto 18" are over, Mubin is able to share the details of what he did to stop these terrorist crimes. He was lucky to find Anne Speckhard. This is a riveting tale, in large measure because of the way it is told. Bracingly honest, and terribly important. May it inspire others to use the whole of themselves – their strengths as well as their weaknesses – to help others.

Jessica Stern
September 25th, 2014
Harvard University

Growing up Between Two Identities

Six-year-old Mubin glanced around him as the white robed children rocked back and forth on wooden benches, their hands piously holding their open Qur'ans. The boys sat separate, segregated from the girls, as they all intoned the Arabic words of their Holy Book. Mubin paused his chanting and listened quietly for a moment. Children all around him struggled to pronounce and memorize whole sections of the Qur'an without having any idea of its meaning. The room was filled with the cacophony of their voices as their sacred verses rose up beyond the snow surrounded building, to an unknown and faraway God. Even though it was Toronto, Canada in the 1980's, the scene could have been anywhere in Pakistan.

Momin Khawaja, the four-year-old boy sitting next to Mubin leaned over and whispered a joke. The two boys guffawed until Issa, their long bearded Islamic studies teacher, intervened.

"You, Momin up here, now!" Issa ordered, his face stern and unforgiving. Momin made his way to the front of the class where Issa whacked his wooden stick hard across Momin's thin back three times. "Take the murga [rooster pose]," Issa instructed, with no pity or humor in his voice. The child didn't dare cry out in pain.

Mubin began chanting his verses again, eyes glued to his Qur'an, anxious not to share Momin's fate. Meanwhile Momin struggled to squat low with his arms looped underneath both of his knees while grasping his earlobes. The "rooster" wasn't an easy pose to maintain, and falling guaranteed another beating from Issa. Momin managed it for the obligatory ten minutes and then—relieved—was sent back to the benches. Neither boy dared glance at each other again that night.

"Ahmed, recite," Issa demanded as he singled out another of the children. Ahmed came to the front of the room to read out his verses in Arabic but poorly pronounced the scriptures he'd been working on. He also received sharp whacks from Issa's stick.

Harsh blows rained down on anyone who didn't recite well—anyone who wasn't progressing—anyone who dared break the archaic rules of the madrasa, the Islamic educational institution. Inflicted pain was to be borne silently. Unlike public school where the teachers smiled brightly, handed out stickers for work well done and praised effort as well as performance, the madrasa rules were strict and exacting and their teacher, Issa, didn't think twice about using his heavy rod to motivate his students into working harder and behaving.

***

"Come, let's read," Abba, Mubin's father, called to Mubin each night after arriving home from work at the Canadian Telecommunications Company where he worked as an electronics engineer. Mummi and Mubin's younger sister, Noor, prepared the evening meal in the kitchen, while Mubin and his father sat together on the living room couch where Abba lovingly opened up the world of books to Mubin. Slowly, over time, Abba showed Mubin how to make out the English letters and read them for himself. Arabic was another matter—that he had already begun learning to recite, without understanding the meaning in the madrasa, under the tutelage of Issa who was neither gentle nor kind.

When Mubin showed up in first grade with Mrs. Scoranio leading the class, Mubin was already good at reading. He excelled in math as well and was surprised to find that unlike the madrasa, no one beat him if he made a mistake.

"Great job! You can go and play with the toys now," Mrs. Scoranio told Mubin on his third day in school as he again finished his lessons before the others. Delighted to receive praise, versus cruel blows, Mubin made for the big plastic construction blocks and began building a hideout.

Kathy Simpson, the girl who would become known as the glue eater of the class, soon joined him inside his newly constructed fort.

"Do you want to see my boobies?" Kathy matter-of-factly asked once she saw that they were alone—isolated from the others behind Mubin's block walls.

Stunned Mubin nodded his head and smiled brightly as his eyes sparkled in delight at her openness. In his Islamic world boys didn't talk to or touch members of the opposite sex unless they were from the same family.

Smiling back Kathy lifted her small dress to flash her flat chest at him.

Oh, okay I have those too, Mubin mused as he gazed silently at her skinny little body before she lowered her dress again. Neither made much of a deal of it although somewhere inside, Mubin knew this would have never happened in the same shameless manner inside his "other" world where female modesty was the norm.

***

That afternoon, crunching home from school on the dry snow Mubin knew that for him and for all the other Indian immigrant kids living in his apartment complex, school was far from over. And there was no way that Mubin could get out of it—his whole family was involved, including some uncles who had very close ties to some of the earliest and now largest mosques in the country.

Mubin's father was one of the founding elders in a leadership position and committed to offering Islamic education to all of the Indian, Pakistani, African, Middle Eastern, and other Muslims students in the area. Their madrasa ran on weeknights after school. Much as he didn't want to go, Mubin knew that for him there was no escaping it.

"Hurry up, eat your supper," Mubin's mother, Zahira, urged as the family gathered in the kitchen after school to eat her dahl, garlic roti and biryani. "Get your robes," Zahira urged clearing their emptied plates from the table as her children went to don their shining white robes. Mubin and his little brother, Umar, returned with their white skullcaps atop their heads and stood still as their mother wiped their faces clean.

"Can't we stay home and watch TV?" Mubin pleaded, thinking about his favorite cartoon—*Roadrunner*—that everyone at school watched and talked about the next day. "I don't want to miss my show!" Mubin begged.

"You children have to learn our religion," Abba answered towering tall and stern in his white robe and skullcap. "To know the Qur'an is the most important thing in life," Abba answered firmly, his brown eyes gentle. "Come now," he said taking Mubin and his sister, Noor's hand. Umar followed alongside them.

Mubin enviously watched the other neighborhood kids play foot hockey with a tennis ball in the yard outside as he and his brother and sister were marched into the madrasa. As they crossed the threshold of their Islamic school, Mubin already understood that entering this world was leaving mainstream Canada to a place where the old world traditions still reigned. Everyone here was dressed in Islamic robes just like the Muslims back home in Karachi, Quetta, Delhi and Lahore, and they all followed an old world mentality shipped straight in from Southeast Asia.

In the madrasa, Mubin was learning what it meant to be a Muslim. Here the community looked up to Abba, and Mubin already understood that his Islamic identity wasn't his alone to mold. He was expected as the eldest son of his Indian family to set the example for his younger brother and sister, to excel in his madrasa studies, and eventually to live up to his father's reputation and ultimately step into his father's shoes as a leader in their Islamic community. Mubin already understood that as a member of this collective community, he had no individual identity of his own other than what the community decreed for him. His future identity was already set and it needed to supersede all else in his life.

In going from a public school during the day to the Islamic madrasa at night Mubin shed his happy go lucky Canadian schoolboy self at the door and became again the immigrant kid from a conservative Islamic culture and Indian family that rejected much of mainstream Canadian culture—the same culture that during the day at school Mubin had been busily soaking up. In madrasa culture, mainstream Canadian culture was understood as nearly synonymous with white Christian culture and here the two were perceived as mutually exclusive. Here, Mubin stepped out of the freedom and innocent openness to the world that the public school nurtured and began to ready himself to take on the heavy mantle of his duties within the "community."

Luckily with all this pressure, Mubin did fairly well. Islamic Studies came easily to him—although he didn't like to follow the strict Islamic rules forced upon him in the madrasa.

As he moved between his two identities, Mubin didn't question which of these very divergent selves was the right one or what either of his selves might mean for him later in life. His existence moved between black and white with no grey in between. When he left school to re-enter his family or the madrasa, Mubin simply shed his Western identity and shifted back into his Islamic self. In the madrasa, he began rocking his small body as he bowed his head over his open Qur'an and started reciting Islamic verses shutting out the voices of the neighborhood kids as they yelled and played right outside the windows. Mubin longed to join them but knew that while the madrasa was in session, he never would.

***

"You can go listen to music now," Mrs. Shellen, Mubin's second grade public school teacher told Mubin when he finished his lessons early the next day. Mubin delighted in plunking the red and blue translucent forty-fives down on the record player and lifting the stylus over to begin the songs. "This old man he plays one, he plays knick-knack on my thumb, with a knick-knack-paddy-whack, give a dog a bone, this old man comes rolling home…" During this time, Mubin felt the easy simplicity and peace of just being allowed to be a child.

It wasn't until third grade that Mubin had a run in with another kid.

It was a minor fight in which Mubin pushed a young boy named Russell. He hadn't meant to hurt him but Russell fell and hit his head on the concrete wall.

"He's bleeding!" the girls shrieked as Mrs. Orano came running.

"You've got to use your words, not your fists, Mubin!" Mrs. Orano patiently explained after taking Russell to the school nurse to be patched up. "You can't fight in school, Mubin, okay?"

Mubin nodded, taking in her rich coffee-scented breath and old lady smell, wondering when the slap was coming to reinforce her words—but no slap came. She also didn't tell his parents. In some ways Mubin noted, the fact that she refrained from violence made a stronger impact upon him than that of Issa or one of his mother's beatings would have. Getting hit didn't always get the lesson across the same way as kind words of concern that kept a child's self-esteem intact.

At such a tender age Mubin was already noticing the distinctions between the strict system of laws within the madrasa and the comparably lax environment of the Western world. So far his young mind found it interesting. But would this innocent recognition of differences turn into something more as Mubin grew up?

In the long afternoons as Mrs. Orano listened to the kids recite their lessons, she'd pull out a packet of crackers, and one by one place a whole cracker on her outstretched tongue. Then in reptilian style she'd pull it back into her mouth to crunch it up and swallow. The students would be fascinated watching her take cracker after cracker on her tongue in this manner. From time to time, she'd call a break and offer to share some peanut butter and crackers with her students. The teacher's generosity and playful personality was a welcome contrast for Mubin.

***

"I know! I know!" Mubin screamed waving his hand in the air. He was in fourth grade with Mr. Young who had the kids practice their vocabulary and spelling by playing *Boggle*.

"Okay Mubin fill in the letters," Mr. Young said, and often enough Mubin was the one to get it right. For Mubin, school was a joy filled and playful place—packed with fun, praise and a growing group of friends from all walks of life. None of them, except those who came from the same background or lived in his neighborhood, had any idea that Mubin lived in a completely alternate identity at home and in madrasa—that in his other world he could increasingly stand and recite from memory, whole sections of the Qur'an in Arabic. They also didn't know that his sister, Noor spent her days after school sequestered from the others with Mummi patiently combing out her hair, working coconut oil into it and braiding it back up into neat order to be dressed up like a doll whenever they went out. Mubin's school friends simply saw Mubin as one of their crowd and Mubin was reveling in belonging.

But on Tuesdays and Thursdays it was always a time of separation.

"You sure we have to go to madrasa?" Mubin cajoled his father after they'd returned home from school, watched a few cartoons and had Mummi's dinner of rice, spiced lamb and roti.

There was no need for a verbal reply as everyone rose from the dinner table under Abba's stern look, to dress up—Mubin putting his white robe over his school pants and placing his white skullcap atop his head. Walking past the kids who were already playing foot hockey, Mubin might give a friendly nod, but it was always the same. By the time madrasa lessons were done it was time for sunset prayers, the benches needed to be put away and then it was time to go home—too late to join in the play. Mubin would always look forward to the next day, however, when he could go to regular school to have some fun with his friends. For now that had to be enough.

***

At home, Abba's relatives through marriage, Uncles Jara and Ishmael, lived in the rooms downstairs. Neither was married. After work, they joined the family for meals. At night, unbeknownst to Mubin's parents, they made the rounds of some of the children's rooms in Mubin's and his cousin Fatima's homes to satisfy their frustrated sexual yearnings. One night Mubin stirred in his bed with a sudden chill. He opened his eyes and leaned up on his elbow wondering why his blankets were not covering him. "Shh my Mubin…It is only me. Lie back and I will be finished in a moment."

Mubin's eyes grew huge as he realized Uncle Jara was crouched over him trying to jerk Mubin's pajamas down past his hips. "Get off of me!" Mubin shrieked as he thrashed out from under his uncle feeling something hard brush his thigh. "What are you doing?"

"Quiet boy!" Uncle Jara ordered as he clamped his hand down hard over Mubin's mouth causing the boy to whimper in alarm. "This will be quick. Now hold still!" he added as he pushed Mubin back down onto his bed. "You won't remember it in the morning," Uncle Jara lied as Mubin struggled to free himself. Unable to escape, Mubin dove into the darkness of the room and concentrated with all his power to forget this shameful violation, just as his uncle had told him to do.

Uncle Jara and Uncle Ishmael visited his cousin Fatima as well and also molested her. "You know, Uncle Ishmael is touching me," Fatima told Mubin some years later.

"Oh Fatima, not you too? I'm going to kill him! I'll slit his throat, I swear it." Mubin answered as rage bubbled up inside of him. Wasn't it bad enough that Uncle Jara visited his room? Couldn't they spare his innocent female cousin? Hypocrites!

But he did nothing. He knew he was powerless because he was still only a boy.

Neither child told their parents until one day Fatima broke down in tears on a visit to their house as she worked with Mummi in the kitchen. "Auntie, I have something I need to tell you. Uncle Jara and Ishmael touched me where they shouldn't have," Fatima told Mubin's mother as her back was turned toward the two youngsters. Mummi was chopping onions for that night's dahl.

"What are you saying?" Mummi asked whipping around to face her niece. Her face was ashen white with shock. "Your uncles are good men! You shouldn't be accusing them like this," she rebuked.

"Uncle Jara touched me also," Mubin suddenly spoke up, backing up his cousin's confession in hopes of his mother coming to their aid. He waited with anticipation and hope.

"You mustn't talk about these things," Mummi answered sternly. "It would make your father so upset to hear it. They don't live here any more. You must forget that it ever happened," she said closing her ears to hear anymore of the details.

Mubin looked sadly over to Fatima as he willed himself to forget again. But how does one forget such a violation of body and spirit? Mubin wished he knew. Fatima wasn't so ready to give up.

"Auntie, it's true!" she cried but Mubin's mother refused to turn back and listen anymore. She knew it would hurt Fatima's marriage prospects if it became known. It was dishonorable to have been molested, and Fatima would be viewed as damaged. It was better to leave it unheard.

Fatima's anger and hurt shone on her face but she was silenced as Mummi remained with her back to them and once again resumed dicing the onions.

"Bring me a candle," Mummi said and Fatima quickly handed her one from the table and Mummi lit it to burn away the acrid sulfur filling the air.

"These onions are making me cry," Mummi complained as she took the corner of her apron to wipe away her tears. It was the only sorrow Mubin would see from his mother and the only acknowledgment that what they had told her had pierced her heart. *Well, at least it was something,* he thought.

The sound of Mummi's knife methodically chopping down hard on the wooden board filled the sad silence that permeated the room and neither child dared utter another word.

"Forgetting," at least momentarily, worked best for Mubin when he joined the other kids out in the courtyard for play. Fleeing the suffocating denial, Mubin ran outside to escape leaving Fatima at home with his sister, Noor, alone to deal with her pain. Unlike Mubin, Fatima, like Noor, wasn't allowed to run free with the other kids after school and she couldn't put all her pain into fiercely kicking the hockey ball toward its goal. But his pain was multiplied by having failed to protect her.

I should have done something! Mubin berated himself as he ran back and forth on the grass. *I should have stopped him. I should go and kill him now!* Mubin raged as he wondered how he could make it right for both of them.

***

"Have some gum Moonbeam!" Alex shouted tossing Mubin a packet of cherry flavored gun.

"I can't believe you did that!" Mubin said laughing in admiration as Alex opened up a packet of his own and Bruce tossed down half of a Mars bar.

Minutes earlier Mubin had been standing in the neighborhood store, his mouth watering at the sight of the neatly arrayed displays of gum and candy bars. Mubin had watched in silent astonishment while Bruce and Alex, two of his classmates, bent down to tuck their trousers into their socks and then quickly stuffed candy bars and packets of gum—treasures that they were now enjoying—into their trousers.

"Free for the taking!" Alex bragged winking as he threw Mubin a candy bar.

It wasn't long before Mubin was in on the shoplifting. A strange feeling of freedom enveloped him making him feel light and carefree. That is until the shopkeeper nabbed him before he got out of the store.

"I know your uncle!" the owner growled. "Let's see what he has to say about this, you little thieves!"

Uncle Ahmed, the oldest of Abba's brothers arrived within the hour, his face darkened with rage.

"Is this your nephew?" the shopkeeper angrily asked pushing Mubin forward to face his six-foot tall, turbaned uncle. "This is what he had stuffed down his pants," the shopkeeper added pointing out a collection of gum packets and chocolate candy bars.

"I'll take care of this," Uncle Ahmed grimly answered, eyeing Mubin with silent rage as he pulled a twenty from within his white robes to lay it on the counter before roughly collaring Mubin to take him home. Mubin's mother had already heard the news and was seated in their darkened living room crying softly when Uncle Ahmed delivered him home.

"My son is going to be a thief!" she moaned upon his arrival. "Where did we go wrong?" she added throwing up her hands to implore Allah.

Shamed to his innermost being Mubin suddenly felt that this was the end of the world. *Why was I so stupid?* Mubin asked as his mind raced for an excuse.

There was none. Muslims are never allowed to steal—not under any circumstances—and being hungry for a treat would certainly never fly.

Ahmed departed after shooting one last look of disgust in Mubin's direction while Mubin, left alone with his shame and hysterical mother, prayed to Allah, *Please make me die now!* He'd never seen his mother sitting there weeping like this. *It's all my fault!* Mubin inwardly wailed as he contemplated his options.

After some time of standing silent in the middle of the room waiting for her punishment, Mubin's mother rose and picked up her cheap Indian sandals with the fake jewelry on them and began using one of them to slap her son on his shoulders, head, back and torso. Being beaten with a shoe was the lowest form of humiliation. Shoes were considered filthy and disgusting since they were worn on the lowest part of the body and used to tread through the dirt and worse.

Mubin didn't defend himself. He took his shots bravely, knowing he deserved everything she doled out. As he flinched behind each strike, a thought burst into his mind. *It should be Uncle Jara standing here taking this beating. Yes, I stole some items from the store. But Uncle stole something of far greater value from me and Fatima. Yet he will never pay for the terrible violations he did to us.* Then strangely he became mesmerized with how the sunlight coming in the living room window sparkled off the red and blue jewels of her sandal as she hit him with it in her flurry of anger. *How beautiful the colors change in the sunlight...*

"Where did we go wrong?" she shrieked as she struck him again bringing him out of his momentary escape. "Our son a common thief? We didn't teach you correctly?" she howled as she slapped him, her personal pain hurting him far more than anything she could inflict with her sandal.

When Mubin's father arrived, seeing his father's face filled with complete and utter disgust worsened the shameful scene one hundred fold. Mubin wished the floor would swallow him up. *I don't deserve to live!* Mubin thought as he tried to disappear into himself.

"He needs more madrasa!" was Abba's conclusion at the end of it all.

***

Mubin's parents left the room; his mother to her bedroom to cry and his father to his den to watch T.V. *I need more madrasa. Madrasa! Madrasa! Is that all there is to life?* Mubin sat on the sofa rubbing the red spots on his leg that were still stinging. His sister Noor came over to him and sat down.

"Mubin, I'm so sorry." She put her arm on his shoulder and he winced in pain. "I know you are not a common thief."

"I knew better. But Bruce and Alex were having so much fun," Mubin looked into his sisters big brown eyes. "So I joined them. Stupid."

"I know, Mubin. It's okay. I know you won't do it again. Mummi told me to leave you alone to think about your crime. I just had to tell you I know it will be okay and you are not a criminal." Noor squeezed his hand and left the room.

I gotta get outa here...

***

"Hey Mubin, how's it goin?'" Mr. Sanders looked up from inspecting the engine of his new Ford Mustang.

"Hi Mr. Sanders. Okay. Brad home?" Mubin walked over to check out the new car sitting in the driveway of the Sanders' two-story home.

"Uh, no not yet. Should be any time now," Brad's dad answered. "Hey can you hand me that wrench?"

"Sure." Mubin picked the wrench out of the toolbox by Mr. Sanders' car and handed it to him.

"So this is the one you had your eye on you told me about. Nice." Mubin ran his hand over the dark blue, shiny finish with a flat palm careful not to put fingerprints on it.

"Yea. Just checking her out." Mr. Sander's gaze went to Mubin's face and down to his neck. "What happened, Mubin? You okay?"

"I'm fine," Mubin said as he touched the still sensitive spot on his neck lowering his eyes to the ground.

"And this?" Mr. Sanders lifted Mubin's chin carefully with the tips of his fingers. "You don't look okay, son. Talk to me."

"I was caught stealing," Mubin whispered, tears welling up in his deep brown eyes. Mubin had become somewhat of a fixture at the Sanders' house. When he visited Brad, Mubin was usually invited for dinner on the weekend nights that he didn't have to attend madrasa. Mr. Sanders always asked him how he was doing in school and was interested in helping Mubin learn Western sports. The boys often invited Mr. Sanders to play video game tournaments with them because he enjoyed the action and competition as much as they did. Mubin had begun to look at Mr. Sanders as a kind of mentor for questions and concerns about Western life, things his own father would have no idea nor wanted to talk about.

"Stealing, huh? What did you take, son?"

"Just some candy and gum. My friends were there too. My parents were pretty upset." Mubin shuffled his feet over the gravel in the driveway. "I knew it was wrong. I won't do it again."

"So you got this from your parents?" Mr. Sanders pointed to the red marks on Mubin's neck.

"Yea, my mom," Mubin answered, his eyes glued to the ground. "I failed them. They took it very hard. I don't know what to do."

"Mubin, you're still very young. It's normal for a kid to try stealing once," Mr. Sanders explained. "The thing is, many kids don't stop at just once. Then you got all kinds of problems all your life. Your parents stop trusting you altogether, you get in trouble with the law, you go to jail. Then it's prison when you get older, you blow any chances for a good life…"

"I know, Mr. Sanders. I'll never do it again. It just seemed fun right then."

"I know you won't, Mubin. You're a great kid. You have a lot to look forward to and you're smart. And your parents love you a great deal or they wouldn't care. They're just super strict because they were raised in a different culture. Life is a lot tougher in India. Tell them you're sorry…it will mean a lot. Hey, there's Brad…"

"Thanks, Mr. Sanders." Mubin looked up at him and smiled. "Hey Brad!"

***

On the walk home, Mubin thought about his parents being immigrants fighting their way in a new society. It made sense that if they didn't care, they would let him do what he wanted. The knot in his stomach reminded him how bad he felt for Mummi; she was so disappointed in him.

He walked in the door and went to the kitchen where Mummi was cooking dinner. She barely turned to see who was home and noticing it was him she turned back around without saying a word. Mubin swallowed and went up to her.

"Mummi," he said softly.

"Yes," she whispered but didn't look at him.

"I'm very sorry for stealing. I'm very sorry to bring you such shame. I know you care and love me." Mubin stood straight and very still, his heart beating wildly, hoping Mummi would forgive him.

Mummi turned around and put her hands on his shoulders, stooping down to look him in the eyes. "Mubin, my son you know a Muslim should never steal. You must live a good life and bring honor to your family and yourself."

"I know Mummi. I'll never do it again. I promise."

***

As they grew closer to puberty, Mubin's madrasa friend and co-conspirator Momin Khawaja were tired of being hit by their Islamic teachers. Momin, joking as usual with the guys, was cut short by Musa, their Islamic history teacher.

"If you guys don't stop talking I'm going to get a stick and hit you," Musa warned the group of rowdy boys with a stern look crossing his face.

While the others—recalling many other times of being hit—quickly silenced themselves, Momin did not. He was fed up with the madrasa violence and conservative led lessons; sick of the harsh punishments doled out to him.

"Yeah, and I'm going to go and get a bigger stick and hit you with it!" Momin fired back.

Shocked by his outburst, the other boys looked away in fear and shame as Musa strode between the benches to grasp Momin's tunic and yank him into a standing position. Silenced, Momin submitted to the beating he received, but years later his taunt would become a reality.

***

By fifth grade, Mubin's family had moved to an apartment complex with four high-rise buildings that surrounded a communal field and playground. His myriad of cousins lived around him in the high-rise building that Mubin's family had their apartment in, and in the townhouses nearby.

At age twelve, Mubin had graduated from the madrasa. He could recite the whole Qur'an in Arabic, had the usual several chapters memorized that are normally recited in Islamic prayers, he knew how to pray and he knew some of the history of Islam. Freed of madrasa, Mubin was now allowed to take his bike out after dinner to be with his friends. Unbeknownst to Mubin's parents, they usually biked over and met up with girls on the Joyce Parkway public school grounds.

And often as not Mubin faced a small argument going out the door at night. "Not coming to evening prayers?" Abba would ask, strong disapproval lacing his voice, as Mubin tried to slip away to join his friends.

"You should come to the mosque," Mummi chided. "I feel so ashamed in front of my friends when their sons are all there praying and you are out on your bike in the neighborhood!" she added staring at her son reproachfully. From time to time Mubin gave in to their demands, but now as a young adolescent the call of his peers was much stronger and more alluring than the muezzin's call to prayers.

When their elementary school graduation was held at Chuck E. Cheese, Mubin was still a bit obtuse about girls. He was playing around with a silver stingray corvette crash-em car at the dance, trying to figure out how it dissembled and reassembled when Linda, a pretty girl from his class strolled up to him. Mubin had a crush on her, but he had no idea she liked him back until she asked, "You want to dance with me?"

"Sure," Mubin answered unsure of why she'd asked him. *Maybe she's afraid or lonely,* he mused. Madonna's *Material Girl* was playing as they made their way to the dance floor. Then as Linda wrapped her arms around him, reality began to dawn on Mubin.

Oh, she likes me! Cool! Nice! Mubin thought as he reciprocated, pulling her close.

What Linda didn't know about Mubin was that in his Indian culture he wasn't allowed to touch or dance with a girl—especially a non-Muslim girl. In fact, any overt sexuality or even physical affection between a man and a woman that was shown on television at home resulted in a quick change of the channel. This real life experience was something he wouldn't be able to tell his father, otherwise Abba's response—as usual, would be shocked indignation followed by, "My kid is corrupted and needs more madrasa."

***

"Coming to our show?" Mubin asked Maria, his sixth-grade crush, in the school hallway with a warm smile.

"What show?" she asked her big brown eyes widening in surprise.

"Break dancing, at the community center on Saturday!" Mubin answered as he made his way to class with his big piece of folded cardboard tucked under his arm. Break dancing was another of his secret Western activities that Mubin engaged in unbeknownst to his parents—and while they would be aghast, Mubin was very proud that he was quite good at it.

The next day a group of about forty kids assembled to watch Mubin and his friends, break dance to Michael Jackson's new song, *Thriller*. Mubin gyrated with the other boys, back flipping across the stage and spinning on first one hand and then the other, finishing off with an upside down head spin.

"That was amazing dude!" Mubin's cousin Faisal shouted as he made his way up through the crowd. Smiling Mubin thought, *Just don't tell our families!*

"You're so strong!" Maria added, shyly eyeing Mubin's chiseled arms and washboard abs.

Suddenly a commotion broke out around them. "Mubin!" someone shrilly screamed from upstairs by the pool. It was a shout filled with terror.

"Mubin, your brother is in the pool!" someone closer by yelled.

My brother in the pool? He can't swim! Mubin thought, panicked as he ran upstairs to the pool area. Umar, Mubin's younger brother, blue faced and unconscious was at that moment being loaded into an ambulance that took off with its red lights flashing before Mubin could intervene.

Racing home to tell his parents Mubin berated himself, *You're the oldest! You should have been watching him! If he dies, it will be all your fault. You shouldn't have been break dancing! You were just trying to impress Maria!*

Luckily, when they arrived at the hospital Umar was recovering in his hospital bed, a tinge of blue still covering his whole body. "The ambulance got him here just in time," the doctor said shaking his head. "Another minute or two and he'd have been brain dead."

Umar it turned out was just as desperate as Mubin to fit in with his Western friends. When his friends had suggested diving together into the deep end of the pool, Umar so wanted to fit in that he dove right along with them—only problem was that being a non-swimmer he sank immediately to the bottom.

"How could you leave your brother alone?" Mubin's Auntie Tahira asked Mubin as they sat near Umar who lay recovering in his hospital bed. Auntie's eyes reproachfully stared him down as Mubin struggled for words. "Thanks to Allah he is alive!" she continued.

Of course there was no way to explain to Auntie how much fun he was having break dancing and that his Western friendships claimed as much a loyalty on his young soul as the family did, so Mubin just hung his head in shame knowing once again he had failed to live up to his family's impossible standards of behavior.

I am the oldest; I should be the one to protect my siblings. Why can't I get it right? Mubin thought continuing a worse berating than anyone in his family could give him.

***

From time to time Mubin would think back to Uncle Jara visiting his room at night. He couldn't remember it all but what he did remember seemed far away and Mubin had the feeling that it wasn't even him remembering. Instead, he, Mubin, was standing twenty feet or so away watching someone else have that memory.

It's another me, Mubin thought as he watched the sick scenes of what had gone on. One day his mind flashed back to Uncle Jara masturbating into the bathtub with a small Mubin watching in horror.

"It's like milk," Uncle Jara was telling him as he ejaculated into the bathtub.

I didn't know milk comes out like that! The young Mubin thought as the older Mubin watched in horror remembering the strange expressions on Uncle's face as the white liquid dripped into the bath water.

Why doesn't he fight back? Mubin would ask himself about the boy he saw in his flashbacks. *Why is he so passive?* When the younger self that Mubin watched in his mind's eye did nothing to protect himself, Mubin was enraged. How he wished he could go back in time and deal with the situation, as he would if he faced it now.

These memories of the younger self that Mubin had disavowed haunted him at odd times—coming like waves, unbidden into his mind. Mubin also had big black spaces in his childhood where he couldn't remember anything. The "other" self that Mubin watched in the flashbacks felt similar to his other discontinuous identities—like the devout boy at the madrasa—as opposed to his modern Western self. They were both selves that he could shed at will, but the emotions he felt when the memories came up from this self were overwhelming and they were harder to dismiss. It was like a game of tug o' war between his Eastern culture heritage and the Western society he lived in, with a vast puddle of quicksand in between, and now this—horrid memories from his uncles. Mubin struggled to understand where he fit in without free-falling into the abyss below.

Mubin was incensed re-experiencing the past. *I want to take my friends to his house and beat the shit out of him with a baseball bat!* Mubin thought, remembering his uncle's sick abuse.

I need to make sure this can never happen again, Mubin decided. In his mind's eye, Mubin vowed, *I'll be a ninja. No one will be able to hurt me ever again. I'll use my ninja powers against them. I'll make things right for Fatima and me because no one else will.* He also signed up for martial arts training and gravitated into a group of street-smart boys at school—learning the ways of intimidation and where necessary, violence. All of these kids also had an inner sense of shame for one reason or another and found honor in bravado and violence.

But learning to protect himself in the here and now still didn't address the past. The flashbacks continued making Mubin crazed with feelings of anger and shame that he didn't know how to work through. Concerned that he was losing his mind and unable to ask his parents for help, Mubin went to his middle school library and turned to books for answers. Unabashedly, Mubin searched out psychology books on rape and molestation and then sat in the library reading texts well beyond his years. As he read, Mubin began to understand what had happened to him.

His mind had sequestered the shameful and horrific experiences and now, he was suffering from posttraumatic flashbacks. Mubin began to understand that he suffered from posttraumatic rage, dissociation and posttraumatic stress disorder (PTSD). He also concluded that his PTSD wasn't as bad as that of many childhood sexual abuse victims.

I'm doing okay, Mubin reassured himself. *I'm figuring it out, giving myself therapy,* Mubin thought as he made his way through the case studies and therapeutic interventions. But reading wasn't true therapy and he never really integrated the experiences into his consciousness nor went through the healing process of having his parents step in and tell him his uncles were wrong and they regretted now not having been aware and able to protect him. Instead Mubin's experiences of being victimized remained sequestered in shame, instilling within him a strong empathy for other victims while they also fueled a growing rage over injustices and the powerful taking advantage of the weak. What Mubin couldn't know was that with this anger and shame boiling inside him—alongside of his cultural message of never being a good enough Muslim—Mubin was ripe for being pulled right into militant jihadi teachings and the "Gangsta Jihadi" subculture.

***

"You joining up?" Brad asked Mubin one afternoon as they took their books for the next class out of their lockers. Mubin was thirteen years old.

"Joining?" Mubin asked. "What are you talking about?"

"Army cadets! What else?" Brad replied. "Camping trips, military drills, shooting rifles and in the summer we get a month out in the forest! You should join!"

A month away from home? No mosque, no overbearing Muslim rules, no not being good enough? Mubin thought amazed at this sudden offer of freedom. "How do I sign up?" Mubin asked, smiling widely. This was like winning a big jackpot. Could it be the answer to the inner rage that continued to boil inside of him?

Years later Mubin would compare how he joined the cadets to how young kids join militant jihadi groups realizing, *This is how they get into radical movements and terrorist groups—their friends invite them into something that offers excitement and escape and they follow right along.* And just like counter-terrorism researcher Marc Sageman argues—for many kids in the West, their primary motivation for joining is that they want to be part of the "bunch of guys" and privy to all the adventures it offers.[1] Mubin was certainly intent on being part of this "gang." He just had to figure out how to get past his parents to do so.

"You want to join the Army Cadets?" Abba asked incredulously that night at dinner. "Whatever for?"

"They teach discipline, they train you in life skills and it helps you get a job!" Mubin argued as he toyed with his roti.

"Well those are certainly fine things, but I don't know that you need to join the cadets!" Abba answered. "You learned those things in the madrasa."

"They pay us!" Mubin added.

"They pay?" Mummi asked her eyes lighting up with newfound pride in her son's potential worldly success. *Now this would be something to tell the community!* Mubin could see she was already thinking to herself.

"Yes, it's a job, as well as training!" Mubin answered enthusiastically seeing that he was clinching his argument.

"Well, give it try then," Abba conceded.

Although they gave in on the Cadets, Mubin's parents still wanted their son to practice their religion in a more serious manner.

"Why aren't you more like Mahnoor?" Mummi asked. "He goes to mosque every night. He's not like you out on the street at night!"

"Yes Son, why don't you come to mosque with us tonight?" Abba asked.

"I don't know what the community thinks when you are never there. Mahnoor is leading the prayers even!" Mummi continued droning on about the insufferable hyper-religious son of her best friend.

"Not tonight, Mummi!" Mubin said pushing his chair back from the table. "I'm going out for a bit," he added heading for the door before an argument could break out.

***

School was finally out and Mubin arrived at the cadet school full of wonder and excitement. He had no worries like some of the other kids who didn't do their best in school. Mubin's grades were always top-notch, he knew how to study, and success was drilled into him on all fronts. Becoming a trained fighter and learning how to survive under any conditions was something he only dreamed about before. And here is where he would fit in without any doubts.

"You are now members of the Royal Canadian Army Cadets!" the sergeant announced as he handed out certificates of matriculation. He was a real Army sergeant and Mubin was in awe as he filed up to receive his uniform and start his training that summer.

"Today we'll start with running and push-ups," the sergeant explained. "You all need to get fit. We are going to push you to your personal limits as individuals and as team-members. You'll be tested on all the skills we teach you—the use of maps and a compass; GPS technology; orienteering; first-aid; camping and survival skills; rock climbing; canoing and mountain biking. And those of you that make the selection will get to go to summer training. So let's get started. Line up over here," he instructed.

Mubin was first in line and no matter how hard the drills were he gave the Army Cadets his all. He was determined to be a fighter and survivor and to fit in. They could test him all they wanted, he was going to make the grade. And he was definitely going to make the summer training selection. There were too many great looking girls in the group and too much fun to be missed by not making it. Besides, no one—NO ONE—would ever mess with him again. That, he was certain of.

Mubin pushed himself, and in doing so he found out that he had an inner strength, and actually did well with discipline when it was fairly and nonviolently applied. He liked becoming strong, independent and empowered—both mentally and physically. And it both soothed the shame and channeled his anger.

Instead of being what seemed like irrationally angry at the world—due to his uncle's sick abuses and the harsh rules of the madrasa with its intolerance for imperfection—Mubin could now express his pent up rage through a strictly regimented system that was both controlled and adventurous. And he was beginning to take on a sense of communal honor that felt real—unlike the Islamic community where there was so much falsehood among those who held themselves out as honorable—like his despicable uncles. This was a different kind of honor system and he felt good here.

And Mubin's parents were proud when they were invited to the graduation ceremony where Mubin wore his uniform with all its badges sewn on. Stopping later at the mosque, an elder even stopped and saluted Mubin as he entered wearing his uniform. "You see, this is good," he said to the others pointing out Mubin's uniform and recognizing the discipline and effort that had gone into earning it.

"Mubin Shaikh," the instructor called his name when the summer training camp selections were announced. Mubin was ecstatic. And it wasn't hard to win his case at home.

"They are paying me and all my expenses!" he told his parents as his face lit up joyfully. "We're going to learn mountaineering and outdoor survival skills!"

Unable to figure it out, Abba just nodded and hoped it was for the best.

***

At summer training Mubin found his voice. No longer shy and introverted he stood up straight and spoke with an authority that was trained into him. And the girls noticed.

"I'm going to come visit you tonight," Pamela whispered to him as she passed him in the afternoon. Mubin smiled at her not fully comprehending her meaning. Later that night when she arrived at their tent and unzipped it to let herself in, he sat up amazed.

Mubin's two tent mates, Brad and Roger, were already fast asleep and Pamela quickly unzipped Mubin's sleeping bag and slid in beside him. It didn't take long for Mubin to lose his virginity. Afterward Pamela threw her clothes back on and disappeared back into the darkness while Mubin relished the feeling of thinking he was in love.

"Hey, who was that?" Brad asked interrupting Mubin's reverie and mortifying him with the realization that his sexual escapade hadn't gone undetected.

"Nah man, that was nothin," Mubin answered quietly, chagrined.

"Yo dog, that wasn't nothin!" Brad answered as Mubin rolled over to face the wall of the tent.

The next morning the Sergeant Major called out for Mubin.

"Shaikh stay here while the others go and do drill formations," the sergeant major ordered. When the others were out of earshot he scolded Mubin in a severe tone, "Shaikh I know what went on last night. Brad told me and you're lucky he didn't blab to the whole camp. I would have had to send you home for this. You can't be fooling around with the female cadets," the sergeant major said wiping his brow. "The last thing we want is to send some girl home knocked up from her time at training!"

Mubin nodded, his eyes glued to the ground. He was too mortified to make excuses. Up till now he knew the sergeant major had been impressed with his performance.

I've really blown it this time, Mubin concluded, but was then surprised to hear the sergeant major conclude favorably in his case.

"Okay, I'll let you stay but knock it off, you hear?" his commanding officer said.

"Yes sir, it won't happen again," Mubin promised daring to make eye contact. After that he kept his distance from the girls—confused between intense pleasure and intense shame.

***

"They're green goblins—LSD," Karen, Brad's older sister told them as she popped one into her mouth. She'd given them each one as well and they both took theirs.

"You'll trip out best in here," Karen added as she led them to the entrance of the downtown Toronto warehouse rave party that she'd taken them to. Inside, the colored laser and strobe lights cut through thick layers of smoke from both cigarettes and the stage smoke machines as the consistent deep thump of the *Deep House* music reverberated off the walls. Mubin looked around at the scantily clad women whose teeth and glimpses of white panties glowed in the dark from the black lights. The red, blue and green of the laser lights swirled above as Mubin felt his consciousness expanding. As he moved deeper into the crowd he moved into actual and chemical ecstasy and a deep feeling of belonging.

Mubin was in high school now—at York Memorial Collegiate—and firmly loyal to his school friends. They were his new tribe and he wasn't willing to risk anything to be kicked out. If they smoked he smoked, if they dropped acid, he did too.

The only exception was that Mubin rarely touched alcohol. "It's haram for a Muslim—forbidden," Mubin explained to Brad while they each snorted up a line of coke together. "We're not allowed to drink," Mubin added completely missing the irony of what he was saying.

"What else does she have?" Mubin asked Brad the next Friday when they got together to party again. Together they tried ecstasy, white cross, speed, mushrooms, weed and cocaine. Of all the drugs they were using Mubin liked coke the best. It made him feel confident and empowered. While high there wasn't anything he couldn't do – he was king. Playing the party line, being away from the watchful eyes of his parents, his first taste of real freedom was as sweet as that ancient apple that started all of mankind's fallen independence.

That summer when they went to Army Cadet training again—this time near London, Ontario—the guys piled into a hotel room—eleven were sharing one room. A bowl of hash was passed around and Mubin—trusting the older guys to watch over him—got blitzed out of his mind. One of the toughest of the older guys walked over to Mubin and put his leather jacket protectively over Mubin, saying, "No body messes with this guy from now on." Mubin was fifteen and loving it all. He was having the time of his young life; he was Superman. And now he even had a more experienced Cadet protector.

Here, it was just laughter and camaraderie with the guys and there seemed no end to it. It was the first time Mubin had his own money, freedom, friends and this time six weeks away from home.

I'm out of my cage and it feels so good! Mubin thought as he laughed at the guys who were homesick. Mubin suffered no such pangs.

Just like the summer before, there were trips into town, beach-side fires with girls, parties and music.

In his inner depths, Mubin had doubts about how he was living. *This is wrong, against my religion,* he knew, but all the fun was too much to miss. *My family would not approve,* rattled around in his mind, but he dismissed it just the same as he dismissed his Islamic identity whenever he was in the company of his Western friends. *If my friends back home could only see me now!* Mubin thought, as he made his way up the ranks. He was promoted to staff cadet and ultimately made instructor.

***

Please Allah, I beg of you, make her convert to Islam, sixteen-year-old Mubin pleaded to the faraway Allah he prayed to daily. He was at Cadet's camp again and in love. The only trouble was the girl was not a Muslim and his parents would never accept that. *Please,* Mubin begged as he knelt and lowered his forehead to the floor, *Please make Sheila convert!*

The love affair didn't last long. "Shaikh, your girl is with some other guy," Brad reported some weeks into their relationship—a look of caring concern covering his face.

"What are you talking about dude, she loves me!" Mubin answered. But later that day, at Brad's prodding, Mubin crept into the common area of the camp to find Sheila there with her arms around the waist of another guy in Mubin's company—one of the superstars of the cadets who Mubin had often admired. When the cadet saw Mubin, he pushed Sheila away—but it was too late.

Mubin had seen enough.

"It's not what you think!" Sheila immediately cried out, but the tears that tumbled down her cheeks betrayed her faster than she had betrayed him.

See, you can't trust anyone, Mubin thought, anger filling his face as he backed away. You have to take care of yourself first and foremost. You think he's your friend but he'll steal your girlfriend the minute your back is turned. Traitor!

To comfort himself Mubin turned to his usual consolations—weed, coke and LSD—blotters. He wasn't interested in Allah for the time being—tripping was much better. After losing Sheila, he was taking a vacation and he didn't care much where.

Returning home from camp and driving the family car on LSD, Mubin noticed the music in his tape player started making strange distorted sounds—oraghhhhh. ARRRGHHHH!

Oh man, I'm having a bad trip, Mubin thought, panicking. A bit later he found out the tape was broken.

A few days after, Mubin was driving again with his father in the car. This time it was a flashback. Mubin's whole area of vision suddenly shifted as he was driving down the highway—making the road and everything on it take a sudden shift to the right. Mubin jerked the steering wheel sideways and then realized, *No the road is still right here,* as he noticed his father jump in alarm.

The next day, balancing on a ladder to hang a picture for his mother, everything went purple and things started coming out of the wall.

I think I better give up the blotters, Mubin realized. *If my parents notice these strange behaviors, all hell will break loose. My hard work as a cadet will be finished!*

***

"We are going to be in the battle of the bands!" Mubin's friend Rocky announced in the fall when school started up again. "You gotta hang with us," Rocky said, smiling. "Rock, drugs and women," he added. "It's all coming together now!"

Mubin hung with his friends—the potheads and the rockers—and Rocky was right. All the girls wanted to know them. Mubin lifted weights everyday now, so he was buff as well, and when it came to fighting he held his own. Everyone knew he was a scrapper—not to be messed with.

"Yo Mubin, a whole bunch of guys are coming to start a beef with you," Brad came to tell him one afternoon. Words had been exchanged with one of them earlier in the day.

"What guys? What beef?" Mubin bellowed in alarm, but it was too late to escape. According to Brad—they were just around the corner.

"Okay my friend, it's going to be back to back fighting," Mubin said as he saw the guys approaching. Most of them were well built.

We're going to get hurt, but we'll go down fightin', Mubin made up his mind. Then he saw among the approaching gang, Jay, a guy he didn't know well but who he worked out with every morning.

"Nah, you can't fight him, leave him alone yo!" Jay said to the others as he came and clapped Mubin in a friendly way on the back. "I work out with him in the mornings. This guy will kick your ass, man!" Jay said to his friends in a mocking tone. "He's good! He's my boy! Leave it alone. Shit, man," Jay laughed.

The guys backed down for then, but later Mubin saw the rest of them following him home from school. He took off running for home and later returned to the street with a machete stuck down his pants. Mubin strutted around chest out, arms held out from his sides, waiting for the guys to surround him. When they did he took the machete out from his pants and wielded it in the air. "Come on mother fuckers!" Mubin smiled as they got scared and all took off running.

***

At seventeen, Mubin's parents decided to make a family visit back to their village in India. The colors, smells, and poverty surrounding them upon their arrival were shocking to Mubin, Noor and Umar. They'd never experienced anything like it.

"Don't give them money," Auntie told him about the begging children. "Don't you see how you get surrounded by even more of them?" she chided. "There's no end to the street urchins here," she said bundling the family off down the street. Mubin looked over his shoulder at the rag-tag collection of children who at first followed but then realizing Auntie's determination, gave up and ran off.

"I have to leave early to register for one of my senior year classes," Mubin lied to his parents after three weeks in their Indian village. "It's very important so I can graduate on time." If his excuse had to do with school and graduating he knew his parents would buy it. He was bored out of his mind and had come up with the idea of arriving home early to throw a house party. It was a sure ticket to solidifying his popularity at high school. He'd been to many such house parties and was determined now to throw one of his own.

Back in Toronto, Mubin put the invitation out among his friends and busied himself readying his house. He stuck a pole into the ceiling in the center of the living room and using sheets sectored off the large room into a "chill-out" area, dance floor, and bar. He set out magic markers in his bedroom to let everyone graffiti one of the walls. His plan was to cover it over later with wallpaper. The only unforeseen hitch in the plans was that Mubin didn't know that Abba had asked Uncle Ahmed to look in on the house, and keep an eye on Mubin.

The revelers soon appeared—girls in short skirts, guys carrying marijuana joints, pills and bottles of hard alcohol—and the party got into full swing. Mubin cranked the music as loud as it could play as couples gyrated on the dance floor and some paired off on the sofas and even snuck away to the bedrooms.

Mubin, already having ingested some magic mushrooms and having drunk a fair share of vodka was out on the veranda smoking a joint when Uncle Ahmed in his turban and Islamic robes strode up the driveway. Mubin's eyes were healing from an irritation problem caused by the pollution in India and he still couldn't see far with his contact lens, so he didn't notice at first—not until Brad asked, "Dude, who's that guy coming up the driveway?"

"Who?" Mubin asked squinting. He could only make out a blur—whoever it was, he was an imposing and tall figure—in a turban and white robes! Mubin recognized the blur immediately—*Uncle Ahmed! Oh shit!*

In a few quick strides Uncle Ahmed strode up to Mubin and without hesitating, struck him hard across the face. "Get out!" he shouted to the others in his loud baritone voice as he proceeded inside. "Get out! This is my house!"

The partiers started running out of the house, some of them jumping from the balconies, some running out through the garage—all of them grabbing bottles and joints with them as they ran. Then Uncle Ahmed turned back to Mubin.

"You, come with me!" Uncle Ahmed roared as he grabbed Mubin by the front of his shirt and hauled Mubin inside the house. Mubin seeing the party through Uncle Ahmed's eyes was mortified as he stared in shock at the residue of discarded beer, wine and hard alcohol bottles, joints, pills, mushrooms and his high school friends still running for the exits—some of the short skirted girls mouthing I'm so sorry! as they backed out of the room.

"Get out! Get out of my house!" Uncle Ahmed roared as he dragged Mubin from one destroyed room to the next. Luckily he hadn't yet seen the stolen car parked in the garage that Mubin's friends had parked there for a joy ride later in the evening.

"I'll run up and chase the others out," Mubin offered when they got to the staircase. But once upstairs and free of his uncle's heavy hand on his chest Mubin felt suddenly panicked. Drugged and boozed up he wasn't in his right mind, but he knew it was better to run, than face Uncle Ahmed again—right at that moment. He would be lucky to get out of the coming beating with his life.

Run! Mubin's inner voice instructed and without thinking, he obeyed. Mubin raced quickly back down the stairs, flew past his uncle and ran into the driveway. Just then, Brad pulled up, his car full of their friends.

"Get in, man!" Brad shouted, and as the girls opened the back door Mubin piled in the back seat on top of the others while Brad hit the accelerator and they tore off down the street.

***

Oh shit! My world is definitely falling apart, Mubin thought as he sat with Brad, coming down from all the drugs and alcohol in a park in a neighborhood far from his home. Dialing his cousin Fatima—Uncle Ahmed's daughter, Mubin talked hurriedly into his phone, "Look, I'm not coming home for a few days," Mubin said as Fatima cried and pleaded with him to return. "No the situation is way too hot to come home right now. I'm going to stay with friends and let things cool down, then I'll come home," Mubin explained. "Don't worry about me."

I think I've been slipping off my Islamic path, Mubin later reflected as he thought about the girls he'd slept with, the drugs he'd been doing and now this. *This is a mess, a real mess…*

Mubin spent the next three days at Brad's house—a place where he always found safety and security as well as Western openness and acceptance—just as he was. He rested and worried, and then he went home to face the uncles.

His seven uncles, some religious and some not, were all assembled in the living room when Mubin arrived. The house was cleaned up—perfectly. *No one would be able to guess a wild party had recently been held here,* Mubin thought. There wasn't a trace of bottles, cigarette butts—nothing—except for the vulgar graffiti on Mubin's bedroom wall not yet hidden under wallpaper—that remained.

The uncles were seated in a circle in the living room and placed Mubin in a dining room chair in the middle of the room. He felt so ashamed he couldn't make eye contact, and sat slumped forward, staring at the carpet.

"Mubin, how could you do this?" Uncle Ahmed started in, his voice laced with disgust and anger. "People pray in here! This is a place of religious worship and awareness of Allah!"

"Have you no shame?" Uncle Faisal asked his voice also filled with repugnance. Mubin didn't dare look up at them as they continued.

"Do you know how many beer cans, cigarette butts and drugs we found in this house?" Uncle Ahmed asked then went on without waiting for an answer, "Forty beer cans! Thirty-five cigarette butts thrown on the floor and tables, and sixteen marijuana cigarettes and five bottles of pills! In our brother's home! In this place where people pray to Allah!" Uncle Ahmed roared, incensed at the pollution of his brother's home.

"These are things that send people to hell!" Uncle Tehsin shouted, causing Mubin to want to sink farther down in his chair and even to hope the chair itself would sink down through the floor at that moment—possibly to hell—rather than face more of this emotional flogging. "You could burn in hell for this!" Tehsin continued, seconding Mubin's thought.

When they finished Mubin was left with overwhelming shame. It was so strong that it physically hurt and Mubin thought in an adolescent manner, *I don't want to be alive anymore. I should take my life now. Who would give a damn anyway?*

In a few more days, the family arrived home. Abba's face said it all— *You failed us!* "You've brought damage to our home and dishonor to the family!" Abba shouted as he also forced Mubin to account for himself while slapping Mubin repeatedly in the face. Mubin was grounded for a very long time.

***

"You can come stay here," Brad offered over the phone, but Mubin knew that moving away from their home at this juncture would dishonor his parents and family even more.

I can't create any more stigma or shame for them, Mubin understood, as he pondered how to regain their positive regard—how to have them once again believe he was more than a stupid teenager that dishonored their family. *I want them to believe again that I'm smart and have a good future ahead of me,* Mubin thought.

You're going to fix your life, Mubin's inner voice instructed. *But how?* he asked himself.

Tablighi Jamaat! The answer suddenly came, unbidden. *That's where all the parents send their wayward sons,* Mubin realized. *I'll join and get into Islamic Studies,* Mubin decided.

In doing so he was returning to the group that his father was most ideologically influenced by—a group that didn't proselytize at all but instead took gently educating and bolstering the faith of already declared Muslims as its main mission. Mubin had already gone to their overnight ijtemas—mosque fellowship meetings—and he knew that the Tablighi Jamaat was the default place for Islamic parents to send their prodigal sons to reform themselves.

They will be my conduit to rehabilitation! They will fix me! And that will make my parent's happy—because I am clearly broken, Mubin mused.

In truth Mubin was a bit burned out from drugs and the fast life and it didn't arouse him intellectually either. It had been really fun hanging with the rock band and having girl friends but since his love affair with the cheating Sheila, he'd been gun shy of girls—he didn't want to be betrayed again. So a young marriage and family wasn't in the picture right now. And he couldn't escape like some kids did, to university, because if he enrolled in college he'd be expected to live at home while studying at a Toronto institution and no university would offer him support for dorm rooms when his parents were in town anyway.

Sitting in the Tablighi Jamaat mosque Mubin listened to the speaker. He was an accomplished engineer, active in the group. Somehow his words resonated with Mubin's need for redemption and restoration of his honor within the family and community. His ideas seemed to offer a clear purpose.

After the talk Mubin went to the brothers and signed up for the first four-month student Jamaat from Canada. It would involve taking part in a regimented program in which Mubin would travel to Pakistan and India for four months and spend at least two and a half hours per day in the mosque doing some faith-related reading or missionary activity. Mubin was sure his father would see it as a huge honor to be part of their first Jamaat.

"I'm going with the Tablighi Jamaat to India and Pakistan for four months. It's the first Canadian outreach team being sent!" Mubin told his parents that night at supper.

"What?" Abba asked dismayed by this news. "What about your studies? You aren't going to university?" he asked his face registering deep disappointment. As an immigrant, his aim was for his oldest son to outstrip him, and education was in Abba's mind, the way to do that.

"I want to do this," Mubin answered earnestly. "I need to do this," he added and slowly talked his parents into what he had convinced himself was his path to redemption. He'd go overseas to India and Pakistan on a mission trip with the Canadian delegation of the Tablighi Jamaat for four months, study Islam and come back stronger and better.

"That's for religious people," Mubin's brother, Umar taunted. "And you ain't religious!"

Grandfather, who was elderly and pious, wasn't completely sold either but his words of advice were, "Mubin, there are two ways to learn your lessons in life—either by your own mistakes or learning from the mistakes of others, so do what you need to do and learn."

Mubin meanwhile began to wear Islamic robes and pants that didn't reach his ankles—in the style of the Prophet (SalAllahuAlayhiWaSallam) and his original companions—and started growing his beard out as well.

The Tablighi Jamaat

"I've heard of you," Mubin told another fellow traveler, Sher who he met at the airport. Sher was well built, had small, street fighting scars on his face and curly, dark hair that hung beneath his earlobes. Sher looked Latino but was Indian Muslim and he was also being sent by his family to clean up his act. As they waited together, Sher pulled out a cigarette, lit it and took a deep draw as he admitted he had heard of Mubin as well—as a fellow ruffian—returning the compliment.

The fellow hooligans boarded the plane and arranged to sit together. Fourteen hours later, in New Delhi a member of the Tablighi Jamaat met and loaded them on a bus going to Nizam Uddin the international headquarters for the Tablighi Jamaat movement.

Dozens of street urchins ran up to the bus when they deboarded. Seeing the sports shoes and fanny packs that gave them away as Westerners, the children mobbed Mubin and Sher begging for money and candies. Overcome with the heat, smells, poverty and the kids, Mubin handed out all the coins he had and then made his way into the compound.

It was summer so the heat was unbearable. At night Mubin learned to soak his bed sheets in water and sleep with the fan blowing directly on him. The evaporating water cooled him somewhat.

"I can't sleep in this heat, sweating, and with bugs crawling on me," Mubin complained to Sher in the morning.

"Yeah, it feels like fans pumping hot air, doesn't it?" Sher said laughter filling his eyes. "We really got ourselves into it, didn't we now?"

***

"Your group will deploy in India first, to Saharanpur," the elderly Tablighi Jamaat leader with his giant bushy beard told Mubin's group as he smiled kindly at them. "You will serve at Mazahir-ul-Uloom, the oldest Islamic madrasa in the Indo-Pak continent, started by Mawlana Ilias," he explained in his large bellowing voice. "There you will meet some of the luminaries of the Saharanpur movement."

Mubin and Sher were assigned to the same group. This time they traveled without a guide and were crammed inside an over packed bus. Mubin looked around as people continued to climb into the bus and take seats above it and even hanging onto the bus sides. Some of the people traveled with live chickens on their laps, some with goats and the smells of both people and animals were overwhelming. Once the bus started its journey Mubin found himself so terrified by the multiple near head on collisions that he was frequently reciting the Islamic statement of faith, *La ilaha il Allah, MuhammadurRasulullah [There is no God but Allah, Muhammad is the messenger of Allah.]*

If he was going to die here on this bus with all of these smelly people and their farm animals he wanted to ensure that he was ready to enter paradise. Indeed as a sojourner in the path of Allah he could count on such a death following after his recitation of the statement of faith bringing him the rewards of martyrdom. These included forgiveness of all his sins and instant entry into the highest realms of paradise, a crown and jewel of honor placed upon his head, an afterlife married with seventy-two beautiful houris and the ability to intercede for seventy of his family members to also enter paradise. The thought comforted him as the bus swerved upon the roads making room for a passing vehicle in lanes that could barely contain the two vehicles that were already nearly colliding.

Finally disembarking the bus, Mubin saw the Mazahir Uloom Madrasa rising up from the dusty city. Their first view of the imposing grand century madrasa was of the old two story pink brick building that took up an entire block of land. Both stories of the main building were made up of colonnaded arches with highly decorated verandas. A large white dome rose up another two stories above the main building with a smaller minaret to the side. This building was itself imposing, but on further inspection they could see the madrasa compound was made up of many more buildings—

most with arched colonnades—that sequestered a huge green courtyard on the interior of the compound. In the distance there were more minarets and decorated buildings with holy Islamic scriptures emblazoned upon them.

Mubin and Sher made their way past the white carved stone gate and pots of blooming red hibiscus into the interior green courtyard. After the hot and dusty bus ride it seemed like a heavenly place to Mubin. He looked around as they were taken to their rooms and laughed as he noticed the classrooms of hundreds of young children seated on long benches rocking back and forth and chanting from their open Qur'ans just as he had in their Canadian madrasa. There were even children who having misbehaved earlier were now squatting down in the "murga" or rooster position.

Our parents and teachers just imported Indo-Pak culture right into Canada! Mubin marveled to himself as he witnessed it all.

***

Mubin's beard had grown out long and square by now and reached his chest. He wore a three quarter length robe and plastic flip-flops on his feet. Mubin was honored to be asked by the leaders to give an exhortation addressing the hundreds of students when all the students gathered around, interested to see the "foreigners." Indeed as he traveled more with the Tablighi Jamaat, Mubin's teachers increasingly selected him to speak and he found himself repeatedly in the prestigious position of addressing large groups of believers.

The Tablighi Jamaat's mission was to support and increase the faith of believers so Mubin's chief task in traveling about the continent was to visit mosques where he typically spent the night in the company of whichever small traveling band he was with. In the mornings they would rise for the sunrise prayers where the jamaat, or brotherhood, would announce how pleased they were to receive the foreign visitors. They would then engage in an hour lecture or talk followed by breakfast. After that, they studied from the hadiths about the virtues of believing in Allah and of prayer.

Most of it Mubin had learned before, but there was always more to learn. Mubin and his fellow travelers were immersed in this glorious Islamic myth-making process in which a utopian point of view of Islam was conveyed. In this narrative, the Prophet (SalAllahuAlayhiWaSallam) and his companions were always portrayed as perfect, and Mubin and the others were lead to believe that if they followed the companions' lives and emulated them, all of life could become perfect, and one would obtain all the promised blessings of this life and the next.

There was no glorification of jihad among the Tablighi Jamaat, although militant jihad was taught in the sense of accurate Islamic history, but only as one of the things the first Muslims did—just like fasting, farming, raising families etc. When there was discussion of the early Islamic history of battles that took place they were interpreted through the lens of self-sacrifice, ethics and faith in God. Jihad was not glorified in a militant sense because the group remained completely apolitical. Jihad in its military sense was only taught as a necessary evil of life, unlike how terrorist groups like ISIS now teach—where jihad by itself and the jihadi is revered—and life is renounced. This was never part of the message.

The group of travelers napped in the hot afternoons, as it was impossible to do anything else. Then they woke before the third prayer, ate, prayed and then went out in groups of three or four on "gusht." "Gusht" entailed going door to door to known Muslim homes where the travelers sought to reinforce the beliefs and practice of those who were already Muslims. The practice of the Tablighi Jamaat was strict in this manner and relied on six points: faith in Allah; prayer; knowledge and remembrance; treating your Muslim brothers as you would want to be treated; sincerity of intention and going out on the path of Allah.

Mubin and his group had memorized their approach and had strict rules to follow. They weren't to look into people's homes from the doorway for instance—lest envy or greed were to enter their hearts. If a woman answered the door they were to ask to meet with the men and keep their gazes down. They were never to ask to be invited into private homes because the owner might not be prepared for a guest and embarrassed to have his home seen. Likewise the fellow listeners were to put their gazes upon their jamaat speaker, not the receiver of the message, so as not to overwhelm the receiver with pressure.

All in all, Mubin could see that it was a good system that respected their fellow Muslims and attempted to gain some resonance with them. A good outcome of conveying their message of the importance of being religious and observant in their faith was that the listeners agreed to return to the mosque for evening prayers and the evening lecture. While the jamaat was to seek to understand the issues of the community and their needs, political discussions were strictly forbidden. The Tablighi Jamaat was solely focused on the spiritual life and the greatness of Allah.

At night the travelers would cook with their mosque hosts simple meals of rice, potatoes and sometimes meat. Once in a while miracles occurred like when one of the brothers joked, "What we really need is some lemonade," and within minutes two men walked in carrying a large pail of sweetened lemonade. That night everyone drank until their bellies were full.

As they traveled to mosque after mosque throughout India, Mubin grew in his oratory abilities and his memorization of the Qur'an and he was frequently asked to address the assemblies. Likewise after he did, many stayed to question him and some men even offered their daughters in marriage to the unique and impressive Canadian. Mubin was beginning to feel good about himself again. *This is who I'm supposed to be,* he concluded as the positive attention and feeling of self-satisfaction grew—honor, erasing shame.

***

"Let's get out of here," Sher said on one of the days they were back at headquarters. "Let's go into the city!"

The two got into a rickshaw and drove to an affluent neighborhood to have a look around.

"Look, it's Wimpy's!" Mubin shouted, signaling to the rickshaw driver to let them out. Wimpy's was a burger restaurant back home. Excited by the rich neighborhood, the two young men disembarked, only to have beggars coming out of nowhere immediately swarm them.

"Baba! Baba! I want food!" they screamed. And seeing that they were in Islamic robes and beards some began shouting, "La ilaha il Allah! Baba Muslim!" Mubin and Sher stared in horror at the sea of beggars, some of them disfigured by disease or amputations. Mubin and Sher tossed off some coins before finding refuge inside the guarded Wimpy's burger shop where the beggars couldn't reach them.

"It's Michael Jackson!" Sher called out, laughing at the life size cardboard cutout of the popular singer who was iconic all over India.

"Ha!" Mubin laughed, adding, "It's air conditioned in here!" Mubin stood relishing the cool air blowing over them as they ordered their burgers. The place was heavenly—clean tiled floors and walls, nicely dressed people, no beggars, no filth, no poverty. After they finished their burgers Mubin whose head was already filled with the Michael Jackson songs that had been repeatedly looping, got up and started to dance. Sher laughed and joined him. Then the two danced their hearts out to their old favorite songs from Canada—*Billi Jean* among them—while a crowd of Indian onlookers gathered, clapping and joining in.

When the afternoon finished the two had received four marriage proposals, two job offers, and a few guys asking, "How can you get me to Canada?"

***

After traveling around India, the groups were dispatched to Pakistan. Again it was harrowing bus trips in overcrowded seats with the heat and scents threatening to overwhelm them. Again Mubin prayed for his eternal life assuming his worldly one was about to end.

"This is the most satiating drink I've had in my life!" Mubin commented on their first stop in Raiwand, where they were welcomed by the jamaat with a red rosewater drink, known as Ruh Afzah. Mubin swigged his down.

This time he noticed there were loads of foreigners gathered at the jamaat—African Americans, Singaporeans, Thais, Europeans, etc. The group here made Mubin—to his shock and surprise—their emir, and he was honored again with a confirmation of his leadership skills. As leader, even two Islamic scholars answered to Mubin—as did everyone else—asking permission to go do things as mundane as use the toilet, which amused Mubin greatly.

"Let's go have a smoke," one of Mubin's traveling companions proposed into a few days of having arrived in Faisalabad, one of the larger Pakistani cities where he was sent along with the others.

"Sure," Mubin said grabbing his cigarettes as the two made their way up to the top of the mosque's minaret. It seemed like a good place to smoke without being noticed. It didn't turn out that way however. Soon an angry crowd gathered below talking, pointing and yelling at them.

"Oh crap, they saw us smoking!" Mubin said as the two extinguished their cigarettes and climbed guiltily back down. "I'm sorry," Mubin said as he faced the angry crowd.

"You can't go up there," a villager explained over the indecipherable shouts of the others. "They think you are trying to see over their walls—to see their women," he added.

"Oh no!" Mubin said, "We just wanted a smoke without offending anyone over our smoking…" Mubin explained.

"You can smoke here, no problem," the villager explained. "But no more climbing up the minaret, okay?"

Mubin nodded, laughing at the unexpected explanation.

***

The more Mubin was thrust into leadership positions and asked to preach the deeper he fell into his beliefs. *This is the real me, who I'm supposed to be,* Mubin began to think. There were more offers of marriage and Mubin found himself immersed in validation, praise and glorification.

"I'm not here for that," Mubin dutifully answered to the proposals—following the Tablighi Jamaat rules, adding, "It would ruin my spiritual journey to be seeking riches or a wife." The Tablighi Jamaat taught them that to accept business, do business, or marry while on their mission were all forbidden. This was solely a spiritual journey.

"You are a good Muslim! Better than we are!" the people marveled after Mubin's talks. Their praise filled a hole that had been drilled into him during his childhood of hearing himself compared unfavorably by his parents to the other boys in his Islamic community.

"Look at these people who were living in the paradise of Canada and came here to share their love of the religion with us!" some said.

It was so much better than hearing his parents ask with derision, "What kind of a Muslim are you?"

***

The groups returned between assignments to the headquarters in Raiwand, just like they had returned to Nizamuddin in India. On one of those returns, two of the guys with affluent relatives in Lahore proposed a night out on the town.

"We'll take you into Lahore and we'll hit the scene," Ahmed proposed.

"Lahore has a scene?" Sher joked.

As it turned out Lahore did have a scene. Dressed in Western clothes the four young men went to dinner at the Copper Kettle and were sitting around chilling out after dinner while the waiters started clearing the tables. Suddenly a disco ball appeared, lights come on and without warning they found themselves in a nightclub. Beautiful women started appearing and the dancing began.

As foreigners, Mubin's group attracted the women's attention as they danced. That caused a fight to nearly break out with the local men whose girlfriends were suddenly distracted. Mubin was flexing his muscles when one of the local guys intervened. "No you can't do this," he said. "You are Tablighi Jamaat. You can't do this! It's okay, you were having a bit of fun, but don't do this."

"Yeah, let's go," Mubin said as he came to his senses, along with the others, and agreed to drop it. The group went back to headquarters and snapping back into their austere personas—suppressing all their natural desires—didn't party anymore after that.

***

Their next deployment was in Quetta, Pakistan. It was 1995 and unbeknownst to Mubin, the group that would later become infamous as al Qaeda was headquartered there.

The trip this time was by train. Mubin sat on a wooden bench with his back to the wall and slept part of the trip sitting up. Again the train was packed full. And it was filthy and smelled—especially the bathroom. The only water for washing was dispensed from the lota, a small water container that one would normally find in the bathroom.

From the train station Mubin and his traveling companions packed into a bus that took them to the Quetta mosque, a sandy brown building which almost appeared to be a mirage upon first seeing it. Inside it had beautiful cool tiles and a giant water reservoir where the people could come to make their ritual ablution before prayers. After the intense heat of the day, the astonishing cool interior of the mosque was more than welcome.

Years later when al Qaeda was making the news, Mubin would be surprised to see CNN's Christiane Amanpour standing outside of the same mosque making her report.

At the Quetta mosque Mubin found the Tablighi Jamaat. They were not the only jamaat active there. The Taliban shura were also there but Mubin had no idea at the time who the Taliban were.

Mubin and Sher were dispatched from Quetta to the Mastoong Shehr mosque in a nearby village. Arriving there they could barely keep up their energy. It was difficult to walk any distance in the heat. The climate here was like a desert and extremely hot.

All this suffering is for the sake of Allah, and by this suffering the salvation of the world is coming, Mubin reminded himself.

"What's that gushing noise?" Sher asked interrupting Mubin's thoughts. Then they both saw it—water pumped up from a well and streaming out in a waterfall from a giant two-foot wide pipe discharging into an irrigation ditch. The area just around it was surrounded by green foliage amidst the desert drought.

"MashaAllah [to the glory of Allah]! " Mubin shouted as both young men stripped off their shirts and joyfully dove into the cold water.

When the local guys from the mosque heard them shouting with glee, they came and were surprised to find their foreign partners lounging in an irrigation ditch.

"What are you doing?" they asked, adding, "People don't do this here!"

"We just needed to cool down brother!" Sher explained as they came back out into the oven-temperature air. Immediately the water on their bodies evaporated away.

"We can't take the heat," Mubin explained putting his Islamic robe back over his rapidly drying pants.

***

Once at the mosque, the usual Tablighi Jamaat routine was repeated starting with morning prayers and the lectures. But when it came to napping in the afternoon Mubin was enthusiastic to go out on "gusht."

"It's too hot to go out," the local leader contended, but when he saw that Mubin was determined to go he agreed to accompany him as a translator. As they walked out of the mosque compound a Pakistani fighter jet coming out of nowhere suddenly flew low overhead creating a wall of wind and dust around them. Mubin's heart jumped to his throat as he asked, "Are we about to be bombed?"

The translator nervously scoffed although he seemed worried as well. After waiting a few minutes he explained, "This happens here at the frontier." Then they continued onward.

Here, when they visited their shops and some homes Mubin found that most people were receptive to their message of invigorating faith practices. But some locals asked, "Why would you come all this way to lecture me? Don't you have your own people to talk to back there?"

"We do this also back home," Mubin responded, adding, "Coming here is our way of learning how to do this from the elders."

After covering the main village area Mubin spotted a compound removed from the village, located in a green oasis.

"What's over there?" he asked his guide who just shrugged. "Let's check that out." Before the guide could comment Mubin was leading them across the sand toward the grove of green trees growing near the compound. *I'm really hardcore now,* Mubin thought as the sand blew filling his nose, ears and mouth and gritted between his teeth.

Mubin and his companion walked around the corner of the compound as they searched for its entrance. There, Mubin was startled to suddenly notice seven military looking guys sitting atop the compound wall. They were crouching in perfect balance, holding AK-47s and rocket propelled grenade guns (RPG's) in their hands, with additional weaponry and ammo belts tied to their bodies. Dressed in Islamic robes of various colors with black turbans atop their heads they were hidden perfectly amid the treetops. The customary tail of cloth hanging down from their turbans was dramatically long and black in their cases, reaching below their waists giving them a particularly swashbuckling look, and their turbans had been twisted rather than folded in the classical manner. They sported shoulder length hair that peeked beneath their turbans and their beards reached to their chests. Their faces were weathered and hardened from the harsh elements and circumstances of the fighting surrounding them.

Mubin glanced at his guide who shook his head signaling that they should retreat but Mubin continued onward. "AssalaamuAlaykum! [Peace be upon you]" he called as the soldiers saw him.

"WaAlaykumSalaam [and upon you peace]," they answered back. Then the soldiers started asking who they were and what they were up to.

They were speaking Dari or Pashto, not Urdu, so he couldn't make it out. "Tablighi Jamaat," Mubin picked out from the translation and "Canada."

Most of the soldiers were scowling but some of them looked interested. Mubin, completely undaunted, picked out the meanest looking scowling face and started in on his Tablighi Jamaat da'wah (Islamic invitation), pausing for the translator to follow his words.

"Our success in life and the life thereafter lies in following the commandments of Allah as exemplified by his Prophet (SalAllahuAlayhiWaSallam) [peace be upon his name] and his companions," Mubin began and continued onward, speaking about the greatness of Allah and going through a shortened version of the six points of the Tablighi Jamaat message. When he got to the last point about going out in the path of Allah, Mubin said, "To bring about change in the world..." but he was interrupted by the scowling soldier who raised his gun in the air.

"Jihad," the soldier interrupted, powerfully raising his AK-47 above his turbaned head. "Jihad is how you change the world," he announced triumphantly.

Mubin stopped in shock, taken aback by the warrior's words. This man was so forceful and so certain of himself—dressed in the strict Islamic style he seemed like an incarnation of the companions of the Prophet (SalAllahuAlayhiWaSallam).

Surely he knows something! Mubin thought as he invited the fighters to join them in evening prayers at the mosque.

The fighters agreed and came to the mosque to pray Asr, the evening prayer. When they arrived at the mosque one of the fighters stood and made the Adhan—the call for prayer—singing in a melodious voice. As always the call for prayer touched Mubin in his deepest being—especially now when it was sung so well and by such a heroic looking being.

Look at these guys! They are warriors! Mubin marveled as he watched the fighters bring their guns unabashedly into the mosque and lay them down on their right side as they prepared for prayers—ready at any moment to pick them back up if necessary.

They recite the Qur'an! Mubin mused in pure awe. *They are the mythic guys I've been reading about—the myth come to life here!* Mubin thought watching their every move.

They appeared, as all Mubin had ever desired to be—prayerful, prepared, and fierce warriors walking in the path of Allah. For him, they were the pinnacles of male religious fulfillment. *Here they are, right in front of me!* Mubin thought as he watched them in amazement. Sher too was deeply impressed.

What both of the young Canadians didn't know is that these were the Taliban who would soon fight in Afghanistan, take over and install an Islamic state that would then host Osama bin Ladin and his nascent al Qaeda movement.[2] To Mubin they simply appeared as heroes.

"Can we stay in your company?" Mubin asked the Urdu-speaking fighter after they finished prayers and the evening sermon. Mubin was completely enamored and wanted to be with them as long as possible.

"You know how to shoot?" the soldier asked as they came out to the courtyard, laughing at the young men's thrall with them.

"I do!" Mubin answered excitedly. The fighters moved to a grassy area that faced the desert and handed over some of their weapons to Mubin and Sher, giving them a chance to shoot the AK-47s. One of them set up a fifty-caliber machine gun on its mount and let Mubin fire off a belt-fed round of ammo. Mubin was beside himself with excitement and admiration.

The fighters lingered till sunset then bid their farewells and vanished into the darkness.

I should abandon the Tablighi Jamaat and follow them now! Mubin suddenly thought. But he knew the shura of the Tablighi Jamaat would never agree and his Pakistani visa was limited to a two-month stay. Yet, Mubin had been impacted in a deep way and this episode marked the first time he would be bitten by the jihadi bug.

***

That night Mubin felt an overwhelming sense of loss. *I want to be in the company of such men always! I belong with them!* Mubin thought as he tossed and turned and debated over whether he should just toss his passport and find a way to join them. *They live like the Sahaba [original companions of the Prophet (SalAllahuAlayhiWaSallam)]*, Mubin mused as he daydreamed about them for the next weeks. *These were the actual manifestations of the religious, honorable companions that also fought! They were dressed like the Prophet (SalAllahuAlayhiWaSallam) dressed! I want to be like them!* Mubin thought. *They're brown and look like me,* he also noticed.

Indeed they appeared as the perfect role models for a naive, young, brown, Muslim man who was searching for his way out of shame into honor. Mubin suffered deeply for not having matched up to the expectations of the literalistic Muslims in his extended family and community. Looking at the fighters he saw that their robes and turbans were as sanctioned for religious Muslims. Their guns, ammo belts and the long tails on their black turbans made them appear particularly dashing and masculine. They fulfilled all of the roles of the original companions—jihad included among them.

And their work in the path of Allah seemed a lot more alluring and fun to a young man than sitting in endless Tablighi Jamaat lectures. It looked all laid out for him—a way to restore his honor.

I wonder how I could get back there? Mubin mused once they had made their way out of the area. *I'd probably have to get married to obtain permission to stay,* he realized, as his mind wandered during prayers and sermons. *Maybe it's time I move beyond my purpose with the Tablighi Jamaat?* Mubin wondered, echoing the thoughts of so many other young troubled men trundled off to Pakistan from England and Canada to clean up their lives by devoting their summer months to the Tablighi Jamaat, but later ending up in Pakistani or Afghan terrorist training camps.

Mubin was only steps away from doing the same and didn't even understand what he was really doing. The only thing that stopped Mubin was that he could find no honorable way to abscond, no way that wouldn't shame his family further.

Even on the plane trip back to Canada, Mubin daydreamed. *If only the plane was headed the opposite direction, I'd be making my way back to them!*

***

"I can't hang around with you guys anymore," Mubin told Brad over the phone once he was back in Toronto. "It's not consistent with my religion," Mubin explained.

He'd returned triumphant and changed, and his family was delighted. The "tribe" had accepted and validated him, and even now gave him a high rank. Mubin now knew the Qur'an well, and could speak and quote from it authoritatively. And he could shoot a heavy duty weapon—but he didn't mention that part.

It wasn't easy to cut off his former friends and one day, just out of curiosity Mubin returned back to his high school to check out what the younger ones were up to. Mubin showed up wearing his long black robes, above the ankle pants and black turban, now tied with the long tail just as the Taliban wore theirs.

"Oh my God, it's Mubin!" one of them shrieked after a moment of non-recognition.

"Holy crap, dude, what's happened to you?" Tammy asked throwing her arms up to hug Mubin. But before she could reach him, Mubin backed away holding his arms up to stop her.

"I can't touch girls. We live separate," Mubin explained.

"What happened to you?" Paul asked.

"I want to be more religious," Mubin explained. "This is how I want to live now. No more partying. No more girls. I can't do that anymore."

Yet the lure of old friendships was strong and Mubin found himself going to their parties once again. But without smoking or drinking along with the others it now seemed empty. Soon he found there was no reason to hang out anymore since he had nothing in common with them now.

Deep inside, Mubin felt he was forcing a new identity onto himself and tried to reassure himself that leaving these friends would be best for him. Somewhere inside however, he knew this wasn't true. They may have had their vices but they were the most loyal and loving friends a person could ever ask for.

This is why I left, Mubin commented to himself as he started to look down on his former friends. *Nothing with them has changed, I've been gone for only four months but it seems like a lifetime! I've changed!* Mubin concluded as he backed away from them.

Mubin's family and religious community were pleased. Now finally his parents had the religious son they had always wanted. He was reading the Qur'an, praying five times a day and no longer hanging with the locals. And now people were holding up Mubin as an example to their sons asking, "Why can't you be more like him?"

Mubin basked in the prestige of being part of the first student jamaat from Canada to have traveled to India and Pakistan. His community and his father, most importantly, were impressed. Mubin's "stock" had improved five hundred percent. No longer were other parents warning their sons to "avoid that guy" but now they were encouraging their sons to "go hang with him," and using him as an example saying, "Remember how he used to be. Look at him now."

Yet inside it felt like a caricature that Mubin had forced upon himself to be what his parents and their Islamic community wanted. There was emptiness still, on the inside – a hollow core that still begged to understand where he really belonged. He still had not won the tug o' war. But now the rope was being pulled three ways – Westernization, conservative Islamism, and the militant jihad.

***

At the Tablighi Jamaat, Mubin quickly became one of the more prolific speakers—and was sent to mosques, college campuses and anywhere Muslim organizations were springing up to speak to and encourage Muslims. Mubin was also tasked with being the supervisor for younger students as he continued his own studies as well.

Yet whenever boredom hit, Mubin reverted to his remembrance of the Taliban fighters. They were in the news now and they had taken over Afghanistan just as they had told Mubin and Sher they planned to.

They did what they said they were going to do! Mubin marveled reading the news. *And they did it by the gun, not by da'wah [Islamic teachings] just as they said they would!*

Seeing their example Mubin began to wonder if this endless work educating and encouraging the believers would really bring about the hoped for changes in the world. As a young man he longed for overnight changes— winning territory the way the Taliban just had.

I want more! Mubin thought but when he tried to talk about jihad or geopolitical politics with the Tablighi Jamaat leaders they refused to enter the debate.

"You are causing problems talking about this stuff!" the leaders said taking him aside as Mubin continued to raise these issues. "You can't be doing this, Mubin," they warned sternly.

That's when Mubin decided—*The Tablighi Jamaat is not for me.*

Getting on the "Jihadi" Path & Getting Married

"It's a bid'ah [a reprehensible innovation to Islam, a sin] to be with the Tablighi Jamaat," Muktar commented one day. Muktar was from a local Salafi group[3] that often hung around the same Muslims the Tablighi Jamaat members ministered to. He was usually argumentative and caused trouble. His group promoted more militant interpretations of Islam. Usually Mubin ignored him, but not today.

"You're right," Mubin answered surprising Muktar. "They don't talk about politics and I'm more interested in how politics and da'wah intersect." Mubin knew how this Salafi group worked—they broke down people's beliefs by challenging their sources—many of which are nonexistent for many common so called Muslim beliefs, especially those based in culture, versus scriptures.

Once they broke down what you thought you believed, they offered a new methodology based on the hadiths and scriptures that went all the way back to the Prophet (SalAllahuAlayhiWaSallam) and his companions. By doing so they had a claim to authenticity that was difficult to argue with. The problem was in the way they interpreted things—they were much more interested in militant jihad and saw jihad as an individual duty of each and every Muslim. Mubin knew that, but he was also yearning for something more active, something that would really bring change in the world—the same way he had seen the Taliban carry through with what they had vowed to do in establishing an Islamic state in Afghanistan.

***

Joining the Salafi group, Mubin was again offered a channel for expressing his inner boiling rage at his uncles—but this time it wasn't channeled into disciplined and responsible military actions as it had been in the Army Cadets. Now it was directed at nonbelievers, Westerners and Jews.

The Salafi group Mubin had joined taught him the al Qaeda narrative in which Muslims all over the world were oppressed by Westerners and Jews who the true Muslim believers were to strike down by becoming active participants of the militant jihad. Learning from this group, Mubin came to believe that he had an individual and personal duty to take up arms and join in jihad—just like the Taliban had told him—to bring the needed changes into this world. Mubin just didn't yet know how to do it, but he was fast on his way to discovery.

Traveling with some fellow brothers from his group Mubin commented on a synagogue they were passing in the bus. "I've wanted to hit that synagogue for quite some time," he raged.

The brothers all stood up and moved to the side of the bus scoping it out. "Yeah we should do it!" one of them said.

"Hell why not?" another enthused until the bus moved further along and Mubin pointed out the police station only a few blocks away.

"Oh, now that's a problem," his fellow jihadi remarked.

***

While Mubin was absorbing the militant jihadi ways of thinking he was also struggling with what he referred to as having become a "born again virgin." To stay celibate, Mubin avoided girls, refrained from conversing with them, deliberately looked away when they were around or kept his gaze on the ground. But he was slowly realizing that what he was demanding of himself was impossible. For instance when he rode the subway he kept his gaze on the floor only to look up to check his stop and then he usually found himself confronted with multiple sets of long naked legs and bare cleavages.

I need to get married! Mubin moaned inwardly. Later the same day Mubin went to visit Benny, an old friend from the rock band—the bass player. At Benny's house he saw Joanne, the same cute Polish girl he'd been attracted to in high school but had never dared approach. She was just as attractive but Mubin didn't approach her now for other reasons.

How could it work between us? Mubin asked. *I'm religious—she's not.*

Joanne was the farthest thing from religious. Blonde and petite, she dressed Goth style, sported multiple tattoos and piercings and wore cherry colored Dr. Martens boots. Not the kind of girl he could bring home to his parents.

How am I going to live without a woman? Mubin asked himself as he found the courage to talk to her. Amazingly, despite their differences, she was receptive.

Meeting Joanne at Benny's led to more meetings in the park and talking on the phone. Mubin was very attracted to Joanne, but he didn't dare touch her—although he intensely wanted to. Instead they just talked. But Mubin knew it could go nowhere—she was an atheist and his parents would never accept her.

***

"I want to get married," Mubin announced at home. "I want to go to England to find a wife. Can you set it up with Uncle?"

"I'll call him in the morning," Mummi answered, thrilled with the news. "I'm sure he can organize it."

Before he left Mubin met with Joanne one more time. "I'm going to London to find a bride. My uncle will arrange it," Mubin confided.

"You want an arranged marriage?" Joanne asked lifting her eyebrows in shock.

"That's how we do things in my culture," Mubin answered smiling grimly. "I need to get married."

"Oh okay, good luck then," Joanne said. Mubin felt he could detect a note of disappointment in her voice.

But what does it matter? he asked himself walking away.

***

It was 1998, and Mubin was in London. Mubin's aunt and uncle had phoned to arrange a series of meetings with the fathers of five eligible girls from families with good backgrounds. As they set out in their London cab for their first meeting, Uncle looked impressive. He was dressed in his finest white embroidered Indian clothes, his turban and full-length beard finishing off his portrait of respectability. Aunt was wearing an embroidered sky blue Indian dress and matching pants topped with a pink hijab. Mubin was also dressed in his best—wearing his white embroidered Indian robes and his usual black turban, with the tail trailing over his shoulder in a fashion statement similar to what he'd seen the Taliban wearing.

The first step in getting married was to pass the "father gauntlet"—meeting and impressing the girl's father enough to be able to meet her. At this first family, Mr. Rashid greeted them. He ushered them solemnly into their living room for tea as Mubin glanced around.

The room was well furnished with lush carpets and comfortable sofas alongside the requisite glass cabinet in the corner filled with trinkets from India that stood in for what would have been the china cabinet in a fine English home. They also had an Adhan clock—ubiquitous to Indian homes—sitting on a shelf pointing out the Qiblah, the proper direction to face Mecca in prayer. This one was shaped like an Islamic arch and had a picture of Mecca during the Hajj depicted on its front. It had all of the prayer times listed for the day and was assuredly programed to automatically make the adhan—the call for the five daily local Islamic prayer times—ensuring that no one in this pious household could forget to pray.

No one else was present as Mubin and his aunt and uncle took their seats. The tea and cookies were soon passed to Mr. Rashid through a closed door by unseen hands. While only the girl's father met Mubin's family in the first hour, Mubin thought *undoubtedly his marriageable daughter has her ear glued to the door listening to it all.* Indeed, now Mubin could hear the whispering of the women in the kitchen as they listened anxiously as he answered more questions.

In the absence of a female hostess, Mubin's aunt helped to serve the tea. After everyone had been served their tea, Mr. Rashid who was himself an Islamic scholar began with asking Mubin all about his faith, testing him to be sure he knew Islamic law.

"How many obligatory actions are there in the ritual prayer," he began at a very elementary level.

"Six," Mubin answered.

"How many obligatory actions are there in the ablution?" Mr. Rashid asked.

"Four," Mubin answered marveling at the lack of challenge in the questions. He would have preferred a seriously hard question about an obscure hadith or some aspect of Islamic law that he'd actually studied. These questions covered the very basics of Islam.

"Who is your favorite companion of the Prophet, Peace be Upon Him?" Mr. Rashid continued.

"Khalid bin Waleed," Mubin answered enthusiastically. *Now we are getting somewhere!* he thought.

Such an answer could have cued an astute observer as to Mubin's increasingly strong support for militant jihad had Mr. Rashid been paying attention for that sort of clue. Bin Waleed was the famous Muslim general who had led various military campaigns from the Prophet's (SalAllahuAlayhiWaSallam) time.

When the Islamic questions were exhausted Mr. Rashid turned to more mundane realities. "What kind of job do you have?"

"I'm a full-time da'ee [caller to Islam]," Mubin answered with a big grin crossing his face. His answer was unfortunately met with a severe frown—So you don't have a paying job? Mr. Rashid's face said in response.

"What is your level of education?" Mr. Rashid asked his scowl growing.

"Real education or school, college or university?" Mubin asked trying to emphasize the importance of Islamic, over worldly education. Meeting another severe look, Mubin answered, "I graduated high school."

Mr. Rashid abruptly stood up. "I think we've heard enough," he concluded as he politely thanked Uncle and Aunt for bringing Mubin.

***

The next three meetings followed the same format with Mubin similarly striking out. In the last meeting, he made it further—to actually meeting a potential bride. In that interview as Mr. Latif finished the questioning, he called to his daughter, "Asma, come to the room."

Clearly she had been right outside the door the whole time as she popped in with no delay. Asma was covered from head to toe in a black abaya with a matching black nikab hiding her face. Mubin could see only her brown eyes as she glanced quickly at Mubin before taking her seat. Then her eyes quickly darted away. She didn't dare look him in the face again. It was impossible in any case, to see if she was pleased or unhappy under her black nikab.

After an uncomfortable silence filled the room Mr. Latif asked Mubin, "So what do you want to ask her?"

"Can I speak privately to your daughter?" Mubin asked.

"There will be no private meeting," Mr. Latif answered as his face showed first shock at the request and then took on a severe scowl.

"Well, I have the right to ask her questions in private and you have the right to be watching to be sure nothing inappropriate takes place. We'll leave the door open so you can see," Mubin bargained. He wanted to be sure the girl wanted this too and knew that if she did not, she could never tell the truth in front of her father.

"You have no rights over my daughter," Mr. Latif answered angrily.

"According to the fiqh [Islamic jurisprudence] I do have the right to speak to her in private to ask her questions you might not be comfortable with—questions that a potential husband and wife might need to discuss," Mubin persisted.

"Thank you, you can leave now," Mr. Latif said standing suddenly.

"MashaAllah!" Mubin said, "You talk about Islamic fiqh, and don't observe it. Thank you for wasting my time also!"

Mr. Latif's brow was furrowed in a storm of anger, yet he managed to politely guide Mubin's aunt and uncle to the door and bid them farewells. He ignored Mubin and closed the door tightly behind them.

"Wow that went really well!" Aunt said when they got back into the car.

"You shouldn't have spoken to him like that," Uncle chimed in. "You should have asked him why are you taking the rights away from her, been more polite."

Mubin shook his head and snorted in disgust. "I'm done looking for a wife in this place," he answered as he sulked in the cab.

Joanne is back home and she is perfectly suitable if only she was a Muslim, Mubin thought. *Better than all this hypocrisy where the families pretend that Islamic virtues are the most important but what it really boils down to is how educated are you and how much money do you make?*

Mubin fumed the whole way home, shame and anger alternating on his face as he replayed all the recent living room scenes of rejection.

"Don't worry, it's a tribal thing," Aunt had said after the second rejection. "They are Gujaratis and they don't like our people. That's okay—it's better you don't mix," she added that time.

"Don't worry," she'd said after the third one. "You know there are many girls out there, and you are such a handsome boy."

Now she was silent and Uncle seemed angry sitting alongside her. They had exhausted their contacts.

I'm done! Mubin thought. *I don't want to ever go through this again. I thought worldly affairs didn't matter as much if the suitor had sufficient religious qualifications—obviously not! This is not Islam!* Mubin fumed. *It's Indian culture and not my religion. I don't need all this cultural baggage in my life. I've had enough of Indian culture!* Again his thoughts reverted to Joanne and he felt ready to go home.

***

`Hey I'm back,` Mubin texted Joanne as soon as he landed. It had been a two-month sojourn ending in failure.

`So are you married?` she texted back.

`No it didn't work out,` he typed.

`Oh well, I guess it's a good thing anyway,` she replied.

Is she interested in me? Mubin mused excitedly. `I want to meet and tell you all about it,` he texted.

"How do you marry a girl you've never seen before?" Joanne asked when they were together. Then Mubin explained how an arranged marriage works in Indian culture. "Wouldn't you want to know if she's had boyfriends?" Joanne asked.

"That's the way they do things in my culture," Mubin replied while secretly thinking *She's so awesome!*

"That's just stupid!" Joanne answered laughter lighting up her eyes.

"Yeah, it is," Mubin agreed, thinking how glad he was that he hadn't said yes in desperation to the last girl he'd met in London. Joanne was so much cooler than any of them. They continued meeting regularly after this.

***

He was reading Rumi and she was reading Raji Yoga by Swami Vivekananda.

"You should read this book—it's amazing!" Joanne told him. Mubin smiled back in reply.

Sharing Rumi with Joanne had reopened her heart to a belief in God—something she had given up on years ago. She'd begun admitting there was likely some loving presence, perhaps even a God. But now she was into Hinduism and Yoga.

Mubin now encouraged her to put her legs up across his or he'd rest his arm on her legs. They were getting much closer physically, but still there was no sexual intimacy. Yet, it had the feeling of the comforts of marriage.

"Okay, give it to me, I'll read it at home," Mubin said taking the book from her.

At home Mubin's parents asked in dismay. "Why would you be reading this author?" they asked. Being Indian they were familiar with his ideas.

"I'm studying Mummi! How can I be a Muslim scholar and not know what other religions teach? Relax, I'm not going to convert, okay?" Mubin told his mother. But he could see that clearly it was not okay.

"Don't buy into that stuff," Abba warned.

"I'm just educating myself," Mubin said and exited the room, book in hand.

Later meeting with Joanne again, this time downstairs in the family room of her home, Mubin sat with her and discussed what he had found in the book. They spent the whole afternoon and into the evening discussing philosophy and life as Mubin fell deeper into love.

At one point Joanne's father came downstairs, "I forgot my screwdriver," he said pretending to look for his tool. Seeing them seated at a distance and Mubin looking reserved with his beard and Islamic robes, her father seemed reassured that nothing was going on. Although he did give Mubin a strange look that seemed to say, *What the hell is your deal?*

After an enthusiastic day of sharing, Mubin wistfully told Joanne, "If your views were a little different about the oneness of God, I would propose marriage."

It was suddenly silent in the room. Then looking strangely at him Joanne came over and sat on his lap.

"Okay, I'll do it," she said smiling into his eyes.

"Wait, you need to understand!" Mubin countered, suddenly worried that she might be thinking that converting was a simple thing. "There are expectations based on what my family would be comfortable with—I couldn't bring someone home that was not a Muslim, not in hijab," he explained. "And there are the five pillars of Islam—faith in Allah, prayer, charity, fasting and the pilgrimage to Mecca if you are able to do so. We pray five times a day," Mubin explained as his face filled with tension, worried that she had no idea what he was proposing.

"It's fine, I agree!" Joanne reassured him. Suddenly Mubin felt joy melting his whole body.

MashaAllah! was all he could think as he kissed her whole-heartedly for the first time. It had been years since he had experienced such a warm, naturally satiating feeling. This was true love—not the fake love of teenage kids anymore. Their eyes still closed and the kissing continuing, he touched her soft face. *She smells yummy!* Mubin thought. *I have finally found her through Allah and not through the old-world cultural constructs of arranged marriage!* It was a strange reconciliation for Mubin between Islam and living in a Western society.

***

At home Mubin first told his parents about a "friend" who wanted to marry a white European convert.

"There's so many instances where it doesn't work out," Abba said shaking his head. "They get married and have children, then the one who converted isn't happy. It becomes a big mess . . . better to stay within the community, in our culture," he warned.

"Abba, the guy is me!" Mubin finally admitted. "I want you to meet her."

When Joanne arrived at their house, even Mubin was caught off guard. He'd never seen her like that. Her hair was all put up and hidden under her hijab and she was dressed in a nice blouse and flowing skirt. She looked elegant and dignified.

My Dad is going to drill her about her Islamic beliefs, ask if she knows her scriptures, Mubin groaned inwardly dreading the conversation as he introduced her to his folks. But it turned out Abba was far more interested in how she would fit into their family and raise his grandchildren.

"How would you raise your children?" Abba asked. "Would you send them to madrasa or school?" he inquired.

"School is very important," Joanne answered confidently. "You can do the religious training at home, but school is too important to miss."

Satisfied, Abba asked her, "What do you think about how Muslims live?" So it went for five hours. Joanne answered everything to his satisfaction. Then the women went out for a shopping trip.

"She's great!" Mummi said when they returned, "Where did you find this one?"

Abba however was still cautious. He had seen numerous mixed-marriages fall apart because of culture clashes and false expectations. "Why don't you stay with us for a while and make sure you like how we live?" he suggested as Mubin nearly fainted from shock at the suggestion. "Make sure this is really how you want to live," Abba added.

In the next days Joanne moved into Mubin's sister's room and cooked, ate and lived with the family. Mubin was ecstatic. Joanne too warmed to Mubin's family. Both of her parents had worked outside the home leaving her alone a lot in her childhood. Now she was surrounded by the warmth and activity of a huge Indian family.

***

Mubin announced the nikah (marriage contract) for the first Friday in Ramadan. "I want to get the full blessings of Ramadan," he told his friends and relatives about the unusual choice of getting married during the fasting month.

Joanne's family were not thrilled that she was marrying a Muslim but there wasn't much they could say—Joanne had made up her mind. After the wedding Joanne and Mubin made their way to Medina and Mecca arriving in time to celebrate the Muslim holiday of Eid while in Mecca. They went first to Medina, a city known for a place where love is to be found. After all these years of living celibate Mubin was in heaven. He'd used ecstasy, as a drug before, but now he knew true ecstasy was spending most of his time in the room with his new wife and blissfully sleeping in each others arms, their lovemaking now considered to be acts of charity before God.

"What a great system," Mubin grinned looking at Joanne. Sex between married couples was not just lawful and encouraged. It was free of the shame and guilt that haunted him from prior experiences.

In Mecca, they joined the crowds of people from all over the world – Asians, Africans, Europeans – doing the Umrah, an out-of-season pilgrimage similar to the Hajj and at the Ka'bah originally built according to Islamic tradition by Abraham (Peace be Upon Him) in Mecca. There, Mubin and Joanne slipped out of their worldly clothes and wrapped themselves into the plain white sheets—the Ihraam—that made clear that all people—rich and poor, distinguished and humble, are equal before Allah. Circling the Ka'bah seven times in a counter clockwise direction they joined the thousands of others doing the same.

Next they reenacted the frantic search for water of Abraham's wife Hagar as they walked rapidly seven times back and forth between the hills of Safa and Marwah ending at the well of Zamzam, believed to be the water Allah provided for Hagar and her son Ishmael (Peace be Upon Him) after they were left alone in the desert. They also climbed the mountain where the Prophet (SalAllahuAlayhiWaSallam) first received his contemplations.

She's my girl, Mubin thought watching Joanne climb the mountain like a soldier. While distracted by his wife's beauty, Mubin was also deeply moved as he sat in the same space where the Prophet (SalAllahuAlayhi-WaSallam) had contemplated and he felt humbled by the honor of it.

After Mecca they traveled to Egypt where they finally ended up in the Cairo Sheraton after bad experiences in cheap hotels. "Let's go for the halal Italian dinner on the Nile river," Joanne suggested, resorting to their credit card. The next day they toured the pyramids and the Sphinx on horseback. Seeing Joanne in her hijab atop her horse Mubin thought, *It's just like*

Sahaba times. She's like my own Muslim warrior princess in hijab!

Next they decided to tour Israel taking a bus through the Rafah crossing into Gaza and then taking the settler's road onward into Israel. In Jerusalem, Mubin and Joanne checked into a hostel and began making the rounds of all the famous sites—many shared holy places between religions. They even visited the Jewish Wailing Wall. It was 1999, just before Ariel Sharon made his infamous trip to the al Aqsa mosque just before the second intifada. As Mubin gazed up at the al Aqsa mosque built upon the ruins of the Temple of the Prophet Solomon (Peace Be Upon Him) his hatred for Jews that he had absorbed earlier from the militant jihadi groups was now calmed—perhaps by the bliss of new marriage. Mubin began to see things in a more harmonious way and he marveled at the continuity between the three Abrahamic faiths and how he believed that the al Aqsa mosque had been built to continue the worship of the one God.

They went also to the upper room of the Last Supper, the Mount of Olives and the alleged tomb of Jesus, the son of Mary (Peace Be Upon Both of Them). "If you are looking for Him, He is risen," the tour guide told the listeners what the angel had announced to the disciples of Jesus when they came to his grave. Everywhere he went Mubin was touched by the stories. He also found himself an object of interest as tourists often remarked, "Look he looks like those people who used to walk these places!" Sometimes tourists asked to take his picture.

Mubin and Joanne prayed at the Dome of the Rock and in al Aqsa mosque with the imam even offered to allow Mubin to lead the prayers. As he looked at the rock where the Prophet (SalAllahuAlayhiWaSallam) ascended into heaven and where his white winged horse Burak was tied down, Mubin thought, *I feel like I'm living in those days and time,* and he was happy as he immersed himself deeply into the history of the area.

Not everything was smooth sailing however. One day Mubin needed toilet paper and ran with just his tank top and pants to the store. He picked up the requisite supplies and ran back home only to be stopped by a platoon of Israeli soldiers. Their weapons came right up as he rounded the corner and one began shouting "Hamas!"

Recognizing that they thought he was from a local terrorist group, Mubin shouted back, "Canadian!" He understood that they were demanding something of him in Hebrew so he started saying, "English! English!" to prompt them to speak English to him. Finally they did.

"Why are you running?" one of the soldiers quizzed him, his rifle pointed in Mubin's chest.

"Toilet paper!" Mubin answered showing him the roll. "I gotta go!" he added laughing. Then the soldier laughed and gestured with his rifle. "Passport" he said. Mubin walked with him back to the hotel and yelled up to the open window to his wife.

"Joanne, throw my passport down please," he called.

When the Israeli saw it he said, "Okay Canada, go!"

***

Joanne and Mubin had their first child a year after they were married—in December of 1999. Tellingly, Mubin insisted on naming his son Mujahid—which means holy warrior, which was intended to be defined in the context of a Muslim warrior and someone who carried out jihad. Essa, named after Prophet Jesus [Peace be Upon Him] was born the next year in 2000. Mubin worked at odd jobs while he continued to hang with the Salafis, deepening his militant jihadi convictions.

On September 11, 2001, Mubin was back in Canada, driving to work like every other day. He was still hanging with the Salafi brothers and firmly committed to carrying out jihad against Westerners. The news channel was on and began reporting that an airplane had struck one of the twin towers in New York City.

"AllahuAkbar!" Mubin shouted raising his fist in the air. *Finally the U.S. gets what it deserves!* he thought understanding immediately that it was a terrorist attack. Mubin continued listening to the newscast as he pulled into his workplace. To enter his office complex, where he worked servicing student loans, he approached through an underpass that brought his vision up to glance at the tall office building he was about to enter. Mubin was struck by the parallels.

What if another plane strikes this building right now? Mubin asked himself remembering how the Pakistani fighter jet had buzzed low over them in Quetta. *If my brothers were responsible for New York and they struck here as well, they wouldn't warn me ahead of time,* he realized. *They would let me die with everyone else.* Suddenly Mubin was confronted with new questions about militant jihad and its justifications. *If the people I aspire to be like would commit such an act, then what kind of Islam am I following?*

Mubin took the secure elevator up to his floor noticing that everyone on it was giving him the once over. His beard and robes were putting people on guard. He could see their eyes shooting to see if his work badge was prominently displayed, if he even had a badge.

Someone came running out of their office as Mubin reached his floor yelling, "A second plane has hit."

It's a terrorist attack from the brothers, Mubin confirmed as he went to sit down in his cubicle. It wasn't more than fifteen minutes before his supervisor came around with a look of concern on his face.

"Mubin, I'm sure you've heard what's happened," he began. "Please let us know if anyone says anything bad to you," he went on.

The first thing they are thinking about is my wellbeing? They are non-Muslims! And they are worried about me? Mubin asked himself.

A co-worker was crying in a nearby cubicle. Her father was in New York and couldn't be reached by phone.

"They should just fucking bomb these people back to the stone age," another coworker was saying in the next cubicle.

"No all that bombing is why they did this in the first place," another answered the first.

These are non-Muslims! Mubin thought in amazement and was totally confused by their reactions. He also was touched by their suffering and horrified knowing that he would not have been spared had he been in either of the New York twin towers—Muslim true believer, or not.

The attacks had taken place early in the day and Mubin raced home during his lunch break. He walked in the door and found Joanne glued to the television, Mujahid in his diaper on the floor. Joanne stood as he entered, hands on her hips and said, "The phone has been ringing all morning. People are calling to ask what your involvement in this is?" she inquired, her eyes steely with accusation. "Did you have anything to do with this?" she asked, her voice rising in incredulity.

Mubin's non-Muslim friends were also calling, asking if this is the kind of Islam he followed and if it was, they really couldn't accept having a friend who supported it. Mubin was deeply impacted by the events that day and worst of all, the amount of hatred that it was bringing to Islam and Muslims. That especially was too powerful to ignore.

How could it possibly be okay to kill non-combatant civilians? Mubin asked himself. *It is easy to make the argument against combatants, but innocents like this? Do I have a serious deficit in my understanding of Islam?* Mubin wondered.

As the day went on, his doubts in the al Qaeda ideology of promoting militant jihad grew. Yet on another side it excited him to see the reach his brothers in Afghanistan had managed. This time he wanted in.

***

The war is on! Mubin thought. *And I'm not going to miss it! I need to go there and be close to it—if the Great Jihad of the End Time [the apocalypse] kicks off I want to be part of it. I need to get to the Middle East! I need to learn more!* Mubin excitedly concluded.

At home Mubin researched where he could go under the cover of learning Arabic. Mubin was already studying by distance for an undergraduate degree in religious studies. *Saudi,* Mubin thought, *No I won't get past the border with my textbooks, especially the Jewish Jesus! Scratch Saudi.* Egypt turned out too expensive. Syria looked good.

"If you want to study in Syria you can use my place," Jamal, a laborer in the mosque offered when he heard about Mubin's desire. Mubin jumped at the chance. Within weeks, he ordered his wife and their two kids' passports and went ahead to Damascus. Jamal's relatives picked him up at the airport.

Mubin could at this point recite the Qur'an in Arabic but he still wasn't fluent. He enrolled in Damascus University for Arabic language courses to ready himself to take studies in UsuleDeen (Islamic Studies). In his Arabic classes he met others gathered here from around the world—American's, British, Indian, Europeans—all learning Arabic and studying Islam. In the other classes there were Tunisians, Moroccans, and Egyptians, and middle-easterners. Mubin felt intimidated by those with so much Arabic knowledge. He also realized that some of them were militants. He couldn't yet tell who was who.

A year later, in April 2003, he would learn. Asif Muhammed Hanif, age twenty-two from London and Omar Khan Sharif, twenty-seven from Derby, stayed only a short time at the university. In April they left Damascus, traveled to Jordan and then crossed into Israel via the Allenby Bridge traveling to Tel Aviv. In Tel Aviv, they carried bombs to carry out a double suicide attack inside Mike's Place, a local bar located adjacent to the U.S. embassy. Only one of their bombs exploded. It killed Asif, and took three victims while injuring another fifty. The other bomb that Omar carried, cleverly hidden inside a book, malfunctioned. Omar then fled to the sea where he drowned. His body washed up almost two weeks later.

"AllahuAkbar!" the British students of Pakistani descent shouted when they heard the news of the Mike's Place bombing. Mubin wasn't sure how to react.

"I don't know how they can celebrate," Joanne, Mubin's wife complained. "Don't you remember our honeymoon travels in Israel? How blessed it was? That could have been us, blown-up!"

Mubin nodded, his doubts about following the militant jihadi ideology growing. *Yet Israel is guilty of many crimes against the Palestinians who have no army to fight them. If only the former Caliphate were reinstated—if only there were justice restored in this world and it were run as the Prophet (SalAllahuAlayhiWaSallam) instructed,* Mubin thought wondering if bringing the new order through violence could work as his militant brothers believed.

The Syrian government responded to the bombing by canceling many residency permits. Luckily Mubin's was not canceled.

***

"Brother be careful," a Syrian brother at the university warned. "Don't talk about Khilaafah here."

"I'm not calling for anything that is illegal or done by violence," Mubin answered.

"These people don't distinguish," the brother added. "As soon as you say Khilaafah, you are hauled away to prison."

"I'm not here for Khilaafah," Mubin protested. "I'm here to learn Arabic and study my religion." But Mubin realized that many were there for other reasons—like the Mike's Place bombers who had used their university registration simply to obtain short-term residency permits in Syria, making a stopover on the way to their target. Others were here to learn Arabic and to meet fellow jihadis, to prepare for the coming wars.

"Okay, brother just be careful," was the reply.

So free speech is not allowed here, Mubin noted, remembering how freely he could talk in Canada with the Salafis about their dreams for restoring the Caliphate.

"You are too Muslim looking," was the response Mubin got when he applied for English tutoring jobs to supplement the money his father was sending to support his studies. *So I'm in Syria—a Muslim country, but I'm too Muslim looking! Reminds me of when I couldn't get married in England despite devoting my life to Islam because my material prospects weren't good enough!* Mubin thought as he began feeling fed-up with the hypocrisies he was finding in the "Muslim world."

When Mubin needed to get his Royal Jordanian ticket exchanged in Amman he was put into interrogation and had to wait for hours with no success. Only days later did he realize that his ordeal had been caused by the official's desires for bribes that he hadn't clued into. Another lesson learned about how Muslim countries malfunctioned.

Mubin's Syrian neighbors in Damascus had been hauled off for supposedly being "radicals" and Mubin had sat on a bus with a victim of the mukhaabaraat—the secret police. The man was barely conscious when he had been loaded on the bus by the police and looked as though he had been beaten badly. No one dared speak to him and fear filled the bus until he was let off at the next mukhaabaraat center, probably to be jailed and tortured again.

I never really appreciated how free I was in Canada, Mubin mused. *You are not going to disappear if you stand outside a Canadian mosque and rail against the government there, but here if you do that, someone is surely going to grab you and throw you in prison. Maybe the West is more Islamic?* Mubin began to wonder.

***

The U.S. coalition invasion of Iraq broke while Mubin was in Syria and many of his fellow students decided to go from Syria to Iraq to fight jihad against the American coalition invaders. Even though his country's leaders had decided to join the Americans, Mubin was totally against the invasion of Muslim lands by infidel invaders and he longed to join those who were going to fight against them.

Three months into the conflict, Mubin encountered a bus readying to cross the border as he walked to the mosque.

"Abu Mujahid!" one his classmates suddenly shouted from the open bus door using Mubin's Arabic kunya or nickname that meant father of an Islamic warrior. "Come! We are going to jihad!" he added with a big smile on his face as Mubin saw that there were others from his class also on the bus.

SubhanAllah! They are going to Iraq! Mubin thought and for a split second he almost ran to the bus to join them. His classmates looked so elated to go and fight.

Joanne and the kids are back home. Mubin thought, restraining himself. *She doesn't speak much Arabic. I can't leave her to fend for the family alone here,* Mubin remembered and stopped himself from the urge to board their bus as he walked toward it.

"Oh you guys are so lucky!" Mubin said as he walked up to the bus. "In another life maybe, but not this time," he explained. "I'm here to study and I'll be going back home to Canada soon." Bidding them goodbye he tucked his books under his arm and walked away.

This is legitimate jihad, Mubin thought excitedly as he walked home imagining their adventures and regretting his lost opportunity. *This is self-defense from a foreign invasion! They have the right to jihad,* he concluded.

Allah keep them safe! Give them victory in this life and the next! Mubin prayed as he headed home.

He never saw his classmates again.

Deradicalizing

As his Arabic progressed Mubin joined a religious studies class at al Azhar Islamic University campus in Damascus at Masjid Al Fath with several well known Shuyukh (scholars). One in particular stood out. He was a young man—good looking, smelling of perfume. He wore long flowing robes, a bright white turban and he looked angelic—like a living saint. He was so well respected that even the older scholars would come and sit in his class. They called him Shaykh al Bahar, which meant a scholar with the knowledge of an ocean.

After a few weeks Mubin hung around after class to ask some questions from the lesson, on the grounds of Islamic belief. When everyone had gone, Mubin started in, "Shaykh, I wanted to discuss some things with you of who I am and what I believe."

"Who are you and what do you believe?" the Shaykh said in reply.

"I'm Abu Mujahid" Mubin stated referring to himself as the father of a holy warrior. It was a very clear statement for the Shaykh to understand, but Mubin went further saying, "I'm a jihadi."

"Oh, you are a jihadi are you? Good!" the Shaykh replied his face lighting up with an indulgent smile. "What is jihad? What does it mean?" he asked.

"It means to fight in the path of Allah," Mubin answered confidently.

The Shaykh smiled again, nodded and put his hand on Mubin's shoulder, "No, fighting in the path of Allah is qitaal," he corrected. "Tell me what jihad means," he asked again.

Mubin was suddenly mortified. He knew no other shades of the meaning of jihad other than what he knew of the Taliban, al Qaeda, and the former glories of the companions of the Prophet (SalAllahuAlayhiWaSallam). But the Shaykh was making it clear he didn't know the real meaning of jihad.

"What is the root of the word jihad?" the professor continued.

"I don't know," Mubin answered dumbstruck.

"The root of jihad means to struggle in a particular context," the Shaykh explained. "You have to show where the context supports fighting," he continued. "You can't just declare jihad on whim—on whose authority does one do so, their own? Where was this ever allowed in Islam?"

"What about the Mujahideen fighting all over the world?" Mubin asked excitedly.

"How do you know they are all fighting for Allah?" the Shaykh asked. "Some are fighting for land, some for power, some for name and fame. Do you know the Hadith (statement) of the Prophet (SalAllahuAlayhiWaSallam)," he asked and then masterfully quoted it in the Arabic, quoting line by line and then quoting the statements of the classical commentators (Mufassireen and Muhadditheen) as well. It spoke of the first person whose deeds would be judged by Allah; the one who claimed to have died as a shaheed (martyr). "The one who does so for name and fame, will be thrown into hellfire," he explained.

Mubin felt suddenly bewildered. *How could that be?* He had always thought if Muslim fighters claimed it was jihad, it must be true. *After all, these Islamic brothers were willing to sacrifice their lives for the cause!*

As he and the Shaykh discussed things further Mubin realized that all these years he had been sucking up their ideology he had never questioned or had any inkling that these very same people could be fighting for superficial, non-Islamic reasons.

Mubin was twenty-eight, but somehow he had kept his childhood beliefs intact. He was truly shocked to realize the people who looked like the fantasy of Islamic history that he had been fed in the madrasa mythology of Islamic unity and glory were not necessarily the heroes he imagined them to be. In fact even the heroes from long ago were far more nuanced than he'd believed—they'd fought amongst themselves and even killed each other.

"What do you do on Tuesdays and Thursdays after you are done with your classes?" the Shaykh asked, interrupting Mubin's thoughts. "Meet with me in the main area and come back to my house and we'll discuss these things further," he offered. Gratefully, Mubin accepted and thus began another line of learning.

***

The Shaykh's house was very nondescript on the outside, one of many row houses but when Mubin entered the first thing that hit him was the scent of sandalwood and jasmine oils. The Shaykh's children played on the main floor, but the Shaykh led him downstairs through a narrow corridor that opened up to take the full length of the building. It was like a double master bedroom but from the floor to the twelve-foot ceilings it was wall-to-wall books. There were books scattered all around the room as well. The only furnishings were a prayer rug, a wooden bench and a small table with a pen and teapot.

"Welcome to my study," the Shaykh said inviting Mubin to take a seat on the ornate carpet covering the floor. Soon after Mubin arrived the Shaykh's children came carrying a big plate of fruits and nuts. "Help yourself," he offered while Mubin gaped at the books surrounding him. There were so many collections of the authentic sayings of the Prophet (SalAllahuAlayhiWaSallam), books on exegesis (Tafseer), logic, and philosophy—including Greek philosophy.

"We are going to go through the whole Qur'an," the Shaykh began. "And every single verse that you think refers to jihad and killing—we are going to go through it word by word and we are going to consult multiple texts until we are satisfied we have discovered its true meaning."

There are one hundred and fourteen chapters and over six thousand verses in the Qur'an! Mubin thought amazed at the opportunity to study those related to jihad in such a manner.

The lesson began with Bismillah (invoking the merciful nature of Allah) as the Shaykh showed Mubin how much the scholars had gone into detail studying the first Arabic letter of bismillah and of how to take the name of Allah and so on. When they finished that day's lesson, Mubin was struck by how little he really knew about what he had up to then believed was his individual duty to carry out jihad for the sake of Islam, Islamic peoples and lands.

"I now see how much I need to learn," Mubin humbly concluded as he offered to pay for these lessons but the Shaykh refused money.

"This is my duty," he said shrugging off the offer to be paid. Perhaps he saw that by showing Mubin how little he actually knew about jihad he could knock down his confidence to act wrongly and he could divert a life devoted to needless and mistaken violence.

As Mubin continued his lessons he began to think back to the extremist Salafis who had been teaching him to embrace jihad. *They were like infants—they didn't even know Arabic and could only quote snippets of texts taken out of context! This narrow reading of scripture was the problem!* Mubin would later come to learn later that this is one of the ways in which radicalization occurs.[4] Here, there were many Salafis who were not extremists and who knew far more.[5]

Indeed Mubin was not the only young Muslim duped by so-called scholars who only cherry picked scriptures in order to justify and brainwash their students into their worldview and dedication to militant jihad. And many others would not be saved by a sympathetic teacher like Mubin had been and they would go on to commit acts of terrorism—as Mubin would soon learn.

***

"There is not just dar al Islam [land of Islam] and dar al Kufr [land of the unbelievers]," the Shaykh taught referring to the lands under Islamic rule and those not under Islamic rule—the latter that the militant jihadis believed they could attack and plunder at will. "There are many distinctions," the Shaykh continued. "Dar al ahad is the place of covenant, where you are given guarantees of safety, security, mobility and freedom of religion. If they don't prevent you from your worship you cannot war against them. If they don't fight you and expel you from your homes, you can not fight them," the Shaykh taught Mubin showing him the scriptures and hadiths proving his words.

Mubin was also pleased to learn that the Islamic ethics of battle as he was now being taught resonated to what he had learned in the Army Cadets. Wanton killing was forbidden. Killing had to be purposeful. Revenge was forbidden. Whereas he had been taught previously that anything goes, particularly if the enemy had already carried it out—based on the verse from the Qur'an (9:36) stating, "Fight them as they fight you"—he now learned that other verses prevented Muslims from lowering themselves to the tactics of their enemies.

The verse (Qur'an 5:8) "Let not your dislike for a nation cause you to be unjust," now informed Mubin that you cannot retaliate to war crimes by enacting them yourself, and you cannot kill civilians just because the enemy has. He also learned history and was struck that in the Crusades Salahuddin did not retaliate in kind to the crusaders who threw decomposing bodies over their firmaments as one of the precursors of biological warfare. Abu Sufyan, one of the greatest agitators against the Prophet (SalAllahuAlayhiWaSallam) was not killed, nor was wholesale slaughter of the people in warfare condoned. Some were executed, but most were absorbed into the victorious party. Abu Sufiyan became a governor in Syria after having fought the Prophet (SalAllahuAlayhiWaSallam), the Shaykh taught.

And Mubin was astonished to learn that Salahuddin's confidante and personal physician was none other than the Jewish sage, Maimonides who remains a pillar of authoritative Jewish teachings and very likely was influenced by the Sufism of Salahuddin himself—a fact that militants tend to conveniently forget when they extol the virtues of jihad against Jews for no reason other than they are Jews.

Everything the Shaykh imparted was conveyed with softness as they approached the texts and everything centered on the merciful nature of the Prophet (SalAllahuAlayhiWaSallam). "We have sent you as a mercy to the world," the Shaykh liked to quote from the Qur'an (21:107).

What does he want of me? Mubin wondered at first, marveling that the Shaykh was taking so much time and putting so much energy into him. *Oh no, is this another "uncle" type setup?* Mubin mused, his guard constantly up from conditioning.

But as the weeks became months it was clear that the loving kindness he displayed week after week of patiently explaining the Qur'an to Mubin slowly began to open Mubin's heart and redirect his inner anger into a force for good.

***

Once the Shaykh pointed out a child in the neighborhood and said, "You know a very bright child, if he gets armed with a little bit of knowledge can be quite dangerous." The Shaykh never asked Mubin about the source of his anger, yet slowly he began to heal it.

Mubin began to realize that he had imposed his own anger on the Qur'anic interpretations that he had believed supported militant jihad and that all along, he had been looking for something to validate his anger. Mubin's anger had been smoldering all these years inside, alongside all the angst of growing up biculturally in a very conservative community. He had never felt "good enough" for his parents and Islamic community and not fitting in, he had been yearning for something to validate the anger simmering just below the surface.

The militant jihadi interpretation of the scriptures had been just that. If he had to fit in the "Muslim" mold to please his parents—then jihad was going to be his way to work out his anger. It gave him an excuse for being totally reactive to any injustice—and there were plenty of them in the Muslim world. But now with total acceptance and loving kindness as his guidance,

Mubin felt freed of all of it.

Mubin had learned the ultimate lesson. It didn't matter what your physical look was, what level of education you had, or how many times you prayed. It only matters what kind of human being you are. And if you are not a human being you cannot be a Muslim. To be a full human being you need to respect the sanctity of human life and to fully embrace the scripture that says "to kill just one human being kills all of humanity," (Qur'an 5:32).

I wonder how many others who actually commit terrorist acts are just like me—angry kids who picked up a book of scripture and turned it into a book of violence and aggression? Mubin mused, thinking he would dedicate himself to helping others when he returned home.

All those kids have is jihadi groups waiting to prey upon their inner hurts and anger, Mubin thought, remembering how the extremist Salafis had welcomed and nursed his anger. They were so unlike the Shaykh whose calm and loving demeanor had rid him of nearly all of his inner cries for violence and revenge.

Mubin realized now that he was no longer dedicated to militant jihad and it was time to go home. Now Mubin could see plainly that Canada and the other Western countries—unlike the propaganda claims of the Khawarij (rebellious Muslims who kill, especially other Muslims unjustly in the name of Islam)—were the most free and blessed places to be a Muslim. Mubin had seen enough of Syria and their secret police, the mukhaabaraat. He yearned for his full Canadian freedoms.

Home Again—Shariah Law Spokesman

Arriving inside the Canadian border, Mubin was delighted to see his brother, Umar handing him a Tim Hortons coffee. It was March 2004.

"MashaAllah!" Mubin shouted accepting the coffee. "Tim Hortons—our national institution!"

Mubin had not been home for even a week and was driving with Abdulhakeem, his brother-in-law who was a Jamaican convert from the Nayabhingi, one of the branches of the Rastafarian way. They drove down Yonge Street in Toronto when he saw a large banner proclaiming, "No to Shariah courts in Ontario!"

"What is this?" Mubin asked his brother-in-law to pull over. "How is there a shariah court and I don't know about it?" Mubin asked. He walked toward the building under the banner and saw another picture on the wall. This one was of a veiled woman with only her eyes showing—depicted behind jail bars. It proclaimed, "Women are imprisoned when they wear veils."

Walking inside the building Mubin was surprised to run into his father with two of his colleagues exiting the building. Mubin's father had been doing faith-based mediation for their community for years and was highly respected for it. "You don't want to go in there," Abba warned. He explained that one of the Muslim groups had made a formal declaration to create a shariah body from these informal mediations and have them be binding arbitrations that would be recognized in Ontario courts but the anti-Muslim activists were going crazy.

"They say we are going to have stonings, chopping people's heads and other nonsense!" Abba warned. "Mubin you are not going to be able to sit in there. The place is filled with hateful rhetoric!"

"There's the mullah!" someone called pointing to Mubin. As it turned out some of the Muslim leaders had not shown up to give their point of view to the press and now Mubin arriving in his white robes and black turban appeared to fill the part. Suddenly Mubin became the "shariah spokesman".

It just so happened that part of Mubin's duties in serving his mosque was to facilitate the legalities of marriages, divorce, inheritance matters and even ritual burial. He had helped Muslim women with their legal forms many times and was very well informed about how the public justice system worked and did not work out for them.

"Women have their rights," he told the reporters. "Most will not go into courts of law anyway—their families view it as shameful and they are ostracized if they do. But if they come to the mosque we give them their rights. We inform them of all their legal rights and we counsel their husbands to respect them."

"Don't you tell husbands that the Qur'an gives them permission to hit their wives?" a reporter asked.

"Don't you believe that you can beat women?" another heckled.

"We teach them to do what the Prophet, SalAllahuAlayhiWaSallam [Peace be Upon Him], did and taught," Mubin answered, unperturbed. "He taught treat your wives as your partners and helpers, not your subordinates and slaves," Mubin explained. "And it is not even possible that the Canadian courts would ever accept any arbitration that would conflict with the Canadian charter of rights and freedoms," he added.

"Don't you believe in stoning for adultery like they do in Iran?" another reporter asked.

"We are not in Iran or Saudi Arabia. Those were punishments that people did in those days. In a desert society, that was the only way to deal with it. We have prisons and better ways nowadays. You don't need to fear this," Mubin explained.

"Are you going to be cutting off people's hands if they steal?" a reporter asked.

Laughing Mubin countered, "We don't deal with criminal law—only family law."

After that appearance Mubin became the face of the shariah courts in Ontario and even though it was a controversial position, he held his own and suddenly he was getting the validation he longed for. Mubin began to appear regularly in the newspapers and was invited to give talks and be on panel sessions across the city, including law schools, government offices and was now fielding phone calls from around the world by reporters, researchers and academics alike explaining how shariah courts would function.

"You are being seen as an extremist and Islamist," Mubin's father complained, but he was nevertheless proud of how well Mubin stood up to the anti-Muslim rhetoric and answered all questions with a calm and level head, using scriptures to explain and bolster his points.

***

While Mubin was gaining in public recognition of his studies and able to defend Islam on par with the intellectuals and activists who challenged him, so too was one of his former madrasa classmates. Momin Khawaja[6]—the boy who had told their Islamic studies teacher he would return his blows with a bigger stick. Momin was also appearing in the news—as a terrorist.

Momin, born to Pakistani immigrants had been arrested for his involvement in a plot to explode fertilizer bombs in the United Kingdom. Momin's alleged part in the plot was designing a cell phone jammer to be used as the detonator for the bombs.[7] When Mubin saw his childhood friend's picture in the paper, he couldn't believe it. It was April 2004.

There must be some mistake! Mubin thought remembering the kid who had played pranks alongside him on the madrasa bench. *A terrorist? No way!*

The news article reported that the Canadian Security Intelligence Service (CSIS) was the agency responsible for having caught Momin.

I have to tell them it's a mistake, Mubin thought. Looking up the CSIS phone number on the Internet, Mubin gave them a call.

"Canadian Security Intelligence Service," a woman's voice replied upon answering the line.

"Hey, I'm reading the newspaper, and it looks like you've arrested this person, Momin Khawaja," Mubin awkwardly explained. "There must be a mistake. I knew him and I want to give a character reference for him."

There was a slight pause on the other end of the line. "This is a case that is now in the courts," the woman explained. "It's out of the hands of CSIS at this time. Any additional information you'd like to add…"

"I know him. I knew him since he was a child and I just can't believe this is true—what's being said of him," Mubin broke in.

"Oh, well, what I can do is have an agent contact you and you can discuss it further if you like?" the woman offered.

Mubin agreed and gave the woman his name and phone number. Very shortly afterward, the phone rang.

"Hello, this is agent Michael Smith," the voice on the other end of the line began. "So, we understand you'd like to make a statement in support of Momin Khawaja," he probed.

"Yes, I would," Mubin answered.

"Okay, how about we meet at a local place and we can discuss this a little bit further." Agreeing upon a Tim Hortons coffee shop near Mubin's home in an hour's time, they hung up.

***

Mubin went to the coffee shop early. He thought nothing of the meeting—just that it would be a quick chit chat, an opportunity to tell this Michael Smith and the government that Momin Khawaja was from a very good family; that he had a very respectable father and a soft loving mother; that his father was a professor who taught in Saudi Arabia, and that they must have nabbed the wrong guy.

Sitting at Tim Hortons and watching out the window, Mubin saw the blue government car pull up in front and the CSIS agent get out of the car. Michael Smith was wearing a blue pinstripe suit, a brilliant white shirt and nice tie with dress shoes. His brown hair was cut short and he wore "white guy" glasses. Mubin sat calmly waiting in his Islamic robes, turban and glasses.

"Mr. Shaikh," Michael said extending his hand. "How are you Mr. Shaikh? We spoke on the phone. I'm interested to hear what you have to say," Michael said as he slid into the bench opposite Mubin.

"When I was in the madrasa in our neighborhood, long ago, Momin was in the madrasa with me," Mubin began. "And he lived in our apartment building. He was on the eighth floor and I was on the fifth. He lived in apartment 801. There must be a mistake!"

"This is in the courts now, and I can't really say anything about that," Michael demurred. "The courts will decide his fate," Michael replied. Then taking a hard look across the table he added, "I'm more interested in you." Michael was honing in on his trade. "What's your story?"

"My story is I just came back from Syria," Mubin answered, curious that this government man would be interested in his life. Michael was interested, and asked Mubin all about what he had been doing in Syria, what he had studied, who he had studied with and so on.

Mubin told him all about it adding, "I used to agree with blowing up the West, but not anymore—not after what I saw goes on there. I'm very positive about Canada now. And I really appreciate that here in Canada, I'm not going to disappear for holding dissenting opinions to the government from time to time, or put in a jail cell or beat up…"

Mubin's lifelong inner need to belong, to be validated, to be a good guy—to whoever and whichever community he was playing to—was still active and Michael could probably see that and played right into it.

"Sounds like you want to be a part of Canada, be the good guy?" he probed further.

"I served in the Army Cadets," Mubin offered and told Michael about the honors he had earned there. "And my father was the police chaplain in

Toronto for many years," Mubin added. "My grandfather even was a police officer and detective in India. He went on many undercover missions there. We come from good people."

"Would you be interested in consulting with the Canadian government?" Michael asked, his voice tentatively broaching the subject.

"Consulting? What does that mean and what does that entail?" Mubin asked, doubt lacing his voice.

"Well, our job is to make sure Canadians are safe," Michael explained. "You clearly like Canada and want Canada to be safe as well. We would like for you to tell us who you consider to be a threat to Canadian security, and who is not, because we don't want to waste time investigating people who are not," Michael went on. "And I value that you have an appreciation of both cultures. You know the people, the religion, the mindset. If we were to ask you to go and talk to some people are you able to tell us who is, and is not a threat?"

Mubin nodded trying to grasp what Michael was proposing. "These are people that you've arrested, or are interrogating?" Mubin asked.

"No, the mandate of CSIS is not to arrest but to gather intelligence and provide advance warning about activities that threaten national security," Michael explained. "When there is an actual threat we pass it on to the Royal Canadian Mounted Police who make the arrests. We would identify people we are concerned about and we'd send you to these people and you would just give us an assessment of them," Michael explained. "You could see if they held certain views of the world and the trajectory they would likely take—if it warrants further surveillance or not."

"I could do that," Mubin agreed. "I'm certain I could do that. After Syria I really understand the ideology of the militants[8]." Michael and Mubin discussed it further and Mubin was quite certain he was being offered a job, although no money was discussed. Wrapping up their discussion, Michael stood to leave.

"We'll reconvene another meeting, at some other place," he explained. "It's important you don't tell anyone that we had this conversation," he added before shaking hands with Mubin and making his goodbyes.

Going Undercover

Mubin went home and started researching CSIS on the Internet. *Oh they are a security intelligence organization,* he realized reading their description. *They send spies into places and to meet people…*

"I may have landed a consulting job," Mubin told Joanne as he waited to hear back from Michael.

"Really?" Joanne asked as she chased Eesa, their youngest for his diaper change. Joanne was pregnant again with their first daughter, Nadhirah and their savings and loans had been quickly depleted since their return from overseas, and so news of a job was welcome.

"What is it?" Joanne asked.

"It's working for Canadian Security to help them figure out who they need to keep an eye on among the radicalized Muslim population," Mubin explained. "I'm not sure how well it will pay, but they want me to help them sort out who might really engage in terrorism, and who is just spouting off ideology."

"Sounds like a worthy cause," Joanne answered from the next room where she had caught up to Eesa.

Meanwhile Mubin read more about his old friend Momin who he had not seen since he was nine years old. According to the newspapers Mubin pieced together that Momin had reportedly gotten radicalized as a young man and even traveled in 2002 for a three month trip to Pakistan under the subterfuge of finding a wife, but had been planning to join the Taliban. Failing to do so Momin returned to Canada and continued deepening his commitment to militant jihad.[9]

He got lucky when he landed a job as a software developer working as a contractor for the Canadian Department of Foreign Affairs. This job essentially gave him an insider track. From there, Momin reportedly joined other "wannabe" extremists in practicing for jihad in the Canadian forests on paintball and pellet ranges. There, he covered his tracks by signing in under pseudonyms.[10]

Just because he traveled to Pakistan and played paintball doesn't make him a terrorist, Mubin thought as he read on. Yet as Mubin continued watching the case unfold he saw that Momin was accused of attending a one-day terrorist training camp in Pakistan and more importantly of helping British extremists make their bomb detonators out of a cell phone jammer and that his counterparts in the UK were deadly serious. They had stockpiled enough of—what they believed was—fertilizer to make some extremely lethal truck bombs. Ultimately Momin received a ten-year sentence from the courts that, much later under appeal, was extended to a life sentence. [11]

Reading his story Mubin remembered his friend threatening their teacher, "I'll get a bigger stick and hit you." *Well, I guess he tried to do it,* Mubin thought shaking his head with sadness.

***

Michael called a few days later and proposed meeting at the Grand Renaissance Hotel, downtown Toronto. Mubin arrived and took the elevator upstairs to the designated room. From the window he smiled to see that the room had a perfect view of a protest demonstration being held that day in front of the U.S. Embassy. *That's not by accident,* he thought.

This time there were two agents, Michael and another who introduced himself as AJ Brown. They were both in white shirts with ties and wore khaki pants and dress loafers.

"Tuna sandwiches okay with you?" Michael asked as he ordered room service. "What would you like to drink?"

"Canada Dry," Mubin answered.

"Our first order of business after today, is to do a polygraph," Michael explained. "You've been overseas in some dicey regions and we need to be sure you are who you say you are. Normally we are dealing with people who are from here and they don't have recent trips," he added apologetically. "That will be our next meeting, okay?"

Mubin nodded.

"Tell us about yourself," AJ prompted, and Mubin began to go back over the territory he had already covered with Michael. They both asked many questions about why he had traveled, to where and whom he had met.

When the sandwiches arrived and he was deep into telling about his travels, Mubin held up his drink and told them, "Once when we were traveling in India for the Tablighi Jamaat, we pulled into this dusty town there was a poster of Canada Dry ginger ale and I was so happy seeing it. And then, they actually had it! You can't imagine how happy I was! A little piece of Canada, way out there!"

After going through all his travels and foreign contacts, the agents seemed satisfied and left shaking hands with Mubin. "We'll be in touch shortly—for the polygraph," Michael repeated upon taking his leave.

It was a few more days before that phone call came and again they met at a hotel room, although a different one than previously. This time the blinds were drawn and the room was darkened. And it was only Agent AJ and another guy who was the polygrapher. The polygrapher was dressed in a navy suit and glasses. He didn't introduce himself other than to say, "I'm from the service and my job here is to conduct a polygraph test and your job is to answer truthfully and honestly to every question I ask you, okay?"

Mubin nodded.

"Ready then?" he asked. Mubin nodded again while he allowed the technician to attach electrodes to his index and second fingers, wrap wires around his chest and waist and attach a blood pressure cuff to his upper arm.

"So, you work out?" the polygrapher asked, admiration tingeing his voice, as he stretched the cord on the chest strap to make it fit.

"Yeah," Mubin answered. Already he could feel his anxiety rising. The polygrapher sat down then at a desk near Mubin's chair. The light from his laptop eerily lighting up the man's face making Mubin even more nervous.

"We'll start with a set of control questions," the polygrapher explained.

Mubin nodded trying to calm his racing heart.

"Is your name Mubin Shaikh?" the man asked glancing at his laptop screen. Mubin's eyes followed, but the screen was pointed away from Mubin's line of vision.

"Yes," Mubin answered.

"Are you born and raised in Canada?"

"Yes."

"Are you of Jamaican descent?"

"No!" Mubin answered, laughter filling his voice. *That's fairly obvious from my Indian complexion,* Mubin thought.

"Are you married?"

"Yes."

"What were you doing in Syria?" the man asked moving into the serious portion of the exam. Again he repeated all the questions Michael and AJ had already asked him. There were many and it took some time.

"Did the Syrian government send you here to work for them?" the polygrapher asked shocking Mubin.

"What?" Mubin scoffed.

"Please answer yes or no," the polygrapher instructed, his voice and face displaying nothing.

"No!!!" Mubin answered.

The polygrapher stared intently at his screen and then looked up. "Let's take a short break," he said. "I can see you are a bit upset at the question. I apologize."

Mubin nodded thinking, *Me—working for the Syrians? Me—counter-intelligence? Man after all the crap I saw there? Don't they know that's why I left Syria? Their government is so corrupt and there are no freedoms like here!*

The polygrapher released Mubin from his bonds and Mubin took the opportunity to use the bathroom. When he returned the technician hooked him back up again and they resumed.

"Did the Syrian government send you here to work for them?" the polygrapher repeated.

"No," Mubin answered calmly this time.

"What do you anticipate doing with the Service?" he asked next.

"I understand I'm to help figure out who in the Muslim community poses a real threat to Canadian security," Mubin answered.

"Will you be truthful and honest in dealing with the Service?"

"Yes."

"Have you told anybody about this meeting?"

"No," Mubin lied. He had told Joanne.

"You are not telling the truth," the polygrapher said turning his chair to face Mubin directly. "I told you that you have to tell the truth."

It felt like a classic police interrogation scene. *How did he read me so easily Mubin wondered? Does my conscience just not allow for dishonesty? But if I'm to be an undercover operative,* Mubin thought, his mind racing, *doesn't that require some ability to be dishonest?*

"I did tell my wife," Mubin admitted. "That's normal isn't it?"

"Did you tell anyone else?" the polygrapher asked without giving any hint of emotion on his face to Mubin's admission.

"No," Mubin answered truthfully.

"Did you tell any member of the Syrian government?"

"Of course not!" Mubin spat out. "I told my wife because I wanted to tell her who I am repeatedly meeting with. If I say I can't tell her, she might start to think I'm seeing another woman!" Mubin nervously chuckled.

"Other than your wife, have you told anyone else?"

"No."

"Okay that's it," the polygrapher said as he rose to pull the wires off Mubin's hand, arm and body. He then carefully wrapped up the wires and placed them back in his bag. He slipped his laptop in next and told Mubin, "You are free to go."

"Please remember don't tell anyone else what you've been doing," AJ added as he shook hands with Mubin. "It's important, for your own safety."

Mubin walked out of the hotel room and down the hallway. *Something's off with that guy, his vibes are weird,* Mubin mused about the polygrapher as he ambled down the hallway to the elevator.

They are probably watching me leave, he thought as he entered the lobby. *I wonder how many of them are here. They've probably been watching me since I left home...*

On the train Mubin went back over the questions. *Oh my God they thought I was working for Syria!* Mubin remembered, still shocked over that.

"So how did the job interview go?" Joanne asked when he returned home.

"Pretty good. They polygraphed me," Mubin replied. "And they asked me if I was working for the Syrian government!"

Joanne burst out laughing. "Are you kidding me?" she exclaimed.

"Seriously, the Syrian government of all people!" Mubin stormed.

"You know honey, you are doing the right thing. After what we saw in Syria on both sides of these issues," Joanne said. "We're on the right page."

"I guess I'll see what happens," Mubin answered sitting down to check his e-mail.

***

A few days later a call came from AJ. "Your interview was successful," he said. "We would like to take our working relationship to the next stage. This time meet me in the Ikea front parking lot. We'll leave your car there and I'll pick you up."

Mubin did as he was told, meeting AJ as planned. AJ drove them to their meeting place, again a hotel. "Wait here for a few minutes until no one is around. Then come up to room 1011. I'll be waiting for you there," AJ instructed.

When Mubin arrived this time he noticed there was already a Canada Dry on ice, waiting on the table for him.

This guy is good, Mubin thought.

AJ held out to him a new phone still in its box. "I put my number on speed dial," he said handing it over. "Don't put any other numbers on this phone and don't show it to anyone else. And never use it for any other purpose." AJ instructed. Then he dialed Mubin to check that it was working and had Mubin dial him back. It worked.

Okay, now we are getting into the spy toys! Mubin thought as he smiled in appreciation.

"We'll need you three days a week, four hours minimum each time," AJ explained. "We'll pay you fifteen hundred dollars in cash per month."

Mubin ran the numbers in his head. *Okay, thirty dollars an hour to put my life on the line,* Mubin thought. *But I'm not doing this for the money,* he reminded himself and nodded his agreement.

"You'll have to claim it on your taxes," AJ added. "Put it under other income. Okay, let's get down to business," AJ continued. "Your first task relates to information that just came in. There is this imam who might be linked to the Taliban and we need you to conduct an eyes and ears verification of what we are getting from guys who are less trustworthy than you. They are passively bringing in information, but we are actively sending you out to collect," AJ explained as he passed Mubin the imam's name.

"I know him!" Mubin exclaimed.

"That's why we hired you," AJ answered with a smile.

"Listen, this is completely false," Mubin started. "There is no way he's with the Taliban. I've heard him condemn the Taliban for some of the things they are doing."

"We want you to go and talk to him and confirm or deny," AJ explained.

***

"Shaykh, I want to come and talk about some fiqh issues," Mubin said over the phone to Imam Khalid.

"Sure, come on Sunday after prayers," the imam answered. Mubin had already been there previously to talk about fiq—Islamic jurisprudence. He knew Mubin well and also knew that Mubin had studied in Syria. As a result he did not appear to suspect Mubin at all and likely never dreamed that Mubin had been sent by CSIS to query him about his opinions of the Taliban, al Qaeda and militant jihad.

Mubin ran the conversation as previously but this time inserted questions about the topics of interest to CSIS. When he asked the imam about the Taliban he answered, "The Taliban position on this point is absolutely wrong. Some of the things they are doing and saying you cannot justify in any law of Fiqh." The conversation continued until Mubin had exhausted all of his maneuvers and was satisfied that this imam would never support militant jihad.

"The content of your report is completely false," Mubin told AJ when they met next. "Who would have said this against him?"

"Well, actually it was another imam," AJ answered not naming the informant.

How could another imam do this to a member of our community? How could he refer them to a non-Muslim agency? Mubin mused saddened to hear it. *It must be jealousy or wanting revenge for something or other,* Mubin concluded.

***

His next assignment was to try to get close to Said Hussain, a leader of a Toronto group that advocated for various political reforms in the Muslim world, including the notion of establishing a Caliphate. "Tell us what he's about," AJ instructed. "What are they up to and what their beliefs are and put that in the context of a risk assessment for dangerousness to Canada."

Mubin was already scheduled to take part in a major Islamic conference that was taking place in Toronto that weekend. "That will be easy," Mubin said. "I'll see him this weekend." AJ smiled in response. "And I can tell you already that group's ideology calls for removing dictators and replacing them with religiously-minded rulers. Whether this guy endorses doing it violently is the question I suppose?"

AJ nodded.

Mubin went with his wife, Joanne to the conference and finding the group's booth, conversed with Said Hussain about the group's aims and objectives.

"The Muslim government should be established, brother," Mubin told Said after listening with interest. "It's just a matter of what mechanisms should be used," he added.

"Perhaps you'd like to have dinner with me and my wife tonight after the conference?" Said asked.

Bingo! Mubin thought. *This is too easy!* After the conference the two couples drove in their respective vehicles to Said's house in the suburbs. It was a stand alone house with no overt Islamic identity to mark it. Inside they all sat together in the same room and had a meal served by Said's wife as Mubin and the leader chatted about the details of what he believed. Mubin was in agreement with nearly all he said.

"May I use your restroom?" Mubin asked later into the night. Said rose and took him upstairs.

"The bathroom is right there," Said said pointing down a long hallway. As Mubin walked to the bathroom he heard Said go back downstairs. Mubin made a look around. There was even a third floor so he quickly crept upstairs to have a look there too. Just as he went back into the bathroom to actually use it and he flushed the toilet he heard Said outside in the hallway again.

"Everything alright?" Said asked.

Mubin emerged, smiled and nodded.

That night after taking Joanne home, Mubin dialed in to AJ and arranged for a meeting.

"I don't think he's a threat," Mubin reported. "I had a look around his house. I didn't see any weapons or evidence of suspicious activity."

"Can you draw a floorplan of the house and all the points of entry?" AJ asked.

"Sure," Mubin answered sitting down to draw the various floors.

***

The assignments kept coming, most of them mundane with Mubin clearing the names of many people in his community without them ever even knowing they had been temporarily under suspicion.

Then Mubin was asked to try to infiltrate a group to learn how guys were going off to Yemen to join al Qaeda in the Arabian Peninsula.

"We know some Canadians have gone and we think these local Salafi guys are arranging their travel and meetings over there," AJ explained. "Can you go and meet them?"

Mubin went to hang with the Salafis at their mosque and sat in on a lesson on one of the books of the Prophetic traditions. The teacher asked the audience a question on Arabic grammar and Mubin's hand immediately shot up. Having studied so long in Syria it was easy for him.

"Brother, your Arabic is good," one of the Salafis, said afterwards, as the others gathered around him. "If you could answer questions like that you should probably go and further your studies somewhere."

"I did," Mubin answered proudly. "I went to Syria!"

"Did you get in touch with Shaykh Abdulwahaab?" they asked referring to a famous Salafi scholar living there.

"Yes I did," Mubin answered. "And I met the brothers around him."

One of the Yemeni brothers came forward as he listened to Mubin. "You know we have some brothers in Yemen," he said. "If you wanted, you could go and study in Yemen."

"Yemen?" Mubin asked pretending to think it over as he thought, *This is perfect!*

"We can get you to Yemen," the brother continued excitedly. "We can arrange a pick up for you at the airport, where you stay, everything. We can even arrange a small stipend for you and your family there."

"That sounds interesting," Mubin deliberated. "How would it work?"

"Well, you get your ticket, and we'll take care of everything after that," the brother explained.

"What do you mean?" Mubin asked. "Because I'm with my family and I have to be sure everything is good on that side."

"You fly in and someone is waiting for you. They will take you from the airport. Then they switch vehicles and you go through the desert a bit," he explained lowering his voice. "We have a place there where our brothers are staying and studying."

"What is the situation with married couples?" Mubin asked trying to stay cool.

"They have residences and there are many Westerners there, studying, who are also married—brothers from Canada, Europe and the U.S. You won't be alone."

Mubin nodded thinking, *Oh yeah!* He already knew this was a jihadi friendly group but it had almost been too easy to get inside.

"It's a disconnected compound, off the radar," the brother went on. "It's a stand alone place. You should go and talk to your wife about it," he encouraged.

Mubin called AJ that night and they met to discuss things. On the way there Mubin thought, *Oh wow, this is a point of no return. What if they want me to actually go and I get caught as a jihadi by the Yemeni authorities?*

"I'm not sure you could even get into Yemen," AJ said as they discussed the possibilities. "But if you could, would you be willing to try?"

Mubin nodded soberly.

"If you could get past the Yemeni authorities we would want you to identify specific individuals we have under surveillance in conjunction with our allies like the Americans, British and Australian," AJ explained as he rubbed his brow. "We would need you to map out the entire area, including the buildings in which weapons might be stored and where women and children might be residing so as to avoid civilian casualties if we were to attack."

This is for real! Mubin thought.

"We would also need you to make contacts with other jihadi recruiters and operatives who might be there at the camp and see where their own links go into Europe and elsewhere," AJ continued.

"And lastly we'd want you to plant an RFID chip in the camp so we could try to locate it—after you left, of course," AJ explained his face suddenly become deadly serious.

"And how would I carry one of those into an al Qaeda camp?" Mubin asked incredulous. "What if they found it on me? What if it fell out of my bag?"

"It's a tiny device," AJ explained smiling wryly.

"And you want me to put it up my butt?" Mubin joked. "You know that's not going to happen!"

"No you'd tape it to your crotch," AJ said his face total serious. "No one would look there. But let's see if you can even get the visa to go before we take this any further."

***

"Honey do you want to go to Yemen?" Mubin lightheartedly asked Joanne the next day.

"Oh Allah! Not again!" she chortled.

"There are going to be other women there," Mubin cajoled. "It won't be like Syria. We are not going to be isolated. There will be other married couples there, English speaking people and they have a married quarters.

Our kids will have other kids to play with."

"Is this for your people?" Joanne asked suspiciously.

"You know I can't discuss details, but yes they want us to go," Mubin answered. "They are discussing it. But I have to know first if you are on board."

"If you want to go, we'll go," Joanne answered smiling.

This is the stuff that movies are made of! He thought. *I notice that I have a natural ability to move as the agents do, but I'm the one on the ground doing the actual operations. This is will show CSIS that I am here to endorse that Islam is not about terrorism and sometimes it takes a Muslim to stop those that think it is.* "Stop your brother when he is the oppressor," Mubin remembered as one of the hadiths of the Prophet (SalAllahuAlayhiWaSallam). Other verses that commanded, "do not spy" (Qur'an 49:12) applied to spying for the purposes of gossip, but not to security. Whereas this was clearly about public safety and extremism in religion—things that the Prophet (SalAllahuAlayhiWaSallam) specifically spoke of and condoned.

AJ had explained that this was an investigation related to Canadians—fellow citizens—who may have been present at the alleged camp. Mubin knew from his studies of the Qur'an that spying was allowed in this case as it was the responsibility of the government to be aware of such threats, especially where individuals had gone over as foreign fighters and were now returning with battlefield trauma due to exposure to brutal acts of violence as well as having possibly acquired terrorist training.

Mubin also knew very few, if any Western intelligence agents had managed to infiltrate al Qaeda. Mubin's fears darted around in his mind, especially of carrying an RFID chip in with him.

After applying for his visa to go to Yemen, Mubin kept returning to the mosque where he told the Salafi brothers that he wanted to join their group. "I just need a bit of time," Mubin told them. "I have to give advance notice to my job and I have to convince my wife's parents. They are not Muslims and I don't want them to think I'm running away with their daughter," Mubin explained.

As it turned out the Yemenis wouldn't grant the visa. "They think you are an extremist after your time in Syria," AJ explained. "The mission is cancelled."

Mubin felt sad but also relieved that he didn't have try to deceive al Qaeda operatives in Yemen that he was the real thing—there was so much risk. Joanne was more than just relieved.

***

"We want you to check out the son of a prominent imam. He's been giving firebrand lectures and railing against U.S. foreign policy for some time," AJ explained. "But now we're concerned about his son, Jamal, as well. He's an engineer and works in a sensitive bio lab. If he adheres to beliefs like his father, he could be a serious danger because of the access he has," AJ explained.

Mubin showed up at their mosque the next week. He already knew both the father and son, but he approached neither. Instead he sat talking to some of the other guys. "I can teach a self defense seminar here," he offered. "I've studied close-quarter combat."

Mubin's offer was well received and soon he was teaching some of the brothers how to fight up close. "Do you think we could ever lure some CSIS agents into a trap?" Mubin asked some of them to try to get a gauge on their thinking. *I don't want to entrap them,* Mubin thought, *but I need to understand what they are willing to do.*

"No, it's not a good idea," the brothers said. But they also made clear that they didn't like the government and were pro-jihad.

"It will just bring more heat," one of them said. "You can't do that without expecting them to come after you. Maybe you should talk to Jamal," they offered. "He's more into your line of thinking."

Mubin relayed his findings back to AJ and asked, "Do you want me to follow up on Jamal?"

"No," AJ answered. "We've got him covered."

Next Mubin was asked to infiltrate some online forums. "We have some online tasking for you," AJ explained. "It's a repository of suicide bombings and beheadings that took place in Iraq since 2005," AJ said opening his laptop to show the sites to Mubin.

"I haven't seen a beheading video since the Chechens in the mid-nineties," Mubin said watching the horrific videos AJ was pulling up. "They've sure stepped up their video productions since then!"

"We want you to use your own computer with no IP bouncing so there's no suspicions raised that you are security," AJ said. "And you'll have to read the comments and develop your own leads. We basically want to know who is really into this."

***

At home Mubin signed into the forum creating the online handle of StealthfighterJ—with J for jihad. As he chatted with the participants he could see they were just kids—most of them boys. Half the time they would joke about the girls at school. Then they would suddenly move from juvenile joking around to talking quite seriously about jihad.

"I hate flags, I hate countries... I hate man made laws.... I hate nationalism with a passion... I love for the Sake of Allah and I hate for his sake," Mubin read one post. The author went by the name of Aleph—signifying the first letter of the Arabic alphabet.

Later Mubin would meet the author in person—Zakaria Amara—one of the leaders of the Toronto 18. "When the islamic [rule] comes back..." Aleph posted, "there will be no palisitne flag, no philipino flag... no pakistani, somali, american, or british flag... it will just be 1 flag [sic]."[12]

Mubin could see here that "Aleph" was experiencing the same frustrations of identity with national citizenship. A lot of these kids felt they did not belong and thought of the Muslim "Ummah" (nation) as their self-identity. The trouble was, it was constructed as if mutually exclusive to Western identity.

In late April of 2004, Zakaria Amara's wife posted in response to a question asking the forum members to share their impressions of what makes Canada unique replying, "Who cares? We hate Canada."[13]

Some of the forums were password protected but Mubin made his way into one through a girl he befriended. She started flirting with Mubin.

"Can you let me into the password forum?" Mubin asked her. "I'd like to download some of the jihadi videos," he explained. Boom—she gave him her password. Mubin downloaded everything he thought the agency would want to see and noted—*she seems quite serious about jihad.*

"If you can find us her address, we'll pay you a bonus," AJ said the next time they met. When he got home from that meeting, Mubin was suprised to receive an inquiry from the Canadian tax authorities asking him to name the source of his "other income."

Obviously, the various branches of the Canadian government aren't so good at communicating with each other! Mubin thought, laughing as he put it in his pile of things to discuss in his next meeting with AJ.

Back on the forums, Mubin wrote to the girl, "I work for a courier company. I want to send you some DVDs that I think you'll be interested in."

Boom—she gave him her address.

AJ was impressed. Much later, Mubin would be involved in the arrest of one of her male associates, Fahim Ahmad—the main leader of the Toronto 18—who was plotting to kill and terrorize Canadians in numerous ways.

Infiltrating the Toronto 18

"**H**i Mubin, I have another project for you," AJ said over the phone. "Meet me at the Sheraton." It was November 2005.

When he arrived there was another agent with AJ. Both were dressed in their khaki pants, dress loafers and bright white business shirts and ties.

"This is Agent Frank, he comes to us from the UK, but he works for us now," AJ explained. Frank had a binder with him.

"There are some guys we want you to get to know," he said opening the binder containing over a dozen color photos of mostly young men. Mubin scanned their faces, as Frank talked about target one, target two, etc.

This is a very impersonal approach to real people, Mubin thought as he tried to follow Frank's monologue. Frank pushed the binder over to Mubin who continued to study the photographs of faces. There were sixteen of them and they ranged from baby faced to adults—all different ethnicities, colors and ages. The room became enveloped in silence as Mubin struggled to remember their faces.

What the hell is going on here? he wondered. *Before there were only four or five targets max. Why are there so many guys this time?*

"Do you recognize any of them?" AJ asked after Mubin had studied them for a bit.

"Nope, never saw any of them before in my life," Mubin replied, looking up. "What's going on here?"

"That's why you are here—to find out," AJ answered. Then pointing to who Mubin would later learn was Fahim Ahmad, AJ said, "He'll be the guy with the Coke bottle glasses."

"What's the mission?" Mubin asked.

"Same as always," AJ answered, closing the book. "Tell us what they are about, what they are up to and if they are dangerous."

"Okay, I can do that," Mubin answered. "Where do I meet them?"

"There's an event taking place November 27th at the North York's Taj banquet hall downtown Toronto," AJ explained. "It's a presentation about some individuals who have been arrested and detained on immigration charges based on secret intelligence. There is this whole issue of detaining individuals based on secret intel and this event will depict their plight,[14]" he said somewhat tiredly.

"Wait a second," Mubin said. "I've been invited to that! I know the place and the organizer!"

AJ and Frank both shook their heads as if to say *what are the chances of that?*

"Yeah I could definitely do this," Mubin exclaimed, his interest in the mission growing.

"It's very important Shaikh," AJ said, using his habit of addressing Mubin by his last name, "that you don't encourage them to do anything they wouldn't do on their own. And you want to be extra careful on this case."

"Is the threat level elevated?" Mubin inquired.

"Don't worry, we'll be close by," AJ reassured.

What Mubin didn't know was that CSIS had already alerted the Royal Canadian Mounted Police (RCMP) on November 17, 2005 (ten days before the event) that Fahim Ahmad was a threat to national security, and that the RCMP had just begun parallel surveillance on the same group. Their surveillance effort was code named Project Osage and in time approximately seven hundred police officers would come to work on the case. And Mubin would become the central figure in it.

Likewise already in October 2005, police in the UK had arrested Younes Tsouli, a young Moroccan, living in west London. Tsouli had become one of the most significant figures among a growing network of cyber jihadis. Using the pseudonym Irhabi 007—which was an Arabic reference to himself as a terrorist James Bond—Tsouli set up websites and forums in support of al Qaeda and distributed propaganda and recruiting films made by the Iraqi insurgents. His encrypted hard drive, captured by intelligence agents, proved to be a treasure trove of evidence leading to extremists around the world who had been using Tsouli's password-protected Internet forums to exchange their views on jihad. Following leads from it, law enforcement officials were finding out who was talking to whom on a serious level and plotting to commit militant jihadi terrorist acts in various parts of the world.

Following the arrest of Younes Tsouli, West Yorkshire Police officers in the UK also began observing the activities of Aabid Khan who had worked in support of one of Tsouli's key websites, at-Tibyan Publications. After Tsouli's arrest—in October 2005—Khan slipped out of the UK in January of 2006, leaving for Pakistan where he was supporting Canadians and Americans who wanted to get into terrorist paramilitary training camps. But unknown to Khan and his followers, the UK authorities were now onto him.[15]

Slowly a noose was closing around a large international group of young and older men—and their wives—who were inciting and planning terrorist attacks in the West and Europe. And Mubin was about to infiltrate the Canadian group.

***

It was November 27, 2005 and Mubin arrived at North York's Taj banquet hall in his van, the tires crunching on the fresh snow that covered the ground—including the parking lot. It was still snowing and freezing cold outside.

When Mubin arrived, he saw that it was still early and the organizers were the only ones there, still setting up. Mubin took his place at the far end of a long table near the presenters. There were many more, still empty, tables behind him. Mubin looked around taking in the room, feeling this time his work was more important than usual.

There's something important but evil going on here. I have to find out what it is, he mused as he glanced around. *The bathroom is there, closet over there, screen set up in front; I came in the kitchen entrance. There is another exit door there.* He was readying himself for anything—just in case.

Soon after Mubin was seated, a young man entered. His face was covered by a red kefiyyeh—a Palestinian white and red-checkered scarf. He walked across the room and sat right beside Mubin, and took off his scarf.

Boom—it's Zakaria Amara, one of the guys pictured in the book! Mubin realized. He didn't yet know his name, but he sure as hell remembered the face—*Target Number Two!*

Alright, it's on! Mubin thought as his body cycled between anxiety, enthusiasm, excitement and fear. For the first time in a while, there were butterflies in his stomach.

"My name is Abu Mujahid," Mubin said, introducing himself to Zakaria Amara by his Arabic kunya or nickname.

"I'm Ilias," Zakaria said using his Arabic kunya as well referring to Prophet Elijah (Peace be Upon Him). "How are you doing? I live close by..."

"Oh Mubin! How are you?" the conference organizer interrupted as he stopped at their table recognizing Mubin. He was obviously pleased to see Mubin at his event.

Ilias watched taking it in as Mubin chatted animatedly with the organizer. Out of the corner of his eye, Mubin noticed Target Number One—Fahim Ahmad, enter with another of the targets—Ameen Duranni and five others, individuals who Mubin wasn't sure if they were in the CSIS book or not.

Mubin politely took his leave of the organizer and turned back to Ilias. The others had come to join him but since there were not enough chairs at Mubin's table they moved to the next table. Mubin followed and joined them.

"Hey brother, AssalaamuAlaykum," he said to Ameen Durrani. "I recognize you," he added, making it up. "Have you been around the Meadowvale mosque?" As it turned out he had and he recognized Mubin as well.

Well that fake worked out well, Mubin thought recognizing that the brothers now accepted him as "safe."

The presentation began with the organizer explaining how convicted murderers in prison are allowed to touch their children, but the Muslim guys picked up on secret intel and being held under Canadian "Security Certificates" were not afforded the same rights as convicts. "They are being kept behind glass and can't even touch their family members," the organizer criticized. "And they are not even convicted yet of any crime! It's not right!"

Mubin looked around the hall during the talk at the many militant-minded and angry young Muslims who had found their way to this lecture. *They are probably unable to grasp the more sophisticated legal points on the subject and feel only a deeply subsiding anger over having Muslims detained in Western penal institutions under what they believe is some kind of conspiracy against Islam and Muslims,* Mubin reflected, recalling how he once felt the same anger inside.

Fahim Ahmad, who introduced himself by his kunya as well—Sinaan, meaning Spearhead, was definitely of this ilk. He kept making snide jihadi related comments for those at his table to hear. As the speaker spoke of the inner jihad, which is not militant, Fahim twisted the speaker's words by adding to his reference to peaceful jihad the ending of "with swords" for those at Fahim's table to hear. And when the presenter spoke about their jihad as a struggle against injustice, Fahim added "with guns" making those at his table snigger with delight.

After it was over Mubin followed Ameen Durrani and Fahim Ahmad outside. Mubin walked over to them near the entrance as he overheard the two speaking about the need for Muslims to defend themselves.

"That's so true," Mubin commented as he joined them. "I took martial arts training for just that purpose." Unsure how to continue, Mubin walked over to his van parked near them and opened the sliding door. Luckily for him his baseball bat fell out—almost on cue.

"You play baseball in the winter?" Fahim asked laughing.

"No this is my alarm system," Mubin said. "If I'm alarmed I give them the system," he joked.

The guys laughed as Mubin threw the bat back into his van.

"Muslims are persecuted here and the world over," Fahim continued and Ameen nodded in agreement. Mubin was now welcomed in their conversation.

"You've always got to have your guard up around here," Mubin said guiding the subject into new territory. "When I tried to get into Yemen, the authorities there kept me for four days and wouldn't let me in—they thought I was too extreme!" Mubin said fabricating a story. "But then CSIS came to my house asking questions. Of course, I didn't want anything to do with them!" Mubin spat, hoping to gauge their reactions to Canadian security. Zakaria Amara had joined while Mubin told his story.

"If the CSIS agents come to my house," Fahim said using his right hand to make a shooting gesture to indicate what he would do.

"You have access to weapons?" Mubin probed to which Ameen and Fahim went silent. "I have my firearms license," Mubin volunteered. Seeing their eyes widen in excitement, he pulled it out to show to them. "And I have military training!"

"Isn't it the great blessing that Allah sends people like this to us?" Ilias (Zakaria Amara) said in amazement.

If Allah sent me, it's not for the reason you think, Mubin thought as he waited to find out what would come next.

***

"Is jihad fard ayn or fard kifaayah? Zakaria quizzed Mubin asking him in Arabic terms whether he believed jihad is a personal or communal obligation—if he believed he should personally take up arms or if it should be done by others. It was a classic jihadi question—and all militant jihadis believed jihad is an individual obligation (fard ayn).

"Of course fard ayn," Mubin answered endorsing the individual duty that al Qaeda and other militant jihadi groups preach. It was not what he in fact believed as he had learned from the Shaykh in Syria that there is an *individual duty* only to one's domestic surrounds and only if people in the affected area are unable to answer the call of defense. And as Mubin had learned, there is *not* an individual duty to militant jihad for fighting in far-away lands as extremist groups preach. Jihad was legitimate, but not as an excuse for power and politics, but instead only when framed in ethics and proportionate responses. But now with these guys Mubin put on the face that he endorsed violence against innocents and that this was an integral part of Islam.

"Hey let's go over here for a second," Fahim said pulling Mubin and Zakaria along with him.

"So are you guys about to rob me?" Mubin joked. "Do I have to defend myself?"

"I don't know can you dodge bullets?" Zakaria asked. Then he hugged Mubin and as he did so, Mubin felt something hard on him.

"Is this something in your pocket, or are you happy to see me?" Mubin joked.

Zakaria put his hand in his pocket and Mubin heard the distinct click of the release of the magazine from his gun. Zakaria pulled his hand back out bearing a magazine of bullets. "You see these," he said holding up the hollow point bullets. "These are cop killers."

"You can see what's happening in the Muslim world," Fahim chimed in. "Don't you agree something needs to be done about it?"

Mubin nodded.

"Have you been anywhere besides Yemen?" Zakaria asked, still cautious.

"Yes, Syria for two years for language study and also I traveled in Pakistan with the Tablighi Jamaat," Mubin countered.

"Did you do anything other than hang with the Tablighi Jamaat?"

Zakaria asked his eyes on fire. They all knew the Tablighi Jamaat is not militant.

"I got around," Mubin countered, knowing Zakaria wanted to know if he'd gotten any terrorist training while in Pakistan.

"Did you train with the mujahideen there?" Fahim asked him straight out.

"Yeah, I met some Taliban guys while I was there and they let us shoot off their AK's, RPG's and even a 50 calibre with a belt of ammo," Mubin replied remembering with vividness those heroes who had impressed him so strongly at the time.

"I've just been to Iraq pretending to be a reporter—to Fallujah," Fahim excitedly related. "The mujahideen there told me, 'Here, you are just another person, but in your home country, you are lion!' They told me that we need to attack in the 'belly of the beast.' Our enemy, the Americans, went into Iraq, and the Canadians are allied to the Americans—so they too are fair game. The Canadians and Americans both need to be hit," Fahim said excitedly. "It's hard to get overseas these days so we need to strike right here—hit the near enemy. But we have to be smart and there are ways to do it. "

"How are you going to do it?" Mubin asked hoping to draw Fahim out further. But Fahim was silent.

"You need proper training," Mubin continued. "I've had some military training," he offered. "I know how to do it properly. You have to be very careful. You don't want to be caught and you want to be sure you achieve your objective."

"You know the American's in Iraq are raping our women," Fahim responded with sadness to his voice and face. "You can see what they are doing to the Muslim world for many, many years." His voice trembled as he spoke and he became agitated.

"Yes there are definitely crimes that are being committed," Mubin agreed.

"We need to do something, and we need to do it here!" Fahim continued. "I fired an RPG there, but I don't really have any weapons training. You have training and that's important to us. It just so happens that we are just about to run a training camp."

"Perfect," Mubin answered thinking, *Oh my God, I'm in!*

"I've already scouted out the location and the guys to go," Zakaria explained. "They need to be trained to a higher level. Do you think you can do this?"

Mubin hesitated for a moment. "Yes," he answered. "I can definitely do that. I can train section level infantry. I've trained youth."

Zakaria went to his car as Fahim and Mubin moved towards Mubin's van. Zakaria returned with a bag. He pulled out a map and showed Mubin.

"We've selected a location and it's going to be in this area," Zakaria said, pointing out the location on the map. Mubin's mind raced but he recognized the general area of Ramara Township and the lakes nearby that Zakaria pointed out as possible sites. Mubin committed them to memory.

"In this bag there are some things I want you to read," Zakaria said as he handed the bag to Mubin. "Get on point with it," he said. "We don't fool around."

Mubin took it to read later as Zakaria added, "And save the last two weeks in December for our camp."

"This camp is very secret," Fahim cautioned. "Don't tell anyone. Don't invite anyone. I know these guys. Don't go beyond that," he instructed.

Mubin nodded.

"Look the ultimate goal here is to conduct attacks," Fahim explained. "What I want to happen is to hit nuclear facilities, electrical grids, and so on—to cause chaos and confusion, to scare the people. We can hit the RCMP headquarters, the CSIS headquarters…"

"It will be way worse than the London underground metro bombings!" Zakaria added referring to the events in July of 2005.

It's clear that these guys really hate the authorities, Mubin thought taking it all in.

"This is why we are going to have these camps!" Fahim continued on in his rant. "JazakAllah [May Allah reward you]!" he exclaimed.

"I had some guys bringing in guns from the U.S. but they got arrested at the border," Fahim continued. "I just need fifty-thousand dollars to arm six hundred men," Fahim added. "Then we can bring some serious chaos…"

"Look," Mubin said feeling it was better to wind things up while they still trusted him. "I know you guys have to leave. Let's do this. Let's meet up in a couple of days when there is no one around," he said furtively glancing at the exiting people. "Then we'll discuss this further."

"You are the 'Sword of Allah' come to us," Fahim concluded, joyously as they started to break up their discussion.

Mubin got into his van and pulled out of the parking lot. What he didn't know was that the Project Osage agents had been nearby and had photographed the whole outdoor meet-up.

When Mubin was far enough down the road he pulled out his spy phone and hit the speed dial. Agent AJ answered immediately.

***

"So how did it go?" AJ asked.

"This guy, their ring-leader, is a time bomb waiting to go off," Mubin replied.

"What do you mean?" AJ asked.

"He wants to blow up your offices and get guns to kill a whole bunch of innocent people," Mubin answered. There was silence on the other end. "You still there?"

"I'm still here," AJ answered, his voice serious now.

"He said he wants to blow up nuclear facilities, the electrical grid, hit the RCMP, the CSIS headquarters and so on," Mubin relayed. "He has a camp arranged and he wants me to come and do training there."

"Okay Shaikh, I'll get back to you shortly," AJ answered. "Keep the phone nearby."

While he waited, Mubin looked over the texts Zakaria and Fahim had handed him. They included *The Fundamental Concepts of Al Jihad*, where the concept of striking the 'near enemy' and the obligation to take on the personal identity as jihadi was elaborated upon. *Blood, Wealth and Honour of Disbelievers*, in which it was made clear that disbelievers and their property are legitimate targets; and the *Millat-e-Ibraahim* (The Community of Abraham) – all well-known jihadi texts. *It figures, that this is what they are following,* Mubin thought looking them over.

In about twenty minutes AJ called back. "Shaikh, this has moved on to the next level now," he said. "The police will soon be investigating this case and when they do, we'd like to transfer you over to them. We'll talk that over soon."

Later Mubin would learn that CSIS knew about the training camp plan a full two weeks before Mubin became involved—an important point because much later, in court, the attorneys for the defense would try to blame him—making it look like he had called for and organized the camp in order to draw the others in and entrap them in a militant jihadi plot against the government. Likewise Fahim had also already arranged for weapons to be smuggled into Canada in a failed effort—this too before Mubin became involved. And both were deep into their militant jihadi beliefs and Fahim had met seven months earlier with Aabid Khan—a UK terrorist plotter agreeing to base international terrorist operations in Toronto. Yet, later the defense would try to accuse Mubin of having incited these young men into terrorism and of entrapment versus following an already active and rapidly unfolding terrorist plot—which was the truth of the matter.

***

"Pick me up on Birchmount and Sheppard," Fahim ordered Mubin three days later over the phone. "I'd like to take our discussion of the other night a bit further…" It was November 30th, 2005. When Mubin drove down Sheppard, Fahim was there waiting. Fahim wore a beige colored salwar kameez, the loose trousers and long shirt traditionally worn by Pakistani and Afghan men, over tennis shoes and had a warm winter parka jacket on top.

"I don't think we should talk about anything important inside your car," Fahim said as Mubin stopped his van to let Fahim in. "Now that you are hanging with us, you are probably going to become a CSIS target as well," he explained. "And your car and your phone will be bugged."

"Nah," Mubin protested. "My car isn't bugged!"

"Let's not take any chances," Fahim insisted. "They probably saw you talking with us at the event the other night," Fahim said glancing about Mubin's van as he warmed his hands on the vents. "Let's drive over to Sunnybrook Park. We can get out of the car there and talk safely."

"Nice clothes, dude," Mubin said as he searched for something to say off the topic of terrorism. "Are you Afghan?"

"Yeah, my family immigrated from the Afghanistan when I was one and we lived as refugees in Pakistan until I was ten. We left at the height of the civil war—after the Russian withdrawal—but before the Taliban took over," Fahim explained. "There was a lot of bad shit going on over there… but loads of mujaahideen victories as well. We saw Russian skeletons in burned out tanks," Fahim said his eyes lighting up with excitement.[16]

"I met some of the Taliban when I was in Pakistan," Mubin said but Fahim clammed up so Mubin changed the subject, asking, "You still live at home?"

"No I'm married," Fahim replied. "I got married in high school when I was eighteen! I'm twenty-one now," Fahim explained. "We lived with my parents for the first three months but they didn't like that my wife and I were religious so I had to move. We went from Mississauga to Scarborough—to live with her family. But now we have kids and our own place," Fahim explained.

Mubin would later learn that Fahim and his family now lived on public assistance. Fahim's parents as he had explained were moderate—although his mother did wear hijab—and Fahim's extremist views hadn't traveled with him from Afghanistan. He'd picked them up here in Canada at the mosques he attended. And with the birth of each of their two children, Fahim's young wife, Mariya, had suffered postpartum depression. Overwhelmed and feeling inadequate to address his wife's needs, Fahim increasingly sought refuge with the "brothers" at the mosque.

"Most of the guys that you met so far—Saad Khalid, Zakaria Amara and Zakaria's neighbor, Asad Ansari are my friends from Mississauga's middle and high school," Fahim went on. "Then I met Ameen Durrani when I had to move to Scarborough. I finished high school at Stephen Leacock Collegiate. You met Ameen at the event," Fahim said. "Durrani was a Salafi even in high school and proselytized among the youth on how to be a good Muslim," Fahim continued.

"The Mississauga group worships at the Meadowvale mosque but I mostly go over to the Eastern Islamic Center," Fahim said. "You know Imam Utaybi?"

Mubin nodded and smiled. Utaybi was a controversial imam, a Yemini immigrant who was known for his alleged connections to militant and fundamentalist Muslims. *No surprise there,* Mubin thought as he listened.

"Zakaria was born in Jordan," Fahim went on as they drove toward the park. "His father is Muslim but not devout, and his mother is Greek Orthodox from Cyprus. She had him baptized in Cyprus on a visit home!" Fahim said, "But Zakaria surpised them all later when he converted to Islam at age ten!" Fahim said laughing sarcastically. "Zakaria lived in Saudi Arabia for a while because his father was working there. Then he moved with his mother to Cyprus but he studied in an Arabic school in Cyprus—so he's pretty tight on Arabic."

Mubin nodded taking it all in.

"Then they moved to Canada when Zakaria was twelve but his parents have divorced." Later Mubin would learn that Zakaria sought to deepen his religious commitment as his family fell apart but his non-devout father wasn't much help in that regard, so Zakaria found his answers at the Meadowvale mosque. There Zakaria and many of the others in that group found a father figure in Qayyum Abdul Jamal, a forty-three year old Pakistani immigrant who worked as a custodian at the mosque. Qayyum spent a great deal of time nurturing the searching younger men in his firebrand views of Islam.[17]

Later, when the Toronto 18 were arrested some would recall that Fahim, Zakaria and the others often frequented the mosque dressed in combat fatigues and were clearly enamored of the Chechen jihadis. Later Mubin would also see them appear at the mosque in their fatigues.

"What about Saad Khalid?" Mubin probed. "He's part of your group right?"

"Yeah," Fahim said. "Poor guy. At age sixteen he came home to find the paramedics trying to revive his mother who had died in the bathtub at home! After that he became ultra-religious. Khalid is totally committed to jihad!" Fahim said and then became silent pointing at the ceiling of Mubin's minivan to indicate the possibility of listening devices inside the van.

Mubin later learned that Khalid started the Religious Awareness Club at school right after his mother's death. He was probably trying to make sense of her senseless death.[18] He began leading impassioned speeches about jihad and martyrdom during the school lunch hour,[19] influencing Zakaria and Fahim to further their knowledge of militant jihad as well.

"We were into gangster rap at first," Fahim told Mubin. "But then we got into Islamic rap."

Moving from gangster to jihadi rap was not much of leap as both involve distrust and disdain for state authority and a call to violence, Mubin thought as he nodded and listened.

As Fahim talked Mubin began putting the pieces together. It was in high school that the group began their first steps onto the terrorist trajectory moving from gangster rap and heavy metal into rap songs with religious themes that later became hardcore jihadi rap, as well as forming an Islamic club and blog that endorsed militant jihadi views. They then moved to joining the militant jihadi Internet forums and now were getting to the point where they were actively pursuing training for terrorist activities and working on acquiring the weapons and supplies to carry out their dreamed up attacks.

"Have you heard Zakaria's *Wake Up* rap?" Fahim asked.

When Mubin nodded that he hadn't, Fahim rapped out Zakaria's lyrics about the "iqama"—the second daily call to Muslim prayer and Zakaria's move into obedience to his newly acquired Islamic lifestyle, or "deen."

"I am filled with peace when at the masjid I hear the Iqama

But when I show more interest they call me Osama

Just trying to practice my deen so they call me extreme

They tell me I am too young, I am only sixteen," Fahim rapped. "He's good, man!" Fahim added, laughing.

"We called ourselves the 'Brothers of Meadowvale' and we got active on all the forums!" Fahim bragged. "That's when we got serious about Islam and started dressing conservatively and living the life," he added.

As Mubin listened, he understood that Fahim Ahmad, Zakaria Amara and Saad Khalid had cemented their relationship in Mississauga's Meadowvale Secondary School and fueled each other's interest in militant jihad as they searched for something meaningful to define their budding identities. *The strong ties among the young men likely also provided a substitute family for Zakaria while his disintegrated around him and for Saad Khalid after his mother was found drowned,* Mubin thought, taking it all in.[20]

As Mubin listened to Fahim explain about each of the guys he could easily relate to them. He could understand from his own experience how Zakaria's hurt and anger over his family situation, and perhaps also over being an immigrant that didn't fit in well with the mainstream culture, made him resonant to the angry messages in the Internet calls for jihad. They were the same messages that had resonated with Mubin's stored up hurt and anger and in which Mubin had also been caught up in at one time. And he could understand Khalid's grief and anger over his mother's senseless death and his search for answers in religious views that allowed him to act out his anger in ways that the militant jihadis claimed were righteous—in that, according to the militant jihadis—they purportedly defended victims of injustice.

Sadly they had no one like I had. No one like the Shaykh in Syria, to step in to tell them that their religious views are way off the mark, Mubin reflected as he listened. *So these guys just kept on moving along the terrorist trajectory from talking tough to envisioning militant actions to finally preparing for an actual terrorist plot! How strange that I ended up here. And now I'm about to hear all about it and stop them in a completely other way!* Mubin thought. In his rearview mirror he noticed a car following them. *I could have so easily ended up just like them, but now I'm tasked to watch them and learn what they are up to,* Mubin thought as he looked again to see if there was really someone tailing them.

***

"We're being followed," Mubin said deciding to point it out to Fahim. He didn't know if Fahim had also noticed, but he decided to reveal it—even if it was likely to be one of the government agencies. Pointing it out would build his credibility with Fahim.

"Yeah, they are always following us," Fahim answered, shrugging it off. "I even had the CSIS guys come question me twice now, but I just blow them off!" Fahim boasted.

Mubin wanted to impress Fahim that they were on the same side and that Mubin was protecting him and he also felt some sympathy for this guy that was going to eventually get arrested. Mubin wanted to get across to

Fahim that what he was dabbling in was not child's play, so he pressed the point.

"Look," Mubin pointed out the surveillance car. "He's in the blue car. He's turned into the gas station to watch us, but he won't get gas—watch," Mubin warned. "Look he'll pull back out when the light changes and follow us again. And see that brown car," Mubin pointed. "He's going to follow us too."

Mubin pulled into one of the project's driveways and said, "He'll go by now, so look—it will be a white guy driving the car. How many white guys do you usually see driving around here?" Mubin pointed out.

Fahim was into it now and jotted down the license number and make of the two cars following them. The brown car then disappeared but the blue car stayed with them. "I've got a guy who can do a background check on those cars," Fahim offered.

Mubin pulled into an industrial area and went around the building. When he exited the ramp onto the street a tractor-trailer pulled in so Mubin did a quick u-turn under the truck's cover. When he pulled back up the ramp Fahim and Mubin laughed to see two agents changing from the brown car to another.

"They were trying to put a new car on us," Mubin cackled as Fahim again jotted down the license plate of the new car. In all they identified six cars that were following them. Mubin outmaneuvered them all and then drove into Sunnybrook Park and parked the van.

"I think we lost them," he said smiling. "We burned them all."

"I'm not concerned about another visit from the CSIS guys," Fahim said as the two got out and walked along a snowy path into the deep woods. "I'll put one [a bullet] in their heads if they come back around," he explained.

"What did they talk to you about?" Mubin asked, although he already knew that CSIS had taken note of the "Brothers of Meadowvale" on the jihadi forums in early 2005, about the same time that Mubin had been researching how young Canadian jihadis make their way to Yemen.

"They were all up into that we'd been talking about jihad on the forums to the American and UK Muslims," Fahim answered.

"Which ones are you on?" Mubin asked.

"I'm in all the serious forums," Fahim bragged, "*ClearGuidance, IslamicNetwork* and *At-Tibyan* I'm the 'Soldier of Allah,'" Fahim said, acknowledging his Internet moniker.

"It's better to talk in person," Fahim continued with a worried look crossing his face. "I don't know if the security guys can break into the password protected ones, but better not to take a chance."

"I'm 'StealthfighterJ'—the J is for Jihad!" Mubin countered. "You've seen their videos?" he asked, pretending to be enthused over the gory beheading and jihadi videos he knew were on those forums.

"Oh yeah!" Fahim replied excitedly. "We have brothers in Canada, the U.S., the UK and Bosnia," he boasted. "And we've had serious discussions about basing an international cell here in Toronto. Then we can mount an attack in Toronto, Washington, D.C., London or Sarajevo with all of our connections!"

"You have Americans?" Mubin asked.

"Yes, last March [2005] two guys from a cell in Atlanta travelled here to meet with us," Fahim admitted.[21] "They travelled by bus and stayed at my place," Fahim added. "And a UK operative came as well."

"Jahmaal James was still here then and we discussed with them about what targets we want to hit—the American and Canadian GPS systems, police and military targets," Fahim confided. "All we need to do is interfere with military and civilian air traffic signals and hit some critical infrastructure and we'll have serious chaos,"[22] Fahim explained, his eyes fiery.

"After our meet-up, the Americans went home and began checking out targets in Washington, D.C. and Atlanta. After they got back they sent us[23] video surveillance they made of the U.S. Capitol, the World Bank, the

Masonic Temple in Alexandria and a fuel tank farm in Virginia," Fahim continued. "Ahmed went last summer to Pakistan to take paramilitary training and Syed went to Bangladesh. They are both back in the U.S. now. They want to come here to hide after their attacks—so we need to establish a safe house. Zakaria is working on that."

Later Mubin would learn the full identities of the two Americans—Syed Haris Ahmed—a naturalized U.S. citizen studying at Georgia Tech University and Ehsanhul Islam Sadequee, also a U.S. citizen. It was now December, 2005 but in eight months time, in July of 2006, U.S. federal prosecutors would charge that Ahmed traveled to Pakistan in July 2005 with the intention of joining and fighting with Lashkar-e-Tayyiba to acquire paramilitary training and both parties would be indicted for conspiring to provide material support to terrorists.[24] But for now both were still free and Fahim considered them part of his international terrorism cell.

July 2005, the time when Ahmed was in Pakistan, was also when the metro bombings in London occurred, likely providing encouragement to like-minded individuals that such strikes were not only possible but would garner worldwide attention.

"Jahmaal James is in Pakistan right now!" Fahim added. "He went in November saying he was going to get married, but he was really trying to get into the camps. He met with Aabid Khan—do you know about him?"

Mubin shook his head no.

"Aabid Khan is from the UK, he's known as Mr. Fix-It.[25] He was here in March also. He's married to Saima, my wife's sister. Saima wants to be a 'martyr'—just like Khava Baraeva in Chechnya," Fahim proudly explained, referring to the first Chechen suicide bomber, a young woman who drove a truck bomb into a Russian checkpoint.[26]

"And Saima is helping us to get wives for the brothers who go to Pakistan to take training," Fahim explained, "wives that are proud to marry a mujahid."

"Aabid Khan gets our guys hooked up in paramilitary camps with Lashkar-e-Tayyiba and Jaish-e-Mohammed!" Fahim said, his eyes lighting up. "Aabid tried to hook Jahmaal up in Pakistan—but Jahmaal got sick once he was over there.[27] He's still there and he'll come back with serious training!" Fahim bragged referring to James.

Mubin and Fahim were deep in the forest now. The sun was shining brightly and reflecting off the still snow covered boughs. From time to time big chunks of snow melted and fell from the trees.

"Aabid was also helping the Americans to get into training camps. Our guys that go over there will learn bomb making skills, VIP attacks, assassination skills and other militant training. We have brothers who are getting their skills," Fahim crowed.

"Now we need to get to the operational level of activities," Fahim said. "Our guys are learning to make chocolate!" Fahim said referencing the brothers in Pakistan and laughing at his code name for bombs. "When they come back we'll be able to actually start and do what we want to do!" he added with a gleam in his eyes.

"Our operation is going to be called Operation Badr," Fahim continued. In choosing that name, Fahim was referencing the Battle of Badr—a victorious battle in the early days of Islam.

"We should be ready by Ramadan," Fahim explained. He was referring to Ramadan 2006, the holy month of Islam, which would occur between late September through late October of the following year. "By Ramadan we should be able to attack critical infrastructure—like the nuclear plant maybe, the intelligence agency buildings, the Feds and their building and military bases nearby." Fahim had a long list.

"Car bombs are the ideal way," Fahim said as they walked alongside the snowy forest. "We'll burst through the gates and blow them sky high," he imagined. "Then we can storm inside."

Wow, this is not simply talking about establishing the Caliphate, Mubin mused as his body filled with alarm signals. *This is guns, bombs, attacks on non-combatants—all clearly and explicitly against Islam!*

"We'll even storm Parliament Hill and behead politicians to force the withdrawal of troops from Afghanistan," Fahim announced waving his arms in the air with anticipation. "I'll be sitting in the Speaker's Chair in the Commons Chamber and demand that Canadians embrace Islam. With all that publicity, it will spark an uprising of Muslims and result in guerilla warfare here—just like in Chechnya! I can see it now!" Fahim stated, going deep into his fantasy of violent attack. "And we could do random drive by shootings as well," he added as an afterthought shaking his head in the affirmative.

Mubin listened thinking, *This guy is desperate to lash out, and at the same time, he's so grandiose!*

"The Americans are looking into conducting an attack during the President's State of the Union address," Fahim added. "That too will get a lot of publicity."

"I am in the process of getting weapons," Fahim continued. "But we have had a serious setback in that department," Fahim confided as he wiped his brow. "I had an M-16 and an AK-47, a few other guns, and a lot of ammo that I buried in a plastic garbage bag in the park here, but when I came back yesterday to check them they were all gone!" he complained.

"Who else knew about them?" Mubin asked wondering if there was a mole already inside their operation.

"Two of our guys knew about them," Fahim replied. "But none of us has been back to check on them for months now. That cache cost me six thousand dollars! And all that was left yesterday was the empty garbage bag with a few of the cartridges!"

"What does that mean for the training camp?" Mubin asked referring to the camp to be held at the end of December. "Will you postpone it?"

"No, we have to keep moving ahead," Fahim replied, his face set in grim determination. "We may have to resort to paintball guns instead of real guns with live ammo, but it's the same set of skills. We need to train on combat readiness, wilderness survival, operational security and anti-surveillance," Fahim explained. "Can you train guys to fire rifles and carry out assassination and VIP attacks?" Fahim asked staring excitedly at Mubin through his thick glasses. He reminded Mubin of the bookworm who was finally finding a way to assert himself.

"Yes," Mubin answered, sobered by the idea of such undertakings, wondering how close Fahim was to actually initiating his pursuits. "Can you get any more weapons?" Mubin asked.

"I had two guys smuggling them in," Fahim responded. "I rented a car for them but they got caught at the border. Ali [Dirie] had two handguns taped to his thighs and Yasin [Mohamed] had his gun tucked in his waistband and bullets hidden in his sock."[28]

Mubin remembered the CSIS guys telling him about that arrest last August —it hadn't been formally linked to any terrorism charges as the security guys were just figuring out now how everyone was linked together.

"Their guns were loaded—they should have opened fire!" Fahim spat. "But they got caught and now they're spending two years in prison and I hear they're enjoying it there!"

"Enjoying prison?" Mubin asked.

"Yeah, they have time to pray, plenty to eat, lots of activities to pass the time and a network of Muslim inmates protects them from any threats inside prison."

But I've got other plans," Fahim continued as he made his way through the snow. "And I'm never going to prison. I'd rather go down as a martyr! I'll never be taken alive!"

"AllahuAkbar!" Mubin replied pretending to admire Fahim's courage.

"I am going to talk to some of the gangsters in the hood," Fahim continued while he gazed into the woods at a cyclist that had stopped along the path a ways away and was now fixing his flat tire. "We can get handguns and automatics and I'm trying to smuggle RPGs [rocket propelled grenades], AK-47s, grenades, and sniper weapons from the U.S. I have a Russian guy who brings vegetables across the border. He can smuggle them in!" Fahim threw his head back and laughed. "Isn't it great?"

Mubin nodded trying to take it all in. *They sound so close to operational! This nut is singing like a bird.*

"Listen," Fahim said as they turned to walk back to the car, "we have three cells in the Toronto area so far." Stopping he stared at the cyclist who was still there working on his bike tire. Fahim looked alarmed but Mubin waved it off as unimportant though he knew that it was likely someone from the security forces trying to capture their conversation. "Ilias is the emir of the Mississauga group," Fahim continued. "We also have the Scarborough and West Toronto cells. We also have a cell in Edmonton. They all answer to me. You can also become an emir if you form your own cell," Fahim offered. "We need to grow each of them to about forty to eighty guys each—and train them all for the attacks next Ramadan."

Mubin nodded as they got into his van. The two were quiet as he drove Fahim back home. "Ilias will call you next week," Fahim said when they parted ways.

Later at the Sheraton, Mubin walked in and put the license plate numbers down on the table as he met up with AJ. "What's this?" AJ, the handler asked.

"This is a list of all the surveillance team you had out there today," Mubin answered. AJ's face went red.

"Yeah, we weren't sure if you were with us or not the way you lost them all," he admitted. Mubin debriefed AJ on all that had happened with Fahim, his repeated fantasizing about blowing things up and his very real capabilities if the guys training in Pakistan returned, his gangsters supplied them with more weapons, or his smuggler got them in.

***

"We need to meet up," Zakaria Amara said over the phone a few days later. It was December 4, 2005. "Ilias" had now admitted his real name to Mubin. But the twenty-year-old Zakaria Amara didn't tell Mubin why or what they were meeting for—just told him to meet him at Tim Hortons.

"So what kind of stuff do you think we need before we go?" Zakaria asked when they were together sipping their coffees.

"I say whatever you think your group needs," Mubin answered.

"Do you think we need rifles?" Zakaria asked.

"Who do you expect to encounter?" Mubin countered. "Bears? No, they are hibernating. Wolves? If wolves, yes a rifle would help."

"I know a place where we can buy one," Zakaria offered. "Would you be willing to buy one for us?"

"Okay," Mubin answered knowing that to do so would be illegal and also knowing that to say, 'No, that's illegal,' would make him look silly.

"Good," Zakaria said. "Because that was a test. People were saying that you are a spy." Mubin's blood ran cold hearing it but he remained silent gazing steadily into Zakaria's eyes.

"Okay great, I'm going to pick you up at eight a.m. tomorrow morning and we're going to go shopping," Zakaria concluded as he got up to go.

***

"Zakaria just enlisted me to buy some weapons and I had to agree," he explained to AJ over the phone that evening. "They wondered if I am compromised," Mubin went on relaying the conversation to AJ. "What am I going to say tomorrow?"

"I'll have to get back to you Shaikh," AJ answered. "But try your best to avoid purchasing weapons. You don't want to give the impression that the agent is the one that provided the guns."

The next morning Zakaria arrived. It was December 5, 2005. Zakaria explained to Mubin that he was studying for his hunting license and his instructor had a store where she sold low caliber weapons. He had already preplanned buying a rifle.

"I'll go inside and check it out," he told Mubin when they arrived at the store. Mubin meanwhile opened Zakaria's glove compartment and was surprised to see a nine-millimeter handgun inside. *Does he have other weapons too?* Mubin asked himself as he found his heart racing. *This certainly ups the danger level, although I don't feel under any personal threat—at least not yet.*

"What are you guys looking for in particular?" the shopkeeper asked after Mubin and Zakaria went in together.

"I don't know," Zakaria answered. "Do you have machine guns?" he asked laughing.

The owner bristled and looked uncomfortable. "Anything here you like?" the owner asked running his hands over the glass case displaying his merchandise of pistols, shotguns and rifles.

"No there's really nothing here for us," Zakaria answered and turning to Mubin added, "Let's keep moving."

Back in the car Zakaria explained that he already had his sites set on a twenty-two he'd seen in another shop. They headed to Flaherty's Sport Shop next.

"How many do we need?" Zakaria asked Mubin as they looked over the shotguns. "And what kind of ammo?"

"Probably we need two of them and dozens and dozens of rounds," Mubin answered. "But I don't think these guys can handle a twelve gauge shotgun, unless they've handled one before? You never know what to expect with a twelve gauge and inexperienced handlers." Mubin quizzed Zakaria. "And do you want sounds of shotguns going off in the area?"

Zakaria had Mubin put a deposit down on a Winchester composite shotgun telling the owner they would return to pay the balance on the ninth of December.

"Where do you get the money to purchase these weapons?" Mubin asked once they were out of the store.

"Everyone in the groups contributes," Zakaria answered nonchalantly, "and we have a budget for guns."

At the third place, Ye Olde Sport Centre, the woman who was giving Zakaria hunting classes greeted him. She knew exactly which weapon Zakaria wanted and Mubin could see by his excitement level talking to her that there was going to be no dissuading him.

"I want that one," Zakaria said, pointing out the twenty-two caliber Marlin long rifle outfitted with a scope that lay in a nearby display case, "and get one thousand rounds of ammo," he instructed, handing Mubin four hundred twenty dollars in cash.

What the hell are we going to do with a thousand rounds? Mubin thought as he bought the required gear. Mubin managed to keep hold of the rifle explaining to Zakaria, "Just in case there's a spot check—you don't want to be in possession of it without a license." Zakaria agreed but kept hold of the ammo.

***

"I got a rifle today," Mubin said when he called into AJ that night. Zakaria gave me cash to buy it and he said they have more cash to buy more weapons…"

There was a long pause on the other end of the line, and then AJ spoke, "Okay, Shaikh. We need to get rid of it."

"How are we going to do that?" Mubin asked.

"We need a plan," AJ answered.

"You realize I had to buy it," Mubin explained. "If I had said no, it might have confirmed for him that I'm a spy. He said they suspected me. It looks like the camp is going to happen," Mubin continued. "It's going to be the last two weeks in December and they have at least ten guys coming."

***

The next day AJ called. "Shaikh, I need you to come in," he said. There was something in his voice—worry or seriousness. "We need to discuss this."

Again in the hotel room, AJ launched into his talk, "Look Shaikh, we are really happy with the work you've been doing. In fact we are very impressed with the manner you've been going about this, the skills that you've displayed. We really haven't seen this level of professionalism in anyone else."

What's this? Mubin thought. *What's he buttering me up for?*

"You know you've been doing a really, really good job up to this point," AJ continued. "But the mandate of the service is to collect info and based on your work interacting with this group this has moved out of our hands," AJ said rubbing his hands through his short hair.

"Is the case over?" Mubin asked.

"Oh no!" AJ answered breaking out into a chuckle. "It's just going to the next level. This is now beyond our mandate. We don't investigate criminal matters and based on what you've given us—including the purchase of the rifle—this has now moved to criminal investigations.

"The file will be taken over by the Integrated National Security Enforcement Team [INSET] of the RCMP," AJ said as he opened his folder and took out a business card. "This is the contact info to the RCMP agent," he said handing it to Mubin. "I want to be very clear. I'm not telling you to talk to them, or that you have to. This has to be a voluntary decision that you have to make, but I would like you to."

"Of course," Mubin said.

"Are you sure?" AJ asked. "If you work for the RCMP you will eventually be exposed as an undercover agent and have to testify in court," AJ explained.

"I don't know if I can do that," Mubin answered. "My father has a very prominent place in the Muslim community. That could be a disaster for our family…"

"These jihadis are really serious, Shaikh. We need someone like you on the case," AJ said. "They're up to no good… I think you should meet with the police and see what they can offer you in terms of avoiding going public and having to testify."

"Ok, sure," Mubin answered.

AJ picked up the phone and dialed the number on the card. "Hey Bill," AJ spoke into the phone, "I have our friend here and he wants to meet you guys. Okay, okay," he continued as he jotted down notes.

"And?" Mubin asked.

"And, you are meeting with Bill tonight," AJ answered giving Mubin the sheet of paper. "I'm going to give them your number and they will call you with instructions that you need to follow very, very carefully," AJ explained.

The meeting ended without Mubin asking about pay nor AJ offering any insight into that end of things. Nor were there any real goodbyes, nice working with you—just a cut-off from a very intense relationship that had been nearly daily over the past months. Unfortunately, it had to be this way in order to ensure that the courts could not accuse CSIS of having undue influence over someone who would ultimately become a fact witness in the legal cases involving these actors. Leaving them, Mubin didn't realize how much he would miss AJ and his work with CSIS—but his days and nights would be full, that was for sure.

At home Mubin explained the transfer to Joanne. "Well great," she answered. "Let's see where it goes. Obviously this is moving on. See where it takes you," she encouraged. "Go with it."

"I'm going to be going out tonight to meet with them," Mubin explained. It was hours until the phone rang and by then Mubin had a case of butterflies in his stomach.

***

"Shaikh?" the voice on the other end of the line asked.

"Yes sir," Mubin answered.

"This is Bill."

"Yes Bill, I've been waiting for your call," Mubin said.

"You need to listen to my instructions very carefully," Bill explained. "What you need to do is drive and I'll tell you when to turn. We don't want anyone to know you are meeting with us and we want to see if anyone is following you. Got it?"

Mubin kept the phone to his ear as he went down to get his van. "Go north, go east, make a right over here, pull into this lot, drive across the lot, park your car over there," Bill told him as he drove. "Go into the side entrance and go up to the fifth floor." It was another hotel.

I wonder what's going to go down? Mubin asked himself as he rode in the elevator. *They are really serious about their security protocols!*

The RCMP guys were white, in their forties, clean cut and wearing regular civilian clothes—jeans, t-shirts, running shoes and baseball caps. The one who introduced himself as Bill had a goatie, and George had glasses.

"I'm a practicing Christian," George explained upon meeting. "I want you to know this isn't about being anti-Muslim," he explained in a soft voice while motioning Mubin to take a seat at the table. "This is about working together. They are making your own people look bad and harming all of us at the same time." Mubin could see in his pensive eyes that he was a sincere and good person. Not only that, but this agent, Mubin learned, was also completing a Master's degree in sociology and took a very measured and balanced view of minority communities. He was the intellectual type and this resonated with Mubin.

Bill seemed straight as an arrow and kept focusing on not breaking any laws in his comments as Mubin went through the whole story of what he had already learned. "Shaikh, we don't do that," he'd say when Mubin suggested something a bit off course to lead the jihadis into showing more of their hand. "We follow our protocols. We are the police," Bill explained.

"Our job is to gather evidence that is going to be tested in a court of law. We have to do things correctly"

Bill, Mubin learned was a twenty-year veteran of the service and had spent five years in his initial deployment to the northern regions of the country, frequently living in isolated areas. Bill was predictable in the sense that he would not accept any bending of the rules.

"And you will be required to give testimony in court," Bill added toward the end of their time together. He stood and walked around the room while explaining to Mubin the differences between this assignment and the last one. "You'll be a material witness. This won't be like CSIS where you had your anonymity guaranteed," Bill explained. "If you move forward with us at some point your anonymity will be compromised and your identity will be exposed to the public," Bill continued, "because this case will be tried in court and you will be testifying in court. Are you on board for that?"

Mubin sighed deeply. *Wow this is going to a whole other level. What will this mean for me and my community?* Mubin asked himself. *Once this comes out will my community react negatively and not understand the details of the case—what really happened? If this is going to public prosecution, I'll be in a public courtroom! What will everyone think? What will they say?* Mubin asked realizing that he was echoing the questions his parents had continually asked throughout his development—*what will the others think, what will they say?*

Mubin had no frame of reference to answer his own questions— there had never been a case like this in Canada. *I have a responsibility to see this case through to the end,* Mubin thought while he worried, *Oh man, how is this going to go down?*

"Yes, I'm interested," Mubin answered despite his fears.

"Okay, good," Bill said. "We authorize you to go with this group and to continue to gather your evidence. But our first order of business is to get rid of the rifle." Mubin came up with a plan and called Zakaria a few days later.

***

"You know the cops came to my house asking to see the rifle," Mubin said over the phone.

"Oh shit!" Zakaria answered. "I think they flagged you because you're with me."

"Dude, we need to get rid of it right away," Mubin answered. "I'll go to a gun club and see if I can sell it to someone. We need cash and I can probably get one hundred and fifty dollars more than what we bought it for. Then we can use the cash—buy whatever with it."

"Okay," Zakaria answered tentatively, obviously disappointed to lose his new toy.

"Look, we don't want any heat on us," Mubin continued and Zakaria gave in. Then he called Bill and explained that their plan had worked.

"Look, I'll put it in the back of my van and drive over to Tim Hortons right now," Mubin explained. "I'll leave it unlocked while I go into get coffee and you guys can pick it up. Call me when you've got it and then I'll drive home, but I need the extra money to hand over to them, okay?"

Bill agreed, happy to have the gun disposed of. After hanging up, Mubin called AJ next.

"AJ, I'm still not sure about this—how far I'm willing to go to work with the RCMP," Mubin said. "I think I'd rather just keep working with you guys at CSIS."

"Give it some time, Shaikh," AJ said reassuringly into the phone. "And make sure you tell them all your concerns about testifying and all of that..."

"I got rid of the rifle," Mubin volunteered—trying to keep the connection going. "They wanted to know how that happened while I was with you all. I told them I had to buy it—that the guys were worried I was working undercover and I had to prove myself. They seemed satisfied with that but they asked me a lot of questions about it."

"That's normal Shaikh," AJ confided. "Just give it some time. I'm sure you and Bill are going to develop a close working relationship. You need to keep your contact with him from now on, though—okay?"

"Yeah, sure," Mubin replied sadly, understanding that professionally, it had to be done this way, to keep the evidence intact and to protect the integrity of the case.

"Hang in there, Shaikh. You're doing really important work!"

I wish the hell I could stay with CSIS, Mubin thought, dejectedly hanging up the phone. It was depressing to no longer be able to continue exonerating innocent Muslims and follow up on the ones up to no good. He hung up the phone and stood in silence for a moment, taking it all in.

***

Two days later Fahim and Zakaria came to Mubin's house for lunch. It was December 7, 2005. After eating, the guys sat down to watch some jihadi videos together.

"Some civilian casualties are inevitable in our attacks," Fahim commented as they watched. "Especially with attacking the CSIS headquarters in Toronto—some women and children are going to get killed."

"That's unfortunate," Mubin said and Zakaria nodded his agreement although neither Fahim nor Zakaria seemed too concerned.

"What do you know about the emergency task forces?" Zakaria asked. "What kind of weaponry do they have?"

"I think they have fully automatic rifles and are heavily armed," Mubin replied.

"What's their policy in a shootout?" Amara asked.

"What do you mean policy?" Mubin asked, confused.

"Do they shoot to kill or simply wound?" Zakaria asked.

"To kill!" Mubin answered, again noting that his answer didn't seem to disturb Zakaria or Fahim much. Both seemed resigned to either "martyrdom" or spending time in prison.

"I have a present for you," Zakaria said standing up and handing Mubin his nine-millimeter. Mubin's face clouded in concern as he took it from Zakaria. It was the same gun he'd seen in Zakaria's glove compartment, but Mubin feigned surprise at seeing it again now.

"Don't worry. It's on safety," Zakaria said.

Mubin was trained that any time you take a weapon in your own hands you check. Gazing at his infant son sleeping in the corner he pointed the gun in a safe direction and pulled the slide back to check the chamber— there was a cartridge in one of the chambers. The gun was ready to go off.

"Bro! This gun is loaded!" Mubin shouted angrily.

Amateurs! Mubin thought as his stomach churned in disgust. *They are more dangerous because they are so stupid!*

***

"I told my wife I'm going on Umrah [the pilgrimage to Mecca during the off season]," Zakaria told Fahim and Mubin the next time they met again. "But I'm really sleeping in my car plotting our training trip," he explained. "I've been to multiple locations and I think I've settled on one. It's in a secluded wooded area near Washago, in Ramara Township, near Orillia," Zakaria confided. "I checked with the local OPP detachment and Ministry of Natural Resources about wild animals in the area and there's nothing to bother us. I also fired a few rounds up there last time I went to see if the noise drew any attention. There's no one around for miles," Zakaria reported.

Mubin nodded approvingly and Fahim showed Mubin their "training manual"—a bunch of papers similar to the ones they'd given him on their first meeting. The documents included the *Millat-e-Ibraahim*—a text well known among militant jihadis—so popular that the U.S. military nearly always found it on killed al Qaeda militants in Iraq. The *Millat-e-Ibraahim* laid out a basic understanding of jihad—according to groups like al Qaeda.

There was a second text entitled the *Blood, Wealth and Honor of the*

Disbelievers. Using hijacked Islamic texts taken out of context, it justified killing non Muslims as well as defrauding, stealing from and being duplicitous in daily activities with them.

Fahim's method also outlined how to deal with new recruits:

1) Don't tell them anything, just give them jihadi da'wah [Islamic teachings]
2) Give a false name
3) Keep them on the downlow

As Mubin read through Fahim's materials he realized that their training camp was going to be a bait and switch. They were telling the participants to come for training without fully explaining to them the purpose of the camp.

"Some of these guys don't know why they are going," Fahim later admitted to Mubin, shortly before they headed off to the camp.

"Okay that's my job," Mubin answered.

"Your job is to train these guys," Fahim countered. "And hopefully we'll be able to persuade those who show promise to take more rigorous training in Pakistan."

This is going to be a challenge, Mubin thought, *to come up with a plan that makes it interesting for them but at the same time does not bring them to any operational capability.* As he contemplated it, Mubin's mind wandered off to his Cadet training—how to make a proper fire, military marching, survival in the wild. *Will it be enough to offer them just those things?*

"Friday we'll meet up at the mosque," Fahim instructed Mubin by phone a few days later. "We'll be joined there by the others who are accompanying us on the camping trip. We'll sleep at the mosque and then head out for our camp at first light. We're staying for twelve days."

"It's our anniversary," Joanne said disappointed. But she agreed, knowing how important it was for Mubin to accompany the group.

***

It was late December 2005. Mubin picked up Fahim and Gulshan, a young convert from Hinduism. "We need to get some gear," Fahim explained and they made a stop at the local Canadian Tire where Fahim picked out some snow shovels, a propane heater and some camping gear that they paid for themselves. Then they headed to the Uthman Mosque where they met the others to overnight until the early light when they planned to head out for the camp. In his work with the Tablighi Jamaat, Mubin had often assembled groups of young men for outings and overnights at the mosque and so he knew this would not bring any unusual scrutiny. It was usual to overnight in mosques.

The camping trip brought together the Scarborough and Mississauga participants that Fahim and Zakaria had hand picked for training, uniting fourteen individuals—ten adults and four youth. The youth had been told they were going to a religious retreat. Some of the adults knew more.

Nineteen-year-old Ameen Durrani, a Pakistani immigrant who had arrived in Canada at age twelve was already at the mosque when Mubin and Fahim arrived. He was there along with twenty-four year old Steven Chand, a convert from Hinduism whose parents were from Fiji. Steven had spent some time in the reserves and therefore would also serve as a trainer—along with Mubin.

The group headed out of the mosque at three a.m. Loading Zakaria's car, Ameen Durrani warned, "Don't lock the keys inside," but Zakaria did just that.

They are total amateurs! Mubin thought as they called a tow truck to jimmy the door open and recover the keys.

On the way up to the camp Zakaria, driving the lead car with Ahmad Ghany as his passenger, Ameen spotted a local gun store and called Fahim on the telephone to say, "Let's check this out!"

Fahim alerted Mubin who pulled his van into the gun store parking lot. Steven Chand, Ameen Durrani, Gulshan and Fahim piled out of Mubin's car. But before they went into the store, Zakaria brought his nine-millimeter over to show Mubin the make and model so they could buy bullets for it. Inside the store Fahim was beside himself with excitement—like a child in a candy store.

Oh, let's get this one and that, Fahim elatedly exclaimed, pointing out a few models, while Mubin thought, *This will be a disaster!*

"Look, I know you have the hundred and fifty dollars to spend," Mubin said attempting to dissuade them. "But, I'm worried about having more than one gun at the camp with so many inexperienced guys. I don't want them shooting each other!" Mubin protested. "It's better to just have one piece for now—that way I can keep track of it, okay? Come on, let's get the ammo for the one we have. I'll set up a firing station and teach everyone basic gun safety this time and we'll practice with that one," Mubin said.

Disappointed, Fahim went over to look at the ammo and ordered bullets for Mubin to buy with their cash. Later, arriving at the camp Mubin saw that it was a rural part of what Fahim believed was a national forest.

"This is crown land," Fahim crowed. "See we are already taking over their lands! This is the start of much more in the future!" Fahim boasted.

The snow was already two feet deep this far north. Zakaria who was leading the way got his car stuck in the snow nearly immediately and everyone had to help push it out with Mubin instructing them on how to rock the car gently back and forth while trying not to let the tires spin and create ice under the car. *These guys definitely don't fit the stereotype of the hardcore, super trained terrorist! Seems their reach exceeds their grasp!* Mubin thought as he saw how their camp experience was already starting out.

Unpacking the car, Mubin got out his gear and quickly assembled his artic tent, setting up his propane heater outside it. Mubin built a fire pit in the middle of the camping area and gathered logs and kindling. He set up the wood to start a good size fire. Then he went over to see how the others were doing. Ameen Durrani was still fumbling with his tent alongside some of the others.

"These are spring tents!" Mubin said astounded that the guys were so stupid to think their summer gear would hold up to the freezing cold. "Let me see your sleeping bags," he demanded and was similarly disappointed. "Look, we need to go back into Orillia and buy a heater and a big tarp," he said, "Or you guys will never make it out of here."

Later, after buying the additional winter gear, Mubin helped the youngsters set up the tarp and heater so that it circulated warm air around their tents. *Still they are going to be cold,* Mubin thought, worried if any of them could go hypothermic. *I know what my job is here, but I still feel a human responsibility for them,* Mubin mused. He also looked proudly over his handiwork. He had bought a camouflage tarp and it was hard to make out the tents at all, from even a short distance.

"Come and get your gear," Fahim and Zakaria shouted out. They had bought heavy camouflage pants and shirts and were handing them out from a large open garbage bag. "You can wear these over your clothes," Fahim explained. Their camos were green.

Mubin was wearing white camos and thought, *Not so camo in the snow,* but he said nothing. The guys lined up and one by one tried on the camos to see which sizes fit over their outer wear. Ameen put his on and saw the arm only reached halfway down his.

"I can't even get my arm in it," he shouted and laughed as he switched it up. Waleed, the youngest in the group put on a large size that hung over his arms.

"Maybe we can hire him to be scarecrow," one of the guys joked.

It's a powerful move—providing uniforms, Mubin reflected. *It creates camaraderie and they won't have paintball residue left on their clothes when they go home.*

When evening came, Fahim had set up his laptop with an audio lecture entitled *Constants on the Path of Jihad* by Anwar al-Awlaki, the American imam who lived in Yemen and preached hatred of the West. Awlaki, was at that point in time believed to have given spiritual advice to three of the 9/11 hijackers and would later also be linked in 2009 to the Fort Hood shooter and to the Detroit underwear bomber—having cheered on both attacks against the United States. Years later, Tamerlan Tsarnaev, one of the Boston bombers was also strongly influenced by watching Awlaki's Internet sermons promoting militant jihadi attacks against the West.

Fahim invited the brothers into his tent to listen. Mubin knew the lecture as a pseudo-scholarly attempt to elevate militant jihad as one of the foremost Islamic obligations—concepts initially popularized by Osama Bin Laden in his 1998 fatwa.

"You don't need to consult anyone. You just go and do it by yourself," Fahim summarized after they listened to the six-part lecture. Mubin could see that many had become bored listening to it. And everyone was freezing cold, but the brothers—led by Fahim—reassured themselves that they were suffering for the cause and eventually Allah would reward them.

"This is the way for us to get favor from Allah," Fahim lectured. "He is seeing us right now. We are cold—freezing. But we are on a mission. This is what we have to do. Allah will reward us!"

A few days later on December 23, 2005 a third group from Mississauga arrived including Qayyum Abdul Jamal, Saad Khalid, Asad Ansari and Ibrahim Aboud—making the group of guys now a total of fourteen, including Mubin. They also joined in the daily activities, lectures and watching of videos.

Twenty-year-old Asad Ansari who arrived in the later group was an immigrant from Pakistan, although he had spent from seven months old until he was twelve living in Saudi Arabia. Asad had been accepted into the computer science program at the University of Waterloo but couldn't attend due to financial constraints. Mubin knew that he had become suicidal and depressed as a result. *I wonder if Fahim is exploiting his emotional state and whether being suicidal would make him a good "martyr,"* Mubin wondered.

Some of the videos Fahim played were of Taliban-led battles from Afghanistan, others of bombings and explosions, snipers, and beheadings. It was always the Taliban and al Qaeda in Iraq winning against the U.S., ISAF and the coalition forces.

"Watch this!" Fahim shouted excitedly as he showed an American convoy making its way down a booby-trapped road. "Watch! This one gets taken out!" he shouted just before the hidden IED exploded beneath the convoy.

"MashaAllah! What Allah desires is carried out!" Zakaria chimed in as the others joined in with shouts of "AllahuAkbar!"

"We have a responsibility to get our Canadian troops out of Afghanistan," Fahim argued. "This is our duty in jihad—to punish them for invading Muslim lands!"

The group also watched the sniper of Baghdad videos. "Watch this guy," Fahim narrated. "He doesn't even know it's coming." They watched as a U.S. solider came out from the top of his armored personnel carrier. Boom—he was shot. There was a burst of blood as he collapsed back. Others were of soldiers walking on patrol. Boom—they were shot dead.

"AllahuAkbar!" four or five of the most enthusiastic trainees would shout gleefully. The rest looked freaked out and were silent.

"You wanna be on the sidelines or you wanna be on the frontlines?" Fahim chided his "soldiers" as he urged them to embrace militant jihad and potential martyrdom. "Sideliners get no reward and they still die. Frontlines get you rewards!"[29]

Fahim also played the Chechen-Russian Hell videos. Mubin was surprised to see them again—these were videos he'd watched when he'd been in the same mindset back in the nineties.

"Look around you brothers," Fahim said with a feeling of reverence filling his voice as he paused the video feed. "It's just like we're in Chechnya.

The winter snow, we are in the woods. We are living the life, brothers! We are living just like the mujahideen are!"

Mubin listened realizing, *Fahim wants to enter the pure fantasy of those he considers his life heroes—Chechens and Taliban!*

"Look at his blood squirt!" Fahim shouted jubilantly the next day as he showed a beheading video.

It's like jihadi porn! Mubin thought hiding his disgust.

"That's gross," one of the trainees, murmured.

"Wow, I've never seen anything like that," Waleed, another of the teenagers quietly remarked afterwards. He had sat silently watching, white faced.

At meals Fahim pointed out, "Look at how we are eating brothers. The mujahideen do exactly the same thing—they eat simply, and with their bare hands. We're not living large brothers. There's no pizza ordered in thirty minutes or it's free."

Everyone had been instructed not to bring their phones and Mubin had left his regular phone home. The secure phone he had hidden under the floor mat of the driver seat with the ringer turned off and he left it there for the duration of the camping trip.

Some of the younger kids had brought their mobile phones and called home to keep their lies to their parents going. "I'm okay, I've decided I'm staying the whole week at Jamal's house," one lied to his mother.

"This is violating security protocols," Fahim complained to Mubin.

"Yo, what's with the kids calling home to their Mamas?" Zakaria mocked.

The guys also made daily runs into Orillia to a Tim Hortons for coffee, hot snacks and a real washroom—so they weren't really living like Chechens. They also stocked up on tuna and beans at the grocery store, raising eyebrows of the locals who were surprised to see a group of "brown boys" clad in military fatigues. Mubin made a few calls into his handlers from the payphone in Orillia—saying he was calling his wife.

Everyone pitched in for meals, which were mostly just canned foods heated over the fire—tuna, beans and pita bread was the nearly daily fare. During the days and into the evenings the guys kept a campfire going. Gulshan, a convert from Hinduism made a name for himself in the wood chopping business by enthusiastically wielding the axe.

At night, Mubin set up the propane heater to create a bubble of warmth under the tarp around the spring tents, but it was still cold. Finally after the first week of camping, when he saw that some of the younger ones weren't doing so well with the cold, Mubin offered to let them sleep in his heated van. Making sure the exhaust pipe was clear, he left it running all night.

Each night they listened again to the lectures of Anwar al-Awlaki. And five times a day the entire group assembled for prayers. Mubin led them some of the time. Zakaria and the others were the main leaders. And because it was cold they reverted to Tayummum practices to clean themselves before prayers—using dirt or the dust of rocks to wipe their faces and arms. Mubin dug up the dirt area around the fire pit—where the earth had thawed—to provide the dirt for that purpose.

One afternoon Fahim noticed an airplane overhead. "There sure have been a lot of planes each day, I think that's the third one today," he remarked.

It's surveillance, Mubin knew but he answered, "Brother, remember the airport we saw outside of Orillia? They are going to the airport there." Little did Mubin know but there was a team of over two hundred surveillance officers watching them from the ground and the air the whole time.

Mubin set up a paramilitary obstacle course that included a balance bar run, a judo role, jumping from a tall stump, a run along a rocky ridge and a fifteen-foot jump off the ridge into the snow. He also made the guys learn the fireman's carry.

After each physical training, Fahim and Zakaria would take Mubin aside asking, "Who would you say are the 'men' in the group?" or "Who should progress to the next level?" It was clear from their remarks, and Mubin already understood that the purpose of this camp was to select the most appropriate guys and then persuade them to undertake more rigorous training in Pakistan, working through Aabid Khan as Jahmaal James attempted in November 2005.[30]

***

"What we are doing here is trying to decide who is the real deal. Who we are going to send on to the advanced training," Fahim would announce before physical trainings to motivate them.

"Brothers, if you can't take the flag in this forest, how are you going to fight properly in jihad?" Fahim exhorted his trainees during paintball games, as he continually shouted commands to be fearless. "If you are cowardly with the paintball how will you react under real fire?" he shouted.

"Don't be cowards! Don't be cowards!" Fahim goaded the group. "Run for the flag!"

"You attack the enemy wherever you see him," Fahim urged his trainees.

Zakaria and Fahim continued to take Mubin aside from time to time to say, "We want to make men of these boys. Tell us who the real men are." Mubin nodded and just kept training them.

Mubin set up a game to capture the bridge and had the guys imitate the storming of a land target while he and another of the brothers shot at them with paintball guns to simulate live fire. The stormers were not given guns and were in many ways simulating a "martyrdom" mission.

"You need to be brave in the face of fire," Mubin told them as he lined them up to run toward the target. Mubin could see that his trainees were scared. "You may get hit, and it stings a bit, but try and evade—be brave under fire."

"Hey man, this is why you are here—for the training," Fahim told them. "Do it now so you know what its like later. Be fearless."

"Even though you might get hit, you have to keep going," Mubin told them feeling mixed about coaching them for "martyrdom." "If you take a bullet you have to keep going," Mubin repeated. "You have to help your brothers!"

"Some of you will get taken out. Some of you will get hit," Zakaria chimed in. "But some will make it to the target."

One by one they ran to their target and Mubin, acting as a sniper, would try to hit them. They were moving targets but quite a few got hit because Mubin was a good marksman.

"AllahuAkbar!" the trainees would yell as they ran, and especially as they got hit, but some only yelped in surprised hurt—shocked by the paintball pellet.

As the guys ran Fahim urged them on shouting, "Don't you have any honor in your religion? Fight them! Fight them!"

Fahim and Zakaria videoed many of the activities planning to send the video to Aabid Khan and their contacts in Pakistan in the hopes of impressing them about the seriousness of the Toronto cell.[31] Fahim had even made a black flag upon which the Islamic creed was imprinted in white—in complete likeness to the flags displayed by masked mujahideen in Afghanistan and Pakistan. Such flags were always to be found in jihadi training propaganda video.

Zakaria Amara had brought the paintball guns to the camp. While later some would argue that it was benign, innocuous play among young men—Mubin was sure it was not. Their leaders—Fahim and Zakaria—were most definitely training their guys for when they would do the real thing. The commands Fahim shouted made that clear. And Mubin knew the military often does the same thing—using air soft hits to simulate live combat as much as possible instead of using live ammo. Likewise Fahim made it clear to Mubin that he wanted his trainees to learn military maneuvers.

Mubin set up a rifle range as well and instructed the brothers about safe gun handling and how to hit their target. One by one they came up and tried out the rifle. Gulshan had brought pictures of Hindu deities that he hung up and the group used for target practice.

The youngest boy there, Waleed was fourteen. When Mubin had lined them up for rifle practice Waleed fired one round and said, "Oh my God! I didn't expect it to be that loud!" That was enough of gun practice for him. Waleed was freaked out and shivering all the time and was always sleeping in late and difficult to wake up.

He clearly does not want to be here, Mubin reflected. *He must have been dragged along by friends.* Indeed, later Mubin learned that Waleed had been brought there by Gul, the younger brother-in-law of Fahim. Waleed was always the last one up, the last to carry out his duty. *He doesn't want to be ridiculed by the others, but he doesn't want to do it. He follows the group, but just only,* Mubin thought. One night by the fire Waleed was so cold that he put his boots too close to the coals and melted the soles of his boots. *Many in this group are just teenagers, making amateur mistakes!* Mubin reflected. *Yet, how often do these exact kind of teenagers end up joining violent extremist groups, and though amateurs, still take part in terrorist attacks? It has to be stopped,* Mubin realized.

"When we go back you have to put on the *face*," Fahim lectured at night. "You go to your boss and make like everything is okay, but in reality you know now what your mission is. You need to be ready to die for your cause," Fahim exhorted his group. "And you will be selected for the next round—if you earn it."

As they sat eating their evening meal around the campfire, Gulshan, one of the trainees brought a devotional idol that his mother used for prayer. He threw it into the fire and began mocking it. "Oh help me! I'm on fire!" he taunted as his mother's idol was consumed in the flames.

"We are not officially al Qaeda," Fahim explained to the group toward the end of their twelve days together. "But we follow their principles and methods." He urged his trainees to wage war on the West, making an analogy to the fall of Rome—how the West appeared undefeatable but really was not.

"It doesn't matter what trials you face. It doesn't matter what comes your way," Fahim lectured the group. "Our mission is greater, whether we get arrested, whether we get killed, we get tortured—our mission's greater than just individuals. It's not about you or I, or this emir or that emir, it's not about that. It's about the fact that this has to get done. Rome has to be defeated. And we have to be the one's that do it—no holding back—whether it's only one man that survives, you have to do it," Fahim exhorted. "And InshaAllah [Allah willing] we will do it. InshaAllah [Allah willing], we will get the victory!"

Fahim went on telling the group "AllahuAkbar" [Allah is greater] and painting pictures for them of Muslims victorious over the Western governments. "Allah Akbar! [Allah is greater]! It puts fright in their hearts man, it freaks them out. Imagine we're walking the streets of downtown [Toronto] or even Washington [D.C.] or you're in front of the White House and you raise the banner of La ilaha il Allah [there is no God except Allah]! Is anybody ever gonna think of facing us? La ilaha il Allah [there is no God except Allah] in the White House!"

One day Fahim asked Mubin to give a talk—to consolidate the whole purpose of the training. Worried that he was being asked to incite for terrorism as Fahim clearly was, Mubin decided on another tact.

"I'm going to ask each and every one of you in this circle and I want you to tell me what brought you into the group, what you learned while you were here, and what you are going to do when you get back?" Mubin challenged.

"I'm motivated by the suffering that is going on in the Muslim world," a nineteen year old who had emigrated in his teens from Iraq replied. "I'm here to learn the skills to defend them. When I get back that's what I'm going to do, whether it's doing it online or in real life."

That's part of the problem, Mubin reflected, *These guys don't always get the difference between their fantasy online tough guy playing around and the real life terrorism that Fahim has in mind for them!*

"I came here because my friends came," Waleed the youngest confessed. "I have a twenty dollar weekly allowance I'm going to give to this group and its work," Waleed pledged.

"I'm here because I want us to do something real to help Muslims all around the world," forty-three-year-old Qayyum Jamal replied. Qayyum was the oldest participant and had befriended and become a father figure for Zakaria and some of the others at the Meadowvale mosque where he worked as the custodian. "I learned team work. I also learned how to shoot people with paintball pellets," Qayyum continued laughing at himself. "When I go back I'm going to train because I realize I'm out of shape!"

"I didn't really know what this is about," one of the younger teens said. "I thought it was just a camping trip, but now I realize we need to be much more aware of what is happening in the Muslim world. And we need to stand up to defend them and attack those responsible for their suffering. So when I get back I'm going to educate myself more about what's happening and what I can do to carry out my Muslim duty—to protect them."

"I'm going to use my computer skills and help that way," Asad who was overweight and out of shape, volunteered, adding, "I'm fat so I'm not good to you in the field. But everyone needs a computer guy. I'll be that guy. I'll continue my studies and help that way."

"Yes, we need experts too," Zakaria Amara commented approvingly. "I tried to go to Saudi and enroll in Islamic studies but they must have thought I was too extreme when I condemned the war in Iraq—they didn't let me in," he explained. "But I will be putting to good use all that I learned in my semester at Humber College studying fire systems technology," he added.

"I'm going to help recruit others and make our group stronger," Ameen Durrani said.

After each, Mubin said "Mashallah, thank you for your thoughts." All in all, the group was in solidarity with Fahim's thinking, although some were less devoted to actually enacting violent jihad.

Later, Fahim took Mubin aside and said, "I need you to train them on VIP convoy attacks."

"You do need to be trained properly for that," Mubin answered panicked at the thought of imparting such skills to guys who already owned guns. "Let's not do that with these guys *here*. Let's wait until we have the best guys selected out."

When it was time to leave, Mubin ordered the group to do a sweep of the camp. "Collect all the bullet casings, all the garbage. We don't want anyone to know we were here or why," he instructed. Everyone worked together to gather up their stuff. They rolled up the tarps, collected all the bullet casings and Mubin put it all into his van thinking, *That should have nearly all their fingerprints.*

"Don't talk about this when you get back," Fahim lectured. "We played capture the flag and hide and seek," he continued. "There was no jihad talk. Don't invite others until we meet them first."

As they left camp and entered the main road back to the town of Orillia, Mubin noticed a car following them. *Good*, he thought.

"I'm going to dump our garbage in town here," he announced to the others and drove to the garbage bin behind a big store where he unloaded the tarp into the bin—knowing that his handlers would pick it up right after he drove away.

***

"I'm back," Mubin said into the phone after letting the last guy out of his van.

"I know," Bill answered, chuckling.

"Of course," Mubin said laughing back.

"We need to meet up," Bill said.

"Let me get home and shower, because I stink," Mubin said. "It's been two weeks out in the woods there."

When Mubin arrived home Joanne was waiting for him with the kids. "How was camping dear?" she asked laughing.

"It was great!" Mubin answered. "Nothing quite like the bonding experience of sleeping in a tent with a bunch of brothers!"

Joanne came toward Mubin to kiss him but stopped when she got close, "Yeah, you should probably shower now. I could smell you from over there," she said. Joanne followed him into the bathroom and collected his clothes. "What should I do, burn these?" she joked.

"I have to go back out to see the boys," Mubin said from the shower.

"Okay, but don't be too long," she answered. "It's been two long weeks. I have needs," Joanne winked. She had a plate of food warmed up for Mubin to eat before he took off again. It was a far cry from their fire grilled pita bread and beans and tasted heavenly!

When Mubin called Bill again from his van, Bill gave him an address to come to. "Come there and drop off your van," he instructed. "We'll pick you up and show you to the safe house." Mubin knew the general area of the city it was located in and made his way, his mind racing with all sorts of expectations.

Am I being followed? Mubin wondered as he looked in his rearview mirror. He had begun to develop hypervigilance, something that is common while working such investigations.

When they arrived to the hotel in Bill's car, Mubin saw that it was a hotel he'd never visited before. "Here's the key," Bill said. "Count to thirty and follow me, but don't make like you know me," he instructed. Mubin did as he said and soon they were in the elevator together. Bill pushed the buttons for the eighth and ninth floor and when they arrived at eight, motioned for

Mubin to get off. Bill got off at the floor above and took the stairs back down. He walked past Mubin and let himself in the room. Mubin waited and then let himself in.

This time there were four guys present. "Welcome back Shaikh," one of the guys said rising. "I'm Sergeant Yuri. Nice to meet you." Yuri was in his forties, short and stocky, bald and sported a goatee. They shook hands and Mubin noticed Yuri was missing his pinky finger on his right hand.

Where did you pick this guy up? He could be a Russian gangster! Mubin thought noticing he was not the friendliest guy.

"You obviously know my friends," Yuri continued.

"No, I only know Bill," Mubin answered.

"This is David, he's our technical intercept guy, and this is Bill's new partner, Sammy. He's the body builder," Yuri said.

Mubin noticed that Sammy was built and nice looking with brown gel combed hair. David on the other hand, was skinny, and looked like a complete nerd wearing black rim glasses.

You look exactly like what I would expect! Mubin thought as he extended his hand to shake with David. *The only thing missing is tape holding the bridge of your glasses together!*

Then Sammy, the bodybuilder threw his hand into Mubin's, gripping him with an iron grip. No slouch himself, Mubin returned the grip with his own strength.

"Wow, that's quite a grip!" Sammy quipped.

"Coming from you, that's a compliment," Mubin quipped back. "I hope to get to know you a bit better."

"Don't assume anything," Sammy said. "I'm a good guy," he added with a bubbly note to his voice.

They've been here a while, Mubin concluded looking at the glass coffee table surrounded by the sofas they'd probably been lounging on. It had coffee cup rings all over it and there were peanut wrappers strewn about. The sergeant was a chain smoker and the room had the stink of cigarette smoke, even though they had a window open and the overhead fan going.

"How was it?" Bill asked. Mubin launched into a description of the two-week training camp giving them details of all the activities, persons, and conversations they had while the men took handwritten notes. It was clear they were looking for evidence as they had Mubin draw out all the places where they had fired weapons and had him draw the obstacle course, map out the entire camp and locate it physically on the map. They were going to go back and do an investigation of the site.

"There are some serious bad guys among them," Mubin summarized. "They are on the path to committing a dangerous terrorist act," he added.

"So give us your assessment of each of the individuals," Bill instructed.

Mubin broke it into two tiers—the leaders and their followers, "Fahim and Zakaria are the two ring leaders. They are the ones who started this group from the beginning and they are the ones who invited all the others to the camp. They scoped out the location and they visited it previously. These two are serious. They are looking to get weapons to conduct an attack. And if they get them, they *will* attempt something. Whether or not it's the plan as they have described it, or something else—they are *committed and they will act.* Look they already got a long rifle from me. And they have a nine-millimeter and they bought enough bullets for that. And as you already know from the individuals who were arrested in August, they are constantly looking to procure weapons. It's serious," Mubin concluded.

Moving to the followers he told his handlers, "Some of these guys are just kids. They don't belong there. Take Waleed. He's scared shitless, but he's not going to admit it. He got dragged there by Fahim's brother-in-law. I don't know if he'll ever come back. I don't know if they have an actual link to al Qaeda," Mubin explained regarding the group's ideological bent. "In fact, Fahim said, 'We are not officially AQ, but we are with them.' And it's true,"

Mubin continued. "Their ideology is straight out of al Qaeda playbooks. It was prevalent throughout the two weeks. We watched all of these DVDs. I've seen so many heads cut off it's like nothing now—like watching the Sunday morning cartoons," Mubin joked.

The RCMP cops snickered as Bill brought Mubin a cup of coffee.

"Shaikh, we are going to step up our security protocols," Yuri explained. "You'll just continue to monitor the group, but now every time you go out there will be a cover team with you. Rest assured your safety is paramount, but you'll need to be mindful of obeying the speed limits—especially if they are with you. We don't want any other police activity to interfere," Yuri explained. "It could spook some of them. God forbid one of them pulls a gun out on a cop and things go really bad, really fast. And we want to get you a work van—the exact same model you drive now—but fully outfitted with surveillance technology."

Mubin nodded and soon after, the group broke up.

"Go outside and walk down the stairs one floor and take the elevator to the lobby from there. I'll meet you in the parking lot," Bill instructed. From there he drove Mubin back to his car. Mubin hurried home, as there was an anniversary to celebrate.

***

"I sent some of the mujahideen a video clip of our training," Fahim said. Mubin was sitting in his new van with Fahim, listening to him talk, knowing the RCMP was listening as well—perhaps with some time delay.

"Which mujahideen?" Mubin asked.

"The ones in Pakistan," he said referring to the Aabid Khan, the brother who had gone over to Pakistan and was setting about to arrange for others to get into paramilitary training there.

"What does that mean for us?" Mubin asked.

"I want to show our Pakistani brothers that we are serious, that this is what is going on in Canada—we are the real deal—so now support us,"

Fahim said referring to the al Qaeda camp where Aabid had contacts. "I also requested them to send a trainer to us. Someone professional to take this to the next level. Someone who can help us make chocolate," Fahim said smiling.[32]

"Great!" Mubin commented.

"Zak is going to get a place for us," Fahim went on.

"What do you mean, a place?" Mubin asked.

"A place—a house."

"What are we going to do there?" Mubin asked.

"It's going to be set up for training," Fahim answered. "And when they bring back some of the brothers, we need a place for them to live. We need to be ready. And we need a safe place to store our weapons when they arrive."

Mubin nodded.

"Oh by the way, I've made an order for ordinance," Fahim continued.

"Great, what do I get?" Mubin asked.

"For you, I have some special sniper rifles," Fahim promised.

"That's perfect," Mubin responded. "That's my competency."

"Yeah, I got rocket propelled grendades, machine guns, AK-47s and the ammo," Fahim boasted. "I've got a Russian contact. I gave him four thousand dollars down already. He's bringing it all soon."

Mubin nodded thinking, *Man they are getting so close to operational!*

✳✳✳

Zakaria called some days later. "I want to come see you at your house. I'm going to bring my family," he inquired.

"Sure, you are more than welcome," Mubin responded.

Zakaria arrived on the agreed upon date with his wife of one year. Nada, his wife, arrived wrapped in black robes and a nikab covering her face. She held a baby girl in her arms. The women excused themselves to another room leaving Mubin and Zakaria to eat their meal alone.

"So what did you think of the camp?" Zakaria asked.

"Well, there were too many kids," Mubin responded.

"Yeah, I wasn't too happy about that, in fact," Zakaria agreed as he picked up a piece of Joanne's spiced chicken.

"How so?" Mubin asked also helping himself to more food.

"Well first of all like you said—too many kids. We need men. We don't need boys. And there were no security protocols—kids phoning their mommies and daddies. What is this a daycare?" Zakaria spat out.

"Yeah, Operation Potty Training," Mubin said, laughing as he put his chicken bone down on his plate.

"You know, honestly I think Fahim is a big bullshitter," Zakaria complained.

Is he genuine, or is he trying to trap me into talking bad about Fahim? Mubin mused. *Or is he asserting leadership of the group? Is the family breaking up?* Mubin's mind raced as he struggled how to answer.

"You know, it fell short," Zakaria continued letting Mubin off the hook for an answer. "It was supposed to be more than that. We had kids there!"

Zakaria stayed for prayer time and then rounded up his wife, Nada, and left.

"His wife lives in a jihadi fantasy world. And she knows exactly what her husband is up to!" Joanne said when they were gone. "These guys are a bunch of jokers!" she added, asking, "Where do you find these people?"

Mubin laughed in response.

"I *know* he's serious!" Mubin replied. That night Mubin looked around his home at his three little kids and his hero wife. *Man, I've shown this guy where I live and introduced him to my family. I guess I can move if I need to...* Mubin thought as he wondered what would come next.

***

"Hey, I've got some electronics I need to get rid of," Fahim said into the phone. "Are you coming by this Friday?" It was late January 2006.

Mubin was in the habit of meeting Fahim at the mosque on Fridays. *Is this code for something? Is he trying to sell stuff to fund the group? What is this?* Mubin asked himself but knew better than to voice aloud.

When Mubin showed up at the mosque Fahim was there waiting outside.

"I want you to meet someone," he said and took Mubin off to the side where he hugged a brother. "This is Jahmaal James, our brother, the graduate. He's just back from Pakistan," Fahim explained and introducing Mubin to Jahmaal, he added, "This is our brother, the trainer."

Jahmaal was a black Canadian convert from Christianity. His parents had emigrated from Fiji. He was dressed in black robes and sported a beard and turban. Mubin shook hands with Jahmaal saying, "Oh, looks like we are going to be having a few conversations."

"Looking forward to it brother," Jahmaal answered.

After Fahim and Mubin separated from Jahmaal, they began walking toward the mosque for prayers. "I've thought of some ways to fund our projects," Fahim said. "I'm going to rip off the banks. We can take their money anyways—it's fair game," Fahim added referring to the jihadi ideology about the wealth of disbelievers being open for the grabbing.

"How?" Mubin asked.

"I'm still thinking about it, but I want to create a job letter and get a loan from the bank and then cash it out. We'll screw the bank by using a fake identity," Fahim explained. "I've got a guy in the banks who can help me out with this. Steven Chand introduced me to him," Fahim said referencing the Hindu convert who had helped with the training at their winter camp. Steven had spent time in the military reserves.

After Friday prayers were over, Fahim came to Mubin with a plastic bag in his hands. "Come with me," he said looking nervously down at the bag.

"Yeah, let's not do this here," Mubin said looking around them. "Let's go in my van."

"Check this out," Fahim said pulling a camera out from the bag. It was late January 2006

"What is this?" Mubin asked. "You want to sell this?"

"I found this in the exit sign in my hallway!" Fahim explained nervously.

"Oh shit!" Mubin exclaimed.

"They've been watching me *the whole time!*"

"Woah, we don't know that," Mubin said calming Fahim down. "This is just your hallway. What are they going to see—just your mother and father coming and going! What really have you been doing in your apartment? Nothing!"

"Yeah, that's true," Fahim agreed, calming a bit.

"We know that they are trying to find info on us," Mubin continued. "They followed you, but we're one step ahead of them."

"So what do we do?" Fahim asked. "Can you retrieve the data on the camera?

"Yeah, I have a techie guy that could to do that," Mubin answered.

"Can you find out where the receiver is," Fahim asked excitedly. "Are they in my building?"

"I don't think they are in your building," Mubin answered confidently. "I think this is being patched in through the wiring in your building and sent to some remote location. But I can find that out for you. Leave it with me."

Fahim held on to the camera for a bit, hesitating. "Look, I trust you, but don't tell anyone about this," he cautioned, handing over the camera. " I told Zakaria about it. He wants to look at it as well. I don't know if he has anyone that can retrieve the data off it. You have the links…"

"Hey, maybe we can even sell it and make some money off it," Mubin said trying to cheer Fahim up and trying to ensure the surveillance camera ended in his hands rather than Zakaria's. "I bet we could easily get one hundred and fifty bucks."

"Great get the info and sell it!" Fahim said brightening.

"Will do," Mubin answered taking the camera out of Fahim's hands.

Back in his car, Mubin called Bill. "Safe house?"

"Safe house," Bill answered and hung up the phone.

Arriving at the safe house Mubin put the bag on the table.

"What have you got there?" Bill asked. *He doesn't know the conversation that took place in the car,* Mubin realized, then understanding there was some time lag with what was recorded in his van and when the RCMP guys heard it.

"Take a look," Mubin said moving back from the table.

Bill opened the bag and pulled the camera out.

"Oh shit!" he said as his head dropped into his hands. "Okay Shaikh, we need to do damage control on this," Bill added after a few moments of silence.

"Look, he wants me to download the info recorded on it—figure out where it's being received and he wants technical details on the camera, but I told him I can sell it for one hundred and fifty bucks," Mubin explained.

"That's great!" Bill replied. "You can offload it! I'll get you the money and we can retain possession of the camera. Let's do that! If he calls you asking for it back tell him, 'I am selling it right now,' so he knows it's out of your hands."

***

It was the 31st of January 2006 and Mubin was in Lake Aquitain Park in Mississauga with Fahim and Zakaria walking along the grassy area near the lake. It was night and the moonlight was shimmering on the water.

"This is the house I'm looking to buy for us—for our headquarters," Zakaria said handing Mubin a map and a real estate flyer for a residential stand-alone home. "It's in Opasatika, a ten-hour drive north of the city," Zakaria added, pointing out the location. "Abu Mujahid," Zakaria said using Mubin's Arabic kuna, your job is to go check this place out and tell me what you think of it. Is it good for our purposes?"

Mubin agreed and arranged to take the others along. "Look he said, writing down instructions. Tell Ameen to take the bus to this stop and wait for me there on Friday." Mubin wrote separate instructions for Fahim and Steven to be waiting at a nearby subway station. "No phone calls about this trip, okay?" he said handing them the papers.

"Dude, you are really paranoid," Zakaria said taking the paper.

"That's my job," Mubin replied.

"What's in the bag?" Mubin asked noting Zakaria was carrying a white plastic bag. "You have barbeque ribs in there for us?"

"No, it's a detonator I've been working on," Zakaria said as he produced what looked like a circuit board with a battery and some wires attached from the bag. "I haven't completed it yet," Zakaria confessed. "I've been working on it between customers —soldering the component parts into it behind the counter—for months now," Zakaria explained.[33] Mubin knew that he worked at a Canadian Tire gas station in Mississauga and was bored.

Wow he's thinking about using bombs too! Mubin thought as he stared at the device.

"Brother, we need another training camp," Fahim said as the group broke up. "We need to step this up."

"There were just kids there last time," Mubin complained. "You need to select more serious guys."

"Yeah, absolutely," Fahim answered. "Look Zakaria already knows how to make a detonator, so it's for real now," Fahim said.

***

It was February 3, 2006. The roads were icy and the weather was below freezing when Mubin went through his elaborate and seemingly covert pick-up. He picked up Steven, Ameen and Fahim in that order. Mubin wanted to impress upon his comrades in arms that he was very cognizant of them and of operational security. Under the surface however, he was appearing in a rental van that had been fully outfitted for surveillance.

"Where's the other van?" Fahim asked as he hopped in.

"My wife's using it. Anyway I thought it would be better to use a vehicle that no one recognizes. So I rented this one," Mubin explained. "And don't worry I left it at a friend's garage in his house last night. There's no way anyone tampered with it."

Once they got out on the main highway heading north the brothers began joking around. Suddenly, Fahim who was sitting in the passenger seat pulled his pistol out from his pants. "Oh by the way," he bragged, "if we get pulled over by the cops, we are going out in a blaze of glory!"

Man, if we get pulled over by a provincial policeman and he starts shooting, they'll shoot back, the van will be bullet ridden and I'm going to be dead! Mubin thought as his mind raced about how to neutralize Fahim.

"Brother keep it hidden," Mubin said as calmly as he could muster. His heart was thumping as he kept going back over and over the scene of being pulled over and a firefight ensuing. *I'll be dead for sure!*

The brothers joked around but Mubin kept reminding himself not to relax into their banter. *At any moment this could go south. You have to be ready to make your move!*

Later in the day the subject of Abu Sabr and Samir getting arrested for shoplifting camping supplies at a Canadian Tire store for the group's next training camp was discussed. Abu Sabr and another youth had gotten caught for stealing camping utensils, an LED clip light, an axe, and an eighteen-inch machete.

"They were going and stealing stuff for me, for whatever I wanna do," Fahim bragged. Mubin already knew that according to Fahim's militant jihadi principles, stealing from nonbelievers was totally endorsed—even encouraged.

After a full day of driving they arrived in Opasatika and found the house. It was located on 250, Government Road, which Mubin found ironic.

Mubin pulled the van into the driveway. The "for sale" sign was in the yard and the two-story house was uninhabited. The brothers piled out of the van. It was dark but there were streetlights illuminating the area. Mubin and the others walked around the eight-bedroom house checking it out. There were houses nearby on either side, and the town looked like a working class town—and white. There were no drapes on the windows of the house and it had exposed basement windows. The house looked well maintained and spacious inside as the guys walked around and tried to peer inside.

"It looks like even some of the married brothers can come here—at least they'll have a place to stay," Fahim said walking around the house. "It looks like there's plenty of room."

"I can live up here," Steven volunteered, "to maintain the place and make sure everything is okay."

"One of the things we'll have to do is dig a tunnel from the garage for when we bring ordinance up here," Fahim continued as they walked to the unattached garage. "We can't just walk it into the house."

That's ridiculous, Mubin thought but said nothing. *Why wouldn't we just put things in a box and carry it in under cover of night?*

"The kids can play out in the back while we do our thing in the woods," Fahim continued as they walked toward the back. Mubin noted that the yard backed out into to a vast wooded area.

"We could set up a machine gun stand there. And there's a tower here," Fahim said as they examined the large backyard. "We'll set up cameras up there to see in advance if anyone comes. Maybe we'll have to get a tech guy to tap into it to monitor any communications. We need to disrupt all surveillance."

"This is way too close to other people," Mubin commented. His job was to conduct an assessment of the place. "It's affordable—but I don't think it can work," Mubin said referring to the thirteen thousand listing price. "The neighbors can see you from all sides. What do you think they are going to think when a bunch of brown guys with beards and robes move in? We're not going to fit in at all."

"Look," Steven said looking at the map. "There is a logging area close by with old logging roads. If it's accessible through these woods maybe we could hide all of our activities deep inside the forests?"

The brothers gathered around the map and then hopped back in the van to check it out. "Wow, this is actually pretty good," Mubin said as they discovered the multiple points of access and the long abandoned logging roads leading deep into the woods. "You can hide anywhere in here," he said excitedly.

"So the house works!" Fahim concluded triumphantly. "We keep a low profile in the neighborhood and conduct all our activities over here!"

Mubin and the others loaded back into the van as the snow started to fall like crazy—piling up on the windshield almost as fast as the wipers could remove it. While the others had given him some time to rest by taking over the driving from time to time, now Mubin didn't want to yield the driver's seat because the roads were getting dangerous.

"Look, one of the reasons we are getting this place is because we will need to hide out after our big mission at the Parliament," Fahim said as he reentered his grand fantasy of terrorist destruction.

"So what happens at Parliament?" Durrani asked.

"We go and cut off some heads," Fahim answered matter-of-factly.

"Then what?" Durrani asked.

"Then we read about it," Fahim cackled as Mubin pulled the van into a roadside cafe to take a break.

"We'll attack the Parliament buildings of Canada," Fahim continued as they got out of the van for coffees. "First we'll distract the police with car bombs going off all around the city. That will take all the security forces attention away from the Parliament," Fahim fantasized. "And then when they are responding to the car bombs, we will storm the Parliament buildings! I have a guy who has been checking out their security—where the members enter from and what kind of security they have, where they will stand and what weapons they have," Fahim confided.

The others remained silent, sipping their coffees, as Fahim continued describing his vision of their attack. "We will storm the place. We'll take the Members hostage and cut their heads off—one every hour and demand that they bring the troops back from Afghanistan. The Prime Minister's head is definitely going!"

"We'll give the head-chopping job to Gulshan," Fahim said referring to one of the young men that had accompanied them on the camping trip. He had been really into using the axe and splitting logs at their training camp and seeming to enjoy the chore as if he was imagining heads flying instead of logs. "Did you see him chopping the wood?" Fahim broke into laughter. "Can you imagine him chopping necks?"

"What's my job?" Mubin asked.

"You are going to be the sniper taking out the cops and all the guys that come to respond," Fahim answered.

"Alright!" Mubin said pretending to be into the plan. "That's my job!"

"What's my job?" Ameen asked.

"You are going to be the explosives guy, pushing the button while we are storming the place," Fahim replied. Joking, he started mimicking a telephone call, "Hi, calling Parliament building. Enter one if you want to see Members of Parliament with their heads blown off. Enter two if you want to see the walls coming down…"

"We'll go and kill everybody, then read about it, then get victory," Fahim said obviously enjoying his fantasy of success as the guys walked to the van and headed out on the highway again.

The snow was really accumulating—nearly two feet of it by the time Mubin was halfway to Toronto. There were many cars run off the road and the road was slippery beneath their tires. The snowplows and tractor trailers zoomed by creating a maze of snow as Mubin struggled to see his way ahead. *Are we even going to make it home?* Mubin wondered. *And if we do, what's going to follow?*

***

"Anything exciting happen on the way up?" Zakaria asked when they met again at the Ali Mosque past midnight. It was February 5, 2006. "You shoot any cops?"

Mubin laughed. He knew Zakaria hated cops and was quite sure that he was under surveillance. He had even once gotten out of his car and photographed police following him.

"So, do you think the house is useful?" Zakaria asked. "Can we use it how it is?"

"The house is good, but it's too close to some of the neighbors," Fahim answered.

"So kill the neighbors!" Zakaria spat. "Who is going to know?"

"The house itself is not so suitable actually," Fahim went on. "But there is a great wooded area nearby that is very valuable! Man, it's such isolation—like yo, you could be walking around with freakin' guns and nobody will see you. There's nobody there!"

"What do *you* think? Why are you so quiet?" Zakaria asked Mubin. Mubin had been letting Fahim do all the talking.

"He's the emir," Mubin replied flattering Fahim as having the leadership role. "It's just like Fahim said. The house itself is not the greatest, but the areas nearby are perfect."

"So have the 'toys' arrived?" Zakaria asked Fahim as his voice hardened.

"I haven't heard anything from the guy," Fahim replied in his usual nonchalant manner. "I'm still waiting. But don't worry, it's coming. I put four thousand down on them, but we need to figure out how to raise more money."

"Here look at this," Zakaria said pulling out his phone on which he played a video showing his detonator now working—the device sparked powerfully. "See it works!" Zakaria crowed. "I built our first radio frequency remote-control detonator! The only problem is it has a range of only about thirty meters, which is not so good."

"So you'd get blown up? Might as well sit in the car," Fahim joked.

"It's a step forward," Zakaria replied, obviously proud of his invention

"If we can use it from three hundred meters, then we'll do it!" Fahim said with fire in his eyes. "It detonates for sure?"

"Yeah, it does," Zakaria answered, his eyes and voice steely. "When the bomb goes off on Front Street many will be killed and it will be too bad for them!"

***

"So, we've got a bomb detonator," Mubin said when he called into Bill later that night to give his report. "And oh yeah, we're getting sniper rifles and RPGs and..." Mubin began to rattle off the list of weapons Fahim had said were imminently arriving.

"Did you say *bomb detonator?*" Bill cut in, alarm filling his voice.

"Yeah man, that's exactly what I said," Mubin answered.

"Whoa, Shaikh! Slow down! Slow down!" Bill cut in again. "You said you have a bomb detonator already?"

"Yes, we have a bomb detonator," Mubin confirmed, his voice deadpan. "I saw it with my own eyes and it works."

"Holy shit!" There was silence on the line and then Bill continued, "Alright Shaikh, let me call you right back."

Mubin waited for about twenty minutes.

"Ok Shaikh, we need to see you right away," Bill said, "It's a safe house meet."

Bill and Sammy were there, both with looks of concern on their faces as Mubin entered.

"We need to get this info up the chain of command as quickly as possible," Sammy said. They then showed Mubin how to author a debriefing report in which he sat at the computer to write, print, date, and sign it.

"Okay, from here on in you have to author these reports anytime you have a meeting with these folks," Bill explained. "We need to get this fresh after the events—record things as contemporaneous as possible."

Mubin pushed print as he finally finished his write up. He'd been at the safe house typing in his event report until four in the morning. Bill read it and then they both signed it with Sammy witnessing. Bill then filed it accordingly.

"You need to let us know right away when you see any of these weapons," Bill instructed as they began to wrap up their meeting. "Do whatever you need to do. Maintain knowledge at all times where these weapons are coming from. We want to know all the details of when they are arriving and from whom."

Mubin nodded.

"It's obviously getting more serious," Sammy said as they all stood up to leave.

"We are particularly interested in the heavy ordinance," Sammy added. "And under no circumstances Shaikh, are you to blow anything up!"

"I'm not making any promises," Mubin said laughing. The others laughed as well, although uneasily.

***

The next day Mubin returned to the safe house with the rental van and the guys did a sweep of the vehicle for any forensic items they could

find. They turned up a Qur'an, some tissues, and other small items. Bill photographed the items once they were inside the safe house and asked Mubin
to describe who brought what and for what purpose it was used. Then Sammy, Bill and Mubin went over the eighteen actors in this plot and discussed
the risk associated with each one.

"So I'm going to put Fahim, Jahmaal, Steven, Ameen and Zakaria as
all serious threats," Bill commented as Mubin discussed each one.

"Yes," Mubin replied.

"These three teenagers," Bill said pointing to Waleed and two of the
other youngsters, "are low threat, right?"

Mubin nodded.

In a few days, Mubin met Fahim again and asked about the crate of
weapons. It was mid-February, 2006.

"I've made the order," Fahim answered. "I'm just waiting for him to
confirm that he's picked it up. Maybe next month he'll be back."

I wonder if he's making this up? Mubin thought. *Does it take this long
for this stuff to come in? Maybe it does? Maybe the smuggler is being very
careful…*

"There are other guys we have, elsewhere in Canada that we have
told we are looking into a safe house," Fahim continued. "We are thinking of
possibly bringing them our way. And there are other guys out there that we
are going to bring back in—guys in the U.S. and guys in the UK."

He's exposing the network to me, Mubin thought, but then his phone
rang cutting Fahim off. It was Mariya, Fahim's wife. Mubin handed him the
phone. Fahim didn't have his own mobile.

"Abu Hurayrah—he's a former associate of ours—the fucker!" Fahim
exclaimed when he got off the phone. "He was the source of the leak to the
government about the Somalis [Mohammed Dirie and Yasin Mohamed] at
the border—the guys who were bringing us guns last August!" Fahim spouted. "He wants to meet, but I want to pound his face! You in?"

"Sure," Mubin answered. He knew about the guy and that there was more to the story. Fahim's wife's sister had liked him but there had been a fallout after that and Fahim needed to stand up for his sister-in-law's honor.

"I'm going to cut this guy's fingers off!" Fahim fumed.

"Look, if you do something like that the cops will be all over us," Mubin chided. "We have a mission. Stick to the mission. Don't compromise it by doing these emotional things."

When they arrived at the designated meeting place they saw that Abu Hurayrah had arrived flanked by well built friends. Fahim backed off his aggressive plans but still shouted at his former friend. "If you ever call her again," Fahim threatened, "two are coming your way," he said making a shooting motion with his hand. "You know I have it and I can do it!"

Abu Hurayrah just stared back at him while one of his friends warned, "Hey watch what you say!"

Mubin intervened to diffuse the situation and led Fahim back to the van.

***

"We need to step up our assault on the Parliament," Fahim told Mubin in their next meeting. It was February 21, 2006. "Maybe we should attack an armory to get weapons…" he considered.

"We'd get killed for sure doing that," Mubin answered. "They are very highly fortified places."

A week later on February 27, 2006 Fahim told Steven Chand and Mubin that his main mission was to get a hold of weapons and that he wanted to hold another training camp.

"I'm concerned that Islam does not permit a person who has accepted citizenship or official status in Canada to commit crimes here," Steven said, a worried look crossing his face.

Finally! Someone's been reading up on his Islam! Mubin thought. *Looks like Steven is getting disillusioned!*

"Maybe if we left the country and reentered without any official authorization it would be permissible?" Steven deliberated.

"Don't you know Canada spies on its own citizens?" Fahim spat. "What they do cancels any type of Islamic covenants not to commit crimes here. It's our Islamic duty to stop them. Just look at Afghanistan where they are killing our Islamic brothers! Don't you know—if they attack us anywhere in the world then they are subject to our attacks wherever they are found!" Fahim replied. "The laws of Islam are above all other laws! And these national borders were drawn by kuffars!" Fahim spat as he used the Arabic word for a non-believer as a slur.

Steven and Mubin were silent in the face of Fahim's rant.

There is no such cancellation of the covenant! Mubin thought wanting to shout it into Fahim's face. *This only applies when the offense was to attack and expel you from living in their lands for following Islam. It's not true that just any civilians can be attacked in response. These guys manipulate Islam in any way they can to have the means justify the ends,* Mubin thought feeling his body heat rising up around his collar.

"You know, I feel like killing Mufti Waheedullah!" Fahim went on as he fumed next about a well-known Islamic scholar in the community. "Do you know he visited Ameen Durrani's wife and my father-in-law and told them that I'm a *deviant*? Me, a deviant? He probably works for CSIS! We should place a listening device in his office and find out the truth about him!" Fahim ranted.

A few days later on March 3, 2006, Steven Chand introduced his friend, Talib to Fahim and Mubin. "I can help you defraud banks," Talib told them. "There are many ways to do it. One is to obtain an individual's financial profile and then use that information to obtain identification documents."

"But how do you get a person's financial profile?" Mubin asked.

"You can buy it from a credit agency or I can pay a bank employee that trusts me to print it out and give me a copy," Talib answered. "Then we use a 'striker'—usually someone addicted to coke that needs money—to use the false identity papers to file for a ten to twenty-five thousand dollar loan. So far only three or four of the 'strikers' I've used out of fifty have been caught in this scheme."

"Or you can use 'creations.' That's where we invent a person using the Social Identity Number (SIN) of someone who has died or left the country. Then you create ID cards in that person's name and apply for credit cards that we use and pay for over time to create a positive credit score. Then we again use a 'striker' to apply for a mortgage or large loan."

"Awesome!" Fahim said, excited by the idea of stealing so much money from the "kuffars." "This is a global fight by the way," he added. "Soldiers that are training in their military bases here are gonna go to Afghanistan and fight there," Fahim started in. "These same soldiers are fighting you there, so why can't you attack them here? I lived in Afghanistan as a child…" Fahim said his voice fading momentarily.

Then in his customary way, Fahim challenged Talib, "You wanna be on the sidelines or you wanna be on the frontlines? Sideliners get no rewards and they still die!"

Talib was silent listening to Fahim and gave no indication one way or the other how he felt about the militant jihad. Fahim however was oblivious that Talib might not be into it. He was on his rant and continued loudly. "Our thing is going to be on a much larger scale than the London subway bombing that killed ten people."

Two days later, unknown to Mubin at the time, Steven Chand called Fahim to advise him, "Listen you have to approach Talib on a strictly business basis. He will not respond to emotional or religious appeals and he won't give you a dollar if he knows that civilians are going to be hurt." The two discussed whether or not they should be wearing concealed weapons now and Fahim answered that they already had their weapons and that the involved youth certainly didn't need them.

"I know you might not be too down with the beheadings, but it's terror," Fahim told Steven who was vacillating in his commitment to killing Canadian civilians. "It strikes fear into their hearts," Fahim said trying to reassure his fellow plotter.[34]

***

"These are atrocities being committed in Afghanistan by Christian soldiers!" Fahim spouted on March 11, 2006 to Mubin, Steven Chand, Fahim, Ameen Durrani and two of the youth gathered in a restaurant together. Fahim was playing a DVD that depicted gruesome decapitations and dismemberments—claiming that Christians were carrying them out.

One of the youth who Mubin had not met before seemed to be Afghan and Mubin wondered, *Is Fahim particularly targeting him for recruitment?* As Mubin watched the group he felt alarmed that none of them showed any reaction to the video. *Are they just completely desensitized to jihadi violence at this point?* Mubin thought.

"You need to be careful who you show these DVD's to," Mubin warned Fahim when they left the restaurant. [35]

"I'm giving these out at the mosques!" Fahim answered. "I've got my *Reality Series* nearly finished," Fahim bragged referring to the video collection that he was compiling of jihadi videos and a montage of pictures depicting scenes of Muslims being brutalized all around the world. "It's going to be great for recruiting!" Fahim continued.

"I was thinking we could hit different mosques and give my *Reality Series* out," Fahim said a few days later, showing Mubin how he had taped his MSN chat name and phone number to the DVD cover.

Mubin nodded thinking, *He has no sense of operational security—none at all!*

Fahim then took Mubin around to some of the mosques looking for the most receptive and fiery youth to which he would ask, "Hey brother do you know what's happening in the Muslim world—what's happening with our brothers and sisters? We have to do something about it!" Fahim urged. Then handing them the DVD he said, "Take a look at this and call us when you are ready to get serious."

While with Mubin, Fahim handed out his recruitment disk to dozens of young men—all potential fighters for his cause.

"I got a hit on MSN," Fahim reported afterwards. "This brother said his mother wasn't very religious but after she saw it she had tears in her eyes and she told her son, 'Whatever these guys want—go ahead and join them!'"

"Now, I need a copy of our training DVD to show the brothers over in Pakistan what we are doing. I sent a short clip, but Zakaria still hasn't given me the complete training video," Fahim complained.

"Who did you send it to?" Mubin asked.

"I sent a two minute clip of the rough version of our training at the Washago Camp to Mr. Fixit [referring to Aabid Khan] to show the brothers in Pakistan how serious we are. I want him to see that we are still on track with our objective of being involved with them in a series of coordinated terrorist attacks," Fahim explained.

"How did you send it?" Mubin asked.

"By e-mail," Fahim answered, again seemingly oblivious that the security folks would have picked up on that. "It's taking Zakaria and Asad [Ansari] so long to produce our training video!" Fahim complained. Asad was the group's computer whiz. "It seems like he's stalling on giving it to us!" Fahim griped.[36]

He's probably scared to put it out there, Mubin thought.

"You go and get it from him," Fahim told Mubin. "They know you are a serious guy—they respect you," Fahim added, meaning Mubin could physically threaten them.

"Okay, I'll go and pick it up," Mubin replied.

"I also reached out to Ali Dirie and asked him if he has a contact in the city that could provide guns for the group," Fahim admitted referring to a call he had put in to Dirie in prison in early February—a month earlier. Again with no sense of operational security.

Ali Dirie, Mubin knew, was one of the Somali gun smugglers who were serving his two-year sentence at Collins Bay Penitentiary.

Man, this guy takes risks! Mubin thought, knowing surveillance was nearly one hundred percent guaranteed to pick up a call from Fahim Ahmad to Ali Dirie in prison.

Indeed, the exact phone call made on February 6, 2006, in which Fahim inquired to Dirie in prison about "links to wives"—thinking he was using some amazing code, was recorded by surveillance and later used in court against him. Dirie, who had in other intercepts expressed his desire to stay involved in Fahim's cell and terrorist activities, was confused at first when Fahim asked about "wives," but when he realized that Fahim was using their prior agreed upon code, gave Fahim the phone number of a potential clandestine arms supplier.[37]

"I also sent him our *Reality Series One, Return of the Crusaders* and *Constants on the Path of Jihad* videos and told him, 'Remember us in your prayers,'" Fahim smirked like he thought his plan was unfolding flawlessly.

You're an idiot! Mubin thought but said nothing.

***

"How do foreign fighters get to places like Iraq?" Gulshan, one of the youth, a young Sri Lankan immigrant, asked Mubin on March 24, 2006. "Should you go to India, then Pakistan and on from there?" he asked.

"You need contacts," Mubin answered, feeling sorry for the youngsters who were getting dragged deeper and deeper into this. Mubin already knew it was going to end badly for them.

"You can't just present yourself in a foreign land and declare your purpose!" Mubin answered, with his anger of the waste of a young life perhaps coming out in his sarcasm.[38]

"It's just the suffering of our fellow Muslims," Gulshan answered. "I'd like to go for jihad in Iraq and help out."

You are too young to be caught up in this garbage, Mubin thought shaking his head but said nothing, as he didn't want to blow his cover as a fellow jihadi. Mubin recalled how Fahim had pointed out Gulshan some months earlier, saying that he'd like to groom him to become a suicide bomber for the group. And for his part, Gulshan was young and impressionable and as a new convert to Islam, very eager to prove himself.[39]

***

In a few days, in March 2006, Mubin traveled across Toronto to meet with Zakaria.

"Hey, do you think the government will forgive us for what we've done?" Zakaria asked Mubin while they were hanging out.

Are these guys onto me? Mubin wondered as he startled at the question. His heart started to bump wildly inside his chest.

"Look, I don't want to be in Fahim's group anymore," Zakaria continued.

"What do you mean?" Mubin asked.

"We think he's a big bull shitter," Zakaria complained. "He keeps talking about weapons that don't materialize. People are giving him money—but where is it going? Will you leave his group and join ours?" Zakaria asked.

"I'm new to the group," Mubin stalled. "You guys know each other for a longer time. He's supposed to be our emir—now he's not? What's the deal?"

"He's not security conscious," Zakaria complained. "Did you know he sent our training video—the rough one he had—overseas without editing any of our faces out of it? He's going to get himself, and us, busted if he's not more careful!"

Mubin listened, nodding, remembering that Zakaria had done a lot of the filming himself. "Yeah, he's giving out disks at the mosque too."

"He's just plain stupid!" Zakaria said, disgust filling his voice. "I'm moving ahead without him. And I don't have the disk for you either, right now," he added. "The brother who is compiling the disk—I haven't been able to get in touch with him. He's not returning my calls," Zakaria said wrapping up their conversation. "Tell Fahim I don't have it."

"I'm not going to keep coming back here like a yo-yo," Mubin complained. "Who knows what kind of cops are watching? I take a lot of precautions before I leave, but still…" Mubin said.

"Come next week and I'll give it to you," Zakaria said. "Tell him it's being developed. And don't tell him what we talked about."

***

"Safe house?" Mubin asked when Bill called him.

"No, I want you to be aware that tomorrow a newspaper article is going to run and I want you to bring it up with Fahim."

What could this possibly be? Mubin wondered. The next day, March 23rd, 2006, Mubin saw that it turned out to be the arrest of Syed Haris Ahmed, one of the American jihadis that had been in Canada meeting with Fahim and Jahmaal James the previous March of 2005.

"Hey you need to see this," Mubin said over the phone. "The 'Atlanta Cell' has been arrested. Let me come meet you." Later in the van Mubin read the article aloud as Fahim listened. Mubin could see how agitated it was making Fahim—his leg was jumping.

"Oh my God!" Fahim burst out. "What kind of information have they given up to the authorities? They are talking about me!"

"How much do the Atlanta guys know about our plans?" Mubin inquired calmly.

"They don't know anything, just that we wanted to do something big," Fahim replied, his voice filled with worry.

"But they don't know specifics?" Mubin continued.

"No," Fahim answered.

"Who knows about our plans here?" Mubin continued.

"Just us," Fahim answered, his eyes filled with panic.

"The guys who went up, any of these other smaller guys know?" Mubin asked referring to the youth and Qayyum Abdul, the custodian at the mosque.

"Abdul Qayyum! You think I'd trust him enough to give him specifics, screw him!" Fahim spat.

"Okay, what do we do from here?" Mubin asked.

Fahim remained quiet, pensively staring out the window. "I was very, very tight with one of them and both stayed at my house for two weeks," he finally said. "I know jail time is so close and my days are numbered," he added sadly.

Then looking in the back of the van he perked up asking, "How many barrel bombs can we fit in this thing?"

Mubin just stared at him in silence.

"We are going to go fully out now with our mission," Fahim continued. "We need to act now! We could load this van up with gasoline tanks, nails, glass and ball bearings and detonate it in downtown Ottawa!"

***

Five days later, on March 28, 2006, Mubin arrived in Mississauga wearing reflective sunglasses. "Don't I look like a stone cold killer?" Mubin joked.

"No, you look like a spy," Zakaria replied.

They are on to me! Mubin worried as his heart again began to race. "Why would you say that?" he asked. "Who do you think I'm spying for? I've put my own family at risk," Mubin protested in a hurt tone of voice.

"I don't know," Zakaria answered coolly. "Are you spying for Fahim?" Zakaria asked.

"Listen, I didn't say anything to him," Mubin explained. "Did he say anything to you since our last meeting?"

"No."

"So clearly I kept my mouth shut," Mubin replied.

"Listen, I want out of his group. He's a weak link. I'm going on my own. I'm researching what I need to get to make a bomb—looks like ammonium nitrate fertilizer, fuel tablets and my detonator will do the trick," Zakaria said referring to library research he'd been conducting. [40]

"I'm asking Saad Khalid and Saad Gaya to help me. Gaya is studying science at McMaster University," Zakaria added. "I just have to get him on board."

Mubin nodded, wondering how he would be able to track this part of the operation now if Fahim was being dropped from the plan. Up till now Fahim had been the one mainly keeping Mubin up to date on all their activities.

After Mubin left, Zakaria—always the wily one—called Fahim on a phone line he knew was being tapped. "Everybody in Mississauga, we just quit everything, totally," Zakaria told his former emir. He left a similar message on the MSN Messenger account of Mariya, the wife of Fahim. Zak and the Mississauga guys – we're just done with everything, he wrote.

In reality it was the farthest thing from the truth. Zakaria was going full speed ahead, on his own. [41]

***

Having dropped Fahim, Zakaria began in earnest on his own library research of how to make a vehicle born bomb from commonly available materials. And he began reaching out to contacts to figure out how to obtain what he needed. Zakaria also ordered Asad to destroy the training camp video in order to avoid any incriminating evidence thwarting his plans. [42]

The second RCMP agent, Shaher Elsohemy (now in witness protection under an assumed identity) who had infiltrated Zakaria's trust, learned that Zakaria would either obtain his ammonium nitrate by bulk purchase or if that didn't work he would have two unnamed friends, presumably Gaya and Khalid, buy fertilizer, bleach and household chemicals. In that case, Zakaria's plan was for them to buy the items in small quantities, up to nine times a month, from the Canadian Tire and Home Depot—until they amassed enough to make smaller, yet also lethal, bombs.

After Shaher Elsohemy told Zakaria that his uncle owned a large chemical plant, Amara asked him about getting ammonium nitrate, nitric acid and sulfuric acid through his uncle. Then without telling Fahim, Zakaria made an order for three tons of ammonium nitrate—a common fertilizer—along with a couple gallons of nitric acid, to make his bombs.

Zakaria already had his detonator. He'd tested it and he knew it worked and he had also fixed the thirty-meters range problem. His bombs could now be detonated by remote control, via a phone call from anyone—even from out of town.[43] Zakaria was ready to go—as soon as his fertilizer arrived.

Mubin learned of the explosives the next time he visited Zakaria.[44] "Fahim is moving too slow," Zakaria complained. "I want to get on with it. I've created this fake student farmer card," Zakaria explained showing Mubin his fake business cards that he had ordered via the public library computer. "And I've ordered the fertilizer—three tons of it. Saad Khalid will drive it in a rental van to the CSIS building in Toronto, and we'll have Gaya and one of the others drive to the Toronto Stock Exchange and to hit a military base. It's the base where the Canadian fallen soldiers are repatriated," Zakaria explained. "We're going to kill them twice," he said his voice hardening. "And I'm working on figuring out how to put shrapnel and bits of metal in the bombs so they will kill more people," Zakaria explained.

"You know in the UK the brothers thought they had stockpiled fertilizer but the security guys got on to them and replaced it with inert material," Zakaria said. "That won't happen here. We've sealed the door with wax."

Terrorists learn from the successes and failures of their brothers, Mubin mused. He was glad to have learned in his last meeting with Bill that the other operative had led them to Zakaria's fertilizer purchase just prior to it taking place, and as a result the government had arranged for Zakaria to be supplied with an inert product.

Zakaria also told Shaher Elsohemy that his plan would cost $20,000 for the Canadian expenses and $10,000 for the travel and living expenses in Pakistan for those intending to flee and that they already had $20,000 cash. In his court case it would come out that including the money paid for the purchase of the ammonium nitrate and the money seized at the time of the arrests, Zakaria's cell had access to roughly $30,000.

Zakaria was not just talking but totally intent on his plan as investigators learned, when later, on May 3, 2006 they conducted a covert search (allowed by a warrant) of his residence. There they found an instruction manual and diagrams on how to mix chemicals for making a bomb, an MK-160 circuit board, a black box and a battery pack. They also observed the same video Zakaria had shown Fahim and Mubin in which he triggered his remote-controlled detonator via his cell phone.

The RCMP also had intercepts in late April of Zakaria talking about his exit plan—Sudan figured high in his plans because no passport was required but in the end Zakaria settled on going to hide in Pakistan. From there, he said he planned to enter Afghanistan for war.

Zakaria Amara's plan included using a two-way ticket, not because he was returning, but because he knew law enforcement persons might consider the purchase of a one-way ticket as a reason for further investigation. And he was definitely not planning to "martyr" himself. For now, he was going to murder others and escape in his "live and let die" explosions, planned to occur around nine a.m. November 2006. According to his exit plan, he would have boarded his plane and already be headed out of Canada an hour after they were all detonated.

"You know it only took one ton of ammonium nitrate for Timothy

McVeigh to bring down the Murrah Federal Building in Oklahoma City," Bill told Mubin in their last meeting. "That explosion killed one hundred and sixty-eight people and wounded many more."

Thankfully, Mubin knew the material inside the sacks that Zakaria's team had offloaded into his sealed rental container was inert. The government agencies were one step ahead of the terrorists—although just barely and only *one* step.

The Hammer Falls—Fallout

It was late April 2006. "Fahim is talking about car bombs and Zakaria has his two Saads unloading what he believes is real fertilizer and placing it in a rental unit," Mubin recapped the next time he met with Bill in the safe house.

"Shaikh, the case is now coming to a close," Bill said. "We are shutting it down. The hammer is going to fall."

Mubin sighed deeply thinking, *Okay it's going down—they are all going to get arrested.*

"We are going to facilitate your exit from the city," Bill continued. "We'll put you and your family up in a safe house and the hammer is going to come down on the rest of them."

"Okay, just let them have their Friday prayers," Mubin said feeling suddenly disturbed for the suffering of the others.

"Okay, okay," Bill replied feeling no such sympathy for the terrorist plotters.

Mubin drove home heavy hearted. He knew he couldn't discuss his feelings with anyone, yet he could already anticipate the wrath of the Muslim community if the case was not explained correctly.

I feel bad, people are going to get hurt, Mubin thought, and then argued back with himself, *but they deserve it.* And again, *They are going to get hurt—they're kids. But man they were going operational! They've already committed the crimes—I can't undo that! And if they get armed they are really going to hurt people, and I'm not going to be the one who could have done something and didn't.*

It's just like 9-11, those terrorists didn't care if Muslims also got hurt and died, Mubin mused. *What's to say that in blowing up and shooting people here, the same wouldn't happen? I have to do this!*

And if they aren't rounded up and enact their terrorism plots, there will be a terrible backlash onto the community, Mubin thought. *I need to do the right thing and mitigate the backlash on our community. We have to show that some of us stand up against this shit. I hope they understand,* Mubin worried.

The anxiety and racing thoughts continued all night. Mubin was filled with overwhelming tension, doubt and distress. He felt there was nowhere to turn. He couldn't call the RCMP agents back and say, "Hey can we reconsider? Is there any other way to stop this from happening?"

Mubin tried to sleep but found he just tossed and turned in bed, his thoughts racing. *What about their families, their kids? But they did this to themselves! I didn't bring this on them. What are people going to say about me to my kids?*

Before Mubin and his family left town for the safe house, the tension rose to such a level that Mubin reverted to his old ways. He went to visit Brad—his old friend from high school, the friend whose home had always been a safe haven.

"Some serious shit is about to hit the fan," Mubin told his friend as they sat reminiscing over good times and the partying they had done in the past.

"What do you mean?" Brad asked.

"I'm an undercover operative with the government. I've been working a terrorism case," Mubin admitted. It was the first time he'd breached security but the anxiety of the imminent arrest was too much to bear alone.

"Holy shit man!" Brad replied then he added, "Alright!" and beamed at Mubin in admiration.

"You have any coke?" Mubin asked recalling how in high school coke had always boosted his self-esteem and made him feel confident.

"You sure?" Brad asked.

"Yeah, that's what I need right about now," Mubin replied.

Brad made a phone call and when the dealer dropped it by sometime later, he shook a pile out on the table and arranged a line for Mubin.

"Oh that shit is good!" Mubin said after snorting it. He remembered how it used to feel, how it felt now—bolstering his sense of confidence, the euphoria taking him outside of this bleak existence into a sense of exhilaration that made him feel all powerful.

Shit I shouldn't be doing this, Mubin thought as he took his second line. *I'm a Muslim. I've been here before. I should know better.* But the drug was too good and the relief from his pain was too exquisite to stop now.

"Thanks Brad," Mubin said as he let the drug hit him. "I needed that."

"Hang in there," Brad replied. "You're doing the right thing with the case, but that stuff," he said looking dubiously at the coke still on the table, "don't make it a habit, okay?"

***

The safe house outside of town was a regular detached house. Mubin drove his family there himself taking a few suitcases, his computer and any things the kids would need. Mubin and his wife, Joanne lived frugally so it wasn't hard to decide what to leave and what to take—they didn't own much. The kids thought it was a vacation and that's what Mubin told his parents as well. It was June 2, 2006.

"How are you feeling?" Joanne asked as they waited. They were ensconsed in the safe house—two hours out of Toronto—safe from everything.

Mubin had the radio switched on and felt excited waiting to hear as he wondered, *What's happening in Toronto right now?*

"Wow, it's surreal to me right now," Mubin answered. "It's almost like a dream. I don't believe it's happening—that it's even real. I feel sorry for their families—that they would put them through this. I feel sorry for their kids."

"What kind of man are you that you'd leave your wife and kids trying to be some wannabe hero?" Joanne mocked them. She felt sorry for their families but disgusted with their treacherous antics.

"At least they got to say their Friday prayers," Mubin replied sadly.

Aside from Brad he hadn't shared anything with anyone. No one had any idea what was about to hit the fan—until it did.

Friday prayers had just finished and the tactical unit picked up Fahim and Ameen just outside the mosque. Zakaria was taken down at home. Steven was pulled over on the highway and taken down, while a news helicopter whirred overhead capturing the scene of the arrest and the four lanes of freeway blocked by the police.

Waleed and the other teenagers were picked up at their mosque by another team. The two Saads were caught red handed loading more "fertilizer."[45]

Overall, four hundred police officers participated in the coordinated arrests of fifteen terrorism suspects—the two Somali gun smugglers were already serving time—and the eighteenth member of the Toronto 18 was arrested one month later, due to confusion over his identity.[46]

As the terrorist plotters were rounded up in one fell swoop it started hitting the news.

"A series of arrests have been taking place across the city," a news bulletin interrupted their discussion. Mubin had left the radio news station on nonstop since they arrived. *Finally, it was being reported!*

"There are multiple police units involved and it appears possibly related to terrorism. Standby for more news to follow," the broadcaster read.

"Switch on the television," Mubin directed as Joanne moved to do so. The first scene on all the major local channels was showing Fahim being brought to the courthouse. A police helicopter hovered overhead and snipers were positioned on top of the building.

Oh crap! My life will never be the same again! Mubin thought as he watched the scenes unfold. *Everyone is talking about it! This is REAL!* Mubin realized as his mind raced to imagine the repercussions in his personal and community life. *This is just the start of my life being turned upside down!*

Mubin checked his mobile phone. No one from Mubin's former life had called. No one from the various mosques reached out to him. Mubin felt worried thinking about it. *They must know! I didn't get arrested. I'm obviously the spy! How are people going to deal with it? They are probably going to end up blaming me!*

Mubin had been so engulfed in his work first for CSIS and then the RCMP that he had steadily progressed into further and further levels of deception that he hadn't, until the case moved into arrest mode, taken the time to think about how the community would respond to his involvement in this case as an undercover agent. Now he had too much time to think about it. And he knew that his community was in an unhealthy state of denial—they would be much more likely to see the government as the enemy and also blame him for identifying and having infiltrated the terrorist plotters than to believe they were actually guilty. The more Mubin thought about it the more he wanted to get out in front of the media story—to help shape it to more accurately reflect what had actually happened.

Mubin put a call into a friend who put him in touch with a local producer of a very respectable television show—the *Fifth Estate*. After talking over the phone, Mubin left the safe house to meet with the producer who tried to talk him into giving an interview right then and there.

"I'm staying at a safe house and not even supposed to be here," Mubin said stalling. "I want to wait until things quiet down a bit. I'll get back in touch with you."

Back in the safe house Mubin met with two new agents—Sam and Jerrold—these two from the witness protection program. They were both dressed in formal suits and ties. "We've conducted an initial risk and threat assessment and we have concluded that there is a significant threat to your life," Sam said after sitting Mubin and Joanne down in their new living room. "You'll have to go into witness protection with your family."

"What does that entail?" Mubin asked.

"Well, you'll have to leave Toronto," Sam explained. "Your father will have to leave his job and you have to discontinue all relations and communications with your former circles—at the mosques and elsewhere. You will need to change your identities, take on a new look and start a new life."

Mubin and Joanne looked first at each other and then at the agents and burst out laughing. "That's not going to happen!" they both answered simultaneously.

"I've done my own risk assessment and I respectfully disagree with yours," Mubin explained. "I've communicated with my own contacts and I don't see my life in danger. They may disagree with what I've done and not understand the undercover nature of my work. They may be upset, but there's no threat to my life that I can see."

"You need to take this seriously," Jerrold argued, his face clearly showing concern. "We are quite sure there is a significant threat to your lives. You need to leave, cut everyone off. You have to tell your father to leave his job. You, your wife and your parents won't be able to contact anyone again."

"Look, I haven't done anything wrong," Mubin protested. "I'm sorry we're not going to do that." Mubin got up and began pacing the room. "I have a whole life here," he said. "I can't just up and go and cut everyone off. You do understand that my father is the President and Founder of our mosque?" Mubin asked not waiting for a response. "These are impossible requests!" Mubin exclaimed as he paced back across the room. "You don't understand our links to this community. I was born and raised in Toronto, Canada. That's home enough for me." Standing next to the sofa near Joanne he asked, "*I'm* supposed to go away?"

"I'm not ashamed of what I did," Mubin added, pacing again. "Those others are the ones that didn't find Toronto good enough!" Mubin spat, "We are not going anywhere."

"We can't protect you if you don't cooperate," Jerrold replied firmly. "If you reject witness protection then we have no obligations to you. We can't provide you any protection."

"Look, we'll spend a couple of more days here," Mubin said, "but we want to go back home. How do we arrange that?"

The agents were clearly troubled and weren't sure how to respond. "We can offer you a settlement to use as you see fit," Sam offered his eyes filled with worry. "But there's no going back from here.

"Well, what if things heat up and I have to take my family away—to somewhere safe?" Mubin asked.

"That's going to be up to you then," Sam replied. "That's why we want you to go into witness protection."

"No, we are not going to do that," Mubin answered firmly. Everyone was silent in a short standoff while Mubin tried to calculate what it would take to run away with his family if it were necessary to do so. He had no idea what to ask for in terms of a settlement—this was territory he had never imagined.

"Okay, what about three hundred thousand?" Mubin asked picking an arbitrary number from his head, hoping it didn't sound outlandish. To Mubin it seemed like a small fortune—not realizing it considerably undercut any sum ever provided under witness protection.

"Okay…" Jerrold answered.

"You know, even if you don't pay me, I'll testify," Mubin interjected.

Later he would learn that Shaher Elsohemy, the other informant on the case who had joined only in the last month and who had reported on Zakaria's activities ordering the fertilizer did go into witness protection. His compensation package was nearly four million dollars—although he had requested twelve. Mubin asked for three hundred thousand, but got two hundred ninety seven thousand. That sum divided over four years of subsequent legal hearings turned out to be less than the salary of an average police officer. In hindsight, Mubin's only consolation was he didn't have to pay taxes on it.

***

Mubin complained to his handlers about how the government was controlling the narrative of the case as well. "Why aren't you saying that the Muslim community has assisted you in this case?" Mubin asked the agents that visited him in the safe house. "If you don't, the entire community will come under suspicion as a result!" Indeed, after a few days, one of the mosques had all its windows broken by Canadians angry over Muslims who dared plot against them.

"Look this is what I'm talking about," Mubin complained to Bill. "You are saying nothing and you are leaving the community to explain. As usual you are leaving the Muslims to explain every other act that anyone does, but we don't do this to other communities—treat them as an undivided whole."

No one responded so Mubin decided to give his *Fifth Estate* television interview. Joanne and Mubin also moved back to their apartment. The next day the interview aired. Mubin decided to visit his father that day, as he knew Abba watched the show daily.

"Hey Abba," Mubin said entering his father's den. His father was already seated in his easy chair, the remote near his right hand. Mummi was in the kitchen preparing the evening meal. "Remember that terrorism case—the recent arrests in the community?" Mubin began. "It's going to be featured tonight on your show, the Fifth Estate."

Abba listened impatiently. He was distracted—his show was about to start.

"Abba, I'm the undercover on that case," Mubin blurted out.

"Alhamdulillah!" Abba shouted jubilantly. "Tell them to give you a job!"

"What you are about to watch right now, it's me—I gave the *Fifth Estate* an interview," Mubin explained, his face somber. "I want you to be aware of what went on."

Together Mubin and his father watched the show. As it went on, Mubin could see his father's forehead creasing in concern. Abba looked over at Mubin as he realized the seriousness of what he'd been involved with. And Mubin could see his Abba getting more and more anxious and disturbed.

He's probably thinking 'What will people say?' Mubin reflected sadly realizing that part of his upbringing, family and community life would never change. They were a communal society and he was a member of a larger tribe.

The phone started ringing as soon as Mubin's interview concluded. "Did you see your son on television?" the callers asked.

"Yes my son is right here beside me," Abba answered. "He just told me everything."

Most people congratulated Mubin's father, saying it was good that the Muslim community was stepping up to combat terrorism—that this is how we prove that we are indeed against terrorism. But there were detractors as well.

Mubin went to the mosque but found that most people there shied away from him. Their faces as they turned the other way wore expressions of, *Look, here comes trouble,* or *Wait a second. Oh my God! This has been the agent among us the whole time!* Mubin felt pain deep in his heart as he saw the others shun him.

Even the RCMP guys were angry. "Shaikh, what the hell is going on?" Bill said after the interview was broadcast.

"Well, you didn't want to publicly acknowledge that the Muslim community helped you on the case, so I took matters into my own hands," Mubin explained.

"Yeah, well Shaikh, you're compromising the case," Bill said, anger and disappointment filling his voice. "We need you to stop giving interviews."

"I'll take that under advisement," Mubin answered sad to have alienated yet another of his former supporters.

"You worked so hard for this," Bill continued. "Why would you throw it all away?"

"But you didn't say anything about the community," Mubin protested trying to make Bill understand how in Mubin's world individuals didn't exist apart from their tribes. In Mubin's mind he had gone undercover on behalf of the tribe and he'd acted in their behalf and the tribe needed to be acknowledged for doing the right thing—not ignored or blamed—as if all they did was produce terrorists. "I felt I had to do something about that," Mubin explained trying to get the tribal perspective across to a white Westerner. *He'll never get it,* Mubin realized giving up.

"And what does the community think about that?" Bill needled, knowing many in his community had blamed Mubin versus take responsibility for what had come out of their midst. It was a figurative kick in the groin and it hurt—badly.

Mubin was silent for a bit while Bill hung on the line. "Well, I'm going to do things my way now," Mubin said.

"Shaikh, don't blow it," Bill cajoled. "Don't throw it all away." But he didn't offer to meet or show any other interest in what Mubin was going through—in helping with his acute pain.

It seems the government only cares about winning their case, bringing in their guys, not the personal circumstances of their witness, Mubin thought. Although he also realized that the RCMP were limited by legal strictures. They were an organization that prides itself on doing it by the book and even the appearance of too close an association with the witness could be exploited and manipulated by a defence lawyer as "undue influence." But that was of no comfort now.

"Alright—bye," Mubin answered sarcastically and hung up before waiting for Bill to have a chance to also say goodbye. Then he took the RCMP phone and whipped it hard at the wall. It smashed into pieces.

This was too high a price to pay! Mubin cried out in his thoughts. *Doing the right thing—was it worth it in the end? Was it worth it?*

***

"I need some help here," Mubin told his former spiritual advisors as he visited them one by one, but it was the same with all of them. "I did this for Allah, for us," Mubin explained. But one by one, he saw them come up with perplexed and helpless expressions, unable to formulate a good response.

They didn't know what to say. "Our congregation is accusing you of entrapment," Imam Naazim explained. "I can't be seen to condone entrapment of our youth," he added.

"I did it as a duty to my faith," Mubin answered incredulously. "There was no entrapment. These guys were plotting long before I came on the case!"

"We only know what the news is reporting," Mubin's spiritual advisor answered, sadness filling his eyes. "We can't take sides on that."

They've gotten swept up in the wave of public opinion, just like all the rest! Mubin realized. *It's all about how the media and community spins things—and no one is concerned with the truth!*

So according to them, Mubin Shaikh is to blame! Mubin fumed. *I found these innocent kids, set up the camps and then these things happened! It's my fault entirely!*

Walking away from the mosque he asked himself. *I did the right thing—but was it worth it? Does anyone see the sacrifice in that?*

On the positive side, Joanne's father reacted well. For the first time ever he pumped Mubin's hand in his big Polish one, saying in his gruff voice "Good job!" That was high praise coming from Joanne's normally reticent father. "I'm glad you're on our side. I thought you were a terrorist," he added winking sheepishly.

"Shaikh!" Gary, one of his old high school friends called out when Mubin was walking out in the neighborhood. "Right on," he said as he gave Mubin the high five. The nonbelievers congratulated him, but everywhere he went, the Muslims turned their backs—pretended not to see him and went in the other direction when Mubin came down the street.

Mubin logged onto the Internet and read the chat. The storm of condemnation from the wider Muslim community was more than he could have ever anticipated. Suddenly he found himself referred to as "the apostate." Many wished death to Mubin and his family. `He sold out the Muslim community. He's a traitor,` they wrote.

In the Western papers, Mubin found himself reported as "the extremist we knew from former shariah court days." And journalists speculated, `Did he get in trouble and flip to become a government informer?` Some Canadians were calling for Mubin to be given a medal. But it never materialized.

"Don't read the news," Joanne said seeing Mubin becoming more depressed each time he logged on to his computer.

"I can't show my face anywhere!" Mubin complained when suddenly an escape plan appeared before him.

***

Cast out from his Muslim community and no longer meeting with the RCMP agents Mubin felt an acute identity crisis. If he was no longer an undercover agent and no longer a respected Muslim activist in his community of mosques—who was he?

Searching for something—anything to make him feel better—Mubin again reverted to his prior identity and prior behaviors and sought out Brad, his high school friend whose home he had stayed at for the days while he waited for things to cool down with Uncle Ahmed. Now he sought it out again as a refuge from the heat of the controversy brewing all over town inside the Islamic community.

"Man it's worse than anything I could have imagined," Mubin explained. "However bad I thought it could be, it's ten times worse. I have my own people calling me a traitor, a sellout. They are calling me an apostate and saying that I left the faith because I dared stop my own people from attacking our country. What the fuck? What are they trying to say—that they support terrorism?"

"It's just a minority," Brad consoled. "Trouble makers who are trying to get their point across. Haters."

"They have no respect for the country they live in," Mubin complained. "They take living here for granted and they are running this story. Now everyone is saying I entrapped those kids—when the truth is, they were plotting months before I ever got involved. They had a gun and they had tried to run rifles in months before I ever knew them and they were already planning their terrorist training camp."

Brad listened while Mubin ranted. "I know what will make me feel better," Mubin said. "Get me some blow," referring to cocaine.

Brad looked up in shock. "No, Mubin. You left that shit behind. And you are not in the right head space for it."

"No man, I don't care," Mubin argued. "Just hit me."

"You don't want to do this in this kind of mindset," Brad argued. "This is not the right way to do it. I have a lot of respect for you—changing your life. A lot of us were really impressed with the way you became a new person. You were always a good person but you were leading by example—showing what a real Muslim is," Brad said, trying to dissuade Mubin. "We were all really impressed."

"Well, according to these guys I'm not even a Muslim anymore," Mubin carped. "Get me some shit."

Brad gave in and made a phone call. "I'm not happy with this," he said turning and walking away. Mubin did his first line, and then another after that and more as the hours wore on. Brad didn't join in as Mubin became completely consumed with drugging his pain away.

"Oh Allah, what have I done?" Mubin said hours later. "Will I ever recover from this? Will I ever redeem myself inside my community?"

"You are not going to redeem yourself by doing this," Brad warned and they both burst out laughing.

"Oh man, shut up!" Mubin said falling back on the couch. Mubin knew Brad was right but he didn't want to hear it. He just wanted to escape—to find a fix for all the pain inside his head.

"If you need to stay here for a few days you are more than welcome," Brad offered.

Mubin nodded—happy to have found his safe place. `I'm with friends talking things over. I'm going to stay the night. I'm okay.` Mubin texted Joanne. He spent the next days high—out of touch with the pain.

But when he saw that Brad wasn't interested in being an enabler he moved on to staying in a hotel room and called the dealer himself. Mubin felt totally isolated. And his community was rejecting him as well. He didn't know who he was anymore and he needed something to fill the painful hole inside.

Mubin found himself descending into an isolated pit where he could fill his pain with drugs. Cocaine made him feel powerful, confident and euphoric and it got him out of his acute feelings of never-ending ache and turmoil. It was all he knew right now and it was working.

Mubin started disappearing for nights at a time, then for entire weekends—booking seedy hotel rooms to disappear into his coke-infused high. He had his own dealer who delivered to his hotel room where Mubin holed up from Friday to Sunday.

`Where are you?` Joanne texted, worried by his increasingly frequent and longer absences. It was a very bad time for this kind of crisis because they were also expecting little Luqman to be born in October. Mubin needed to be at home, with her.

`I'm at Brad's. I'm okay,` Mubin texted back. Joanne knew Brad and knew he was safe there. But he wasn't at Brad's. He was alone doping up and losing himself.

Then it became whole weeks. The RCMP had given him the first third of his compensation package and he was spending it fast. There was nowhere to run. This was the best safety Mubin could find—to disappear into a fog of drug-induced escape. Mubin had totally lost any concept of himself. He didn't know who he was anymore or where he belonged.

Soon his habit became pretty much every other day. By the time winter arrived it was "snowing" everyday.

***

"Oh man you look just as bad as I do," the RCMP cop said. It was eight a.m. of the first days of the youth preliminary hearings in January of 2007. Mubin had just emerged from the hotel room the RCMP had him in for protective custody during the hearings.

"I didn't sleep at all," Mubin confessed. He'd been a mess wrestling with his nerves over the grilling he knew he was facing while trying to simultaneously vanquish his cocaine habit while in police protection. He knew there was no getting cocaine here.

"I didn't sleep either," the cop admitted. "That usually happens on the first day," he added.

Mubin had expected his testimony to be difficult, but he had no idea that given that the case rested strongly on his statements alone, that the defense lawyers would see it as their mission to personally discredit him. There was loads of evidence to support what Mubin had witnessed and heard from the Toronto 18. But the defense attorneys—and there was a myriad of them—were now hell bent on trying to discredit Mubin and disparage his reputation while attempting to place the blame back on Mubin to exonerate their clients.

"Isn't it true that you are the one that bought the bullets and taught them to fire the gun and then you are the one that told the police that they were firing the gun?" one of the defense attorneys asked Mubin.

Mubin was shocked at the question. His mind raced as he remembered, *I was trying to keep them safe! I took control of the weapon so they wouldn't get hurt. I taught them safe handling of the firearm so no one would get shot. If they had shot themselves, or the gun had misfired and hurt someone, where would we have gone for help? We were literally in the middle of the wild—miles from a hospital.*

"Isn't it true that you are the one that bought the bullets and taught them to fire the gun?" the defense attorney repeated, ripping through Mubin's reflections.

"They already had the pistol," Mubin answered.

"But you did buy the bullets?" the attorney continued.

"Well, I was told to buy the bullets and he already brought bullets with him," Mubin answered, trying to figure out where this line of questioning would take them.

"But you did the buy the bullets?" the attorney repeated.

"Yes, at Fahim's behest," Mubin answered.

"And you drove them up to the camp," the attorney continued. "You facilitated everything. It was your car that you took them up in. You're the one that bought the bullets?" the attorney repeated.

"They were going to go anyway, they already had their own vehicles," Mubin answered.

"Without your vehicle they would not have gone up." The attorney announced.

"That's simply false! They had their own vehicle and would have gone but since it was my job to remain close, I drove up instead," Mubin protested.

"Isn't it true that you selected the location of the camp?" the attorney asked.

"No I selected the site where the tents were set up," Mubin answered. "The site had already been selected and had been visited ahead of time by Fahim Ahmad and Zakaria Amara. They knew where they were going. I didn't tell them where to go."

"Isn't it true that you are the one that taught them how to fire the gun?" the attorney asked.

Mubin hesitated, confused to have his good intentions twisted into bad ones. "I had already seen from them, bringing the gun to my house, that they didn't know the safe handling of a firearm—safe procedures," Mubin explained. "And I had already heard from them of an accidental firing of the weapon, so there was nothing to tell me that they were able to be trusted with this firearm with that many young kids around."

"So you took control of and taught them how to fire the gun, correct?" the attorney continued.

"Yes, I taught them the safe handing of a firearm," Mubin replied.

"So you are the one that equipped them," the attorney concluded.

"Counselor, I remind you it wasn't my weapon," Mubin protested again.

"I didn't ask you if it was your weapon," the attorney caustically stated.

"You are implying it was my weapon," Mubin complained.

"I didn't imply that," the attorney stated as he smirked at Mubin.

"Okay as long as it's agreed it was not my weapon," Mubin protested. "And Fahim's buddies had been arrested with guns taped to their crotch and bullets in their socks trying to bring more weapons to his group," Mubin added.

Amazingly, the attorney was silenced.

"It's been a long day," the judge interrupted. "Let's just keep this to asking and answering questions."

On trial days the RCMP picked Mubin up in armored cars and housed him in a hotel with police guards posted outside his door. They drove to the courtroom in armored cars as well—an Emergency Task Force car carrying guys armed with machine guns led the way, and a chase car followed.

Yet, Mubin felt that no retaliatory bullet for having gone undercover could have hurt as badly as it hurt facing trained lawyers ripping into his reputation, twisting all his words and redefining his good motives to serve his country as selfish.

And all the while they worked to discredit him, Mubin found himself alone. The RCMP didn't talk to him much—they didn't want to influence the witness. And he was isolated from his community who still believed that perhaps Mubin had entrapped their youth and was to blame. Mubin's parents had no idea how to support him and Joanne was overwhelmed with taking care of their children without his support.

"Man, they are just attacking me!" Mubin told Joanne over the phone on a break from the courtroom. "They are making it out like it's my fault— like I invented the terror plot and everything!" Mubin complained, disgust and despair lacing his voice.

"That's their job," Joanne answered, steady as usual reminding him that the Crown's attorney had warned him about this.

"Yeah?" Mubin replied. "I don't like it. It's their job to lie? Because they are lying! They are fabricating information and feeding the propaganda machine of those who believe I entrapped those kids!"

"This is just the beginning," Joanne replied calmly. "This is just going to get worse."

"Okay, thanks, I gotta go," Mubin answered sarcastically cutting the line.

She's right; it is going to get worse! Mubin realized as he dejectedly walked down the hallway back to the witness waiting room.

Staying at the hotel under police protection, Mubin also got a good hard look at how addicted he really was. Each day of the hearings Mubin would be absorbed with thoughts of cocaine. *God, if I could only get a line here. I really need it! I wonder if I could call my dealer and have him deliver to the hotel tonight? If only there was a line waiting for me when I got back to the hotel!*

Mubin found it nearly impossible to sleep. When he did sleep for short intervals he woke up drenched in sweat. *Did I piss myself?* Mubin wondered when he woke amid pools of sweat. *What's wrong with me?* The pillow was wet, the bed soaked and he had nonstop, horrid nightmares of bad things happening—black figures attacking, evil dogs…

Am I cursed? Mubin asked when he woke up repeatedly in a panic. *That's what the people are saying—they said 'We curse him! We hope he destroys himself!' Oh God, it's coming true!*

After the youth preliminary hearings Mubin couldn't wait to get back to his drug induced fog—trying to bolster his confidence with coke, escape into the exhilaration of the drug and find refuge from the pain of withdrawal and all the other painful emotions he was feeling.

"You look sick!" Joanne said on the rare days when Mubin made it home. If he'd been using that day Mubin saw that his children looked at him with fear and confusion. They knew something was wrong and avoided him. He could see in their eyes the terrifying question of, *Who is this?*

"What are you doing? What's going on?" Joanne asked about his long absences.

"The prosecutor needs me," Mubin lied. "The RCMP has me set up at the hotel under police protection while we prep for the case." In fact he was alone snorting cocaine and now taking sleeping pills to come back down for a few hours of troubled sleep.

Mubin was using up to a half a gram now—two bumps in a half hour whereas when he had restarted on coke in June and used through the summer, a half a gram lasted the whole evening. The sleeping pills helped him get to sleep but they created rebound insomnia so he used the coke again to calm himself. Mubin also found himself "tweaking"—engaging in compulsive behaviors for hours while he was high.

Mubin was so far gone, he was checking out from his family almost completely. `Mom's worried about you. She's asking for you,` Mubin's sister, Noor texted while Mubin snorted another line—ignoring her texts.

He also didn't pick up when Mummi phoned him. He just stared at the ringing phone and waited for it to go to the messages. Then he threw his phone back in his pocket and turned back to the coke. The RCMP couldn't even find him because Mubin wouldn't answer his phone.

"The kids need you!" Joanne said trying to pull Mubin back into the family. But when he came home, Mubin was horrified by the looks on his oldest son Mujahid's face. His son looked afraid of the person Mubin had become. Judging from his crestfallen and frightened face, Mubin thought his son was asking, *What happened to my father? Where is he?*

It didn't help when Mubin got agitated and argued with Joanne and smashed things or punched a hole in the wall. In those moments, his whole family looked at him in shock and fear. This was behavior that was totally uncharacteristic in their family.

How did this happen? Mubin asked himself of the stories circulating that he was to blame for entrapping the terror suspects. *Why doesn't anyone in our community stand up for me and speak in my defense?* Finding no satisfactory answers, Mubin went back to the coke.

***

"I can't sleep," Mubin confided to his doctor. He'd decided he needed to seek help. It was March 2007. Mubin had dug his drug-induced hole deeper and deeper and finally after half a year of snorting cocaine he'd hit bottom. "I'm doing way too much coke. I'm doing a couple of grams a day—everyday," he admitted.

"You should be dead at those doses," the doctor replied as she raised her eyebrows in disbelief. "How long has this been going on?" she asked.

"Hardcore since last August," Mubin answered casting his eyes to the floor.

"You know you are going to die," she answered, summing up his situation. "I'm not trying to scare you—I'm just doing the math and it's clear—if you are doing this much coke, you are going to die. I can't highlight this enough," she continued. "You need to check into rehab."

Do I want to die? Mubin's inner voice asked. *Maybe that's my way of plugging out of this mess? So many of my fellow Muslims want me dead—maybe I should die?*

Mubin went back to the hotel. *I don't know how to get out of this,* he thought, despair overwhelming him. *I can't go home messed up like this. My kids are afraid of me. What can I do? Rehab will get me off the drug, but not out of my pain…*

Meanwhile Joanne was texting him and her texts were becoming less friendly. They alternated between: What the hell is going on? to: You have kids at home that are asking for you. I miss you where are you? Mubin didn't answer any of them. But finally he returned home—terrified by what the doctor had said and his inability to quit.

At home Mubin confessed to Joanne, "I'm really sorry babe, I have to tell you the truth… I haven't been prepping for the case. I've been staying in a hotel room and getting high since summer—all day, everyday. At this point, I'm doing so much coke that I don't know how to get off."

Joanne listened with concern, making no comments.

"I had no idea what an adversarial process this would be," Mubin explained, hanging his head in shame. "I never imagined how they would second guess every single thing I said and did! It's a level of scrutiny I could never have anticipated going into this. I thought I was doing the right thing—going undercover—but you see what the community is saying about me on the Internet. Everyone believes I entrapped those kids…some of them are even cursing me now—hoping I die!" Mubin put his head in his hands. "I needed to escape, but now I'm totally out of control!"

"You've got to get off the drugs," Joanne agreed.

"I went to the doctor," Mubin continued. "She told me to go into rehab. She's right, but I also know that's not going to make the underlying issues go away. I'll go for twenty-eight days and then I'll get out and go right back to it because my pain will still be there—staring me in the face!" Mubin said getting up and flailing his arms in the air helplessly. "I think Allah has cursed me!"

"Allah has not cursed you," Joanne answered firmly. "Allah is testing you and even if you fail the test, Allah will still forgive you. What's most important is that you need to get right with Him and everything else will fall into place," Joanne said, kindness and love filling her voice.

Mubin hung his head as she continued, "Why don't you take a trip? Go on a vacation—go to Mecca! Go to Allah's rehab center in Mecca!"

Mubin looked up in awe at Joanne. "This is the first time in forever that I have felt any tiny bit of happiness!" Mubin answered with tears in his eyes, but laughing.

"I'll take care of everything," Joanne answered. "Go out if you have to," she added noticing Mubin was agitated and probably needed his fix. After he left, she booked the entire trip using the money the government had paid them in case they needed protection.

Making the Comeback

"I'm leaving the country," Mubin told Bill over the phone. It was April 2007 just after the preliminary hearings.

"For how long?" came the exacerbated reply.

"For a little while," Mubin replied.

"Are you coming back?" Bill asked, his voice filled with irritation.

"Of course I'm coming back!" Mubin answered.

"Shaikh, we need you for the case," Bill said, clearly worried that Mubin would back out entirely of testifying—something he didn't legally have to do and that was clearly costing him too dear a price.

"I need to get right—with my God, with my family. Then we can deal with the case," Mubin explained. "That's what's going to help the case."

I need to get my shit together, Mubin thought as he prepared for his trip to Mecca and Medina. *Is this how my kids are going to remember me? I need to make things right with Allah. That's the root of my existence and essence,* Mubin reminded himself, his coke habit bedeviling his inner being.

A few days later Mubin was in Mecca crying out to Allah, *Allah what's happened to me? Am I cursed? Have you rejected me? Everything I've done—has it been a waste completely?* Later Mubin stood in front of the grave of the Prophet (SalAllahuAlayhiWaSallam) begging, *Please, I have no one! You are the only one I can come to and ask for some strength,* Mubin cried out.

Mubin was so moved to be in Saudi Arabia, but his addiction remained gnawing at his insides clamoring for his next fix. There was no way to get coke delivered to his hotel room here, so he basically went cold turkey in the hotel—trusting Allah to protect him and bring him through to the other side. Mubin spent his days agitated without his drug and at night he couldn't sleep. Alternating between staring at the television, pacing the room and praying—beseeching Allah to heal him—Mubin felt he would lose his mind. And if he fell into a short sleep, he woke up drenched in pools of sweat. During the days, Mubin used prayer and the holy sites of Mecca and Medina to take his mind off thinking about how to get his drug.

On the third day of detoxing Mubin spent some time praying at the Ka'bah, the black square holy place where Muslims believe Abraham, with his son Ishmael, constructed the first place to worship the one God. That night Mubin had a dream in which a robed figure came through the door. Others were present whom Mubin couldn't see but he did notice that they respectfully rose when the figure entered. In the dream the man walked right up to Mubin and put his hand on Mubin's shoulder saying, "You need to complete your job. It will not end like this." Mubin woke up—startled and comforted by the real quality of the dream and its message. Somehow it delivered peace finally in his soul.

After Mecca, Mubin traveled to Jeddah where he went snorkeling in the Red Sea and spent hours on the beach meditating. *Look at how we see nothing at the top of the sea and underneath, there is so much going on,* Mubin thought as he contemplated how Allah was working in his life as well. After the cold weather of Canada and the hostile lawyers, it was warm and comforting here and the colors were spectacular. *Don't get caught up with the surface view,* Mubin's inner voice counseled. *Look underneath where there is life and depth.*

Even in Jeddah, Mubin still couldn't sleep well. He was no longer waking up in pools of sweat, but he still had hot flashes and felt agitated and constantly thought about how to get a hit of coke.

One of the days in Jeddah Mubin took the hotel bus to the beach. It was so stunning he stayed the whole day and decided to take his chances on declining the bus ride back in order to watch the sunset. As he sat there watching the sun lower over the water a European came and sat beside him.

"Where are you from?" the fellow asked.

"Canada."

"Can you believe they go topless on these beaches here in these holy lands?" the fellow asked. "It's kind of offensive…"

"Not so bad," Mubin said. "It's a hotel beach."

"I can drive you back into town after the sunset," the fellow offered.

"That would be great!" Mubin answered, smiling.

In the car Mubin asked the stranger where he worked.

"At the Irish embassy," the fellow replied. "I work for the Irish security services," he said meeting eyes with Mubin. "I'm staying in the hotel. If you need anything you just give me a call."

Suddenly Mubin understood. The Canadians were looking out for him—even here in Saudi Arabia. He wasn't alone.

***

Mubin returned from Saudi Arabia free of his drug habit and totally reinvigorated. He was now rededicated to restoring his reputation and was filled with a newfound sense of purpose. The adult preliminary hearings were coming up in September, 2007 and Mubin knew it would be the same old scrutiny—maybe worse this time around.

On his return Mubin gave a press interview and mentioned in an aside to the journalist that he had been battling a cocaine habit. He didn't think the journalist would publish it, but there it was in the headlines, Mounties' man admits a cocaine habit. So now his entire family knew what he'd been up to.

On the extremist Internet forums Mubin saw that his Muslim detractors were actually gleeful. They wrote things like, Oh, look he's been doing this to feed his cocaine habit! Another forum commentator wrote, Oh look Allah has cursed him, rejoice, I hope he dies in his cocaine den!

Even mainstream journalists speculated that Mubin had been in trouble for drug use and therefore helped the RCMP in a plea bargain deal. Everywhere he looked he saw people from all sides denouncing him and accusing him of entrapment, or working for money to feed his drug habit.

No Muslim could be good enough to simply do the right thing, Mubin thought sarcastically. *Don't they see these guys were planning their training camp and amassing weapons way before I was involved? Don't they see I only turned to the drugs after they all rejected me for doing the right thing?* Mubin fumed.

Another newspaper falsely reported that the RCMP checked Mubin into rehab. Mubin's rehab had been of another nature—a trip to Mecca and getting it right with Allah, the source of all life.

Mubin was back now and he began working out in the gym almost daily—lifting weights. Everyday he looked in the mirror and told himself the truth—*they are laughing at you and mocking you!* It made him work harder and lift more. Mubin was gaining weight and becoming strong again.

Mubin also enrolled in the Master of Policing, Intelligence and Counter Terrorism at Macquarie University. It was amazing taking the security studies classes as it began to make clear to Mubin all that he had undergone—why the CSIS and RCMP agents had shared some information and withheld others and why they asked him to do things the ways they had.

Mubin stayed behind the scenes and was silent as the trials approached but he knew he was getting on top of his game. And while he dug his way out of his suffering he realized, *I had to go through this.* And as he became stronger, Mubin felt more and more sympathy for the kids who were up for trial in 2008. Mubin and Joanne's fifth child, Hannah would be born to them in July and Mubin's heart softened for anyone whose children got lost on the wrong path.

Some of them were just dragged along. Fahim Ahmad and Zakaria Amara—they wanted to kill innocents, but the really young ones—they were just scared and going along with the program, Mubin reflected.

***

"Why would you do that?" the prosecutor asked Mubin about his admission of using cocaine, his face was filled with disgust. "Now people will make fun of you and insult you. 'Oh you are a cokehead—a crack head!' The lawyers will have a field day!"

"Well, I'm here to tell the truth," Mubin answered, unfazed. "How could I not tell the truth *about me* if I'm to tell the truth about all else?" Mubin challenged back. "I'd rather preemptively disclose and have them make fun of it rather than have it discovered in court," he added.

The prosecutor was right of course—the lawyers had a feeding frenzy over Mubin's coke habit. Lined up in a row they were ready to take pot shots at him in the courtroom. But Mubin was ready too.

That morning as the police security detail signaled that it was time to go Mubin looked one last time into the mirror and saw that he was no longer the gaunt faced, fearful and unsure of himself witness that he had been in the spring. And he was also no longer worried if he was a "good enough" Muslim. Nor was he any longer asking himself, *What will the community say?*

He had gotten it right with Allah and the facts would now speak for themselves. Looking in the mirror Mubin saw that his robes were bright and clean and his face was shining with the truth.

Bring it on, he thought as he entered into the courtroom.

"So you were addicted to cocaine?" one of the lawyers began—adding, "Please remember you are under oath at this time."

"Yes, I admitted all of this," Mubin answered sitting up proudly in the witness chair. "You are not exposing anything new. I volunteered this information before coming to court. I'm here telling the truth," he added.

"Were you doing it off the table?" the attorney asked trying to sensationalize the story.

"Yeah," Mubin answered sarcastically. "I think lawyers know about lines off of tables."

"So are you clean now?" the attorney asked, unruffled by Mubin's reply.

"Yes, I am," Mubin answered proudly.

"Will you pee in a cup?" the attorney badgered.

"Will I pee in your cup?" Mubin asked trying to give it right back. It went on like this for some time until the attorneys realized they had nothing. Mubin was totally on top of his game and now the case rested on the facts and the facts alone.

Each time hearings were held, Mubin was still being taken into protective custody. In the hotel he slept with a police guard outside his door and a device put inside the door to protect him from anyone trying to break in. Every morning and afternoon the police would escort him to and from his hotel room in an armored vehicle with an advance and chase car loaded with armed policemen inside. On a particularly grueling day of hostile cross-examination Mubin turned to his RCMP escort to ask, "What's going on with my wife and family?"

"I have no idea," the cop answered, obviously surprised at the question.

"But you have them under protection too," Mubin said. "Can't you just ask your buddies?"

"They are not under protection," the cop answered.

"What do you mean?" Mubin asked, his turn to be shocked. "Isn't there someone posted outside my house when I'm here testifying?"

"No, you're the principal," the cop answered. "We don't have anyone for them."

"You mean that you are doing all of these VIP protective convoys, using three bulletproof suburban tactical units, taking me armed in and out of the courtroom and my family are sitting ducks at home? You are using a federal RCMP Emergency Response Force team for me and nothing for them?"

The cop stared back at Mubin, a look of shame crossing his face. Silence.

"I don't want to be in protective custody anymore," Mubin said, his voice filled with concern for his family as he realized no one in the RCMP was doing anything for his family's safety while at the same time they were going to such great lengths to protect him. "I want to go home. If you're not protecting my family, I will." Mubin announced.

"No, you can't go home," the cop answered.

"Call your supervisor," Mubin replied. "I'm done staying in hotels."

"Listen Shaikh, please reconsider," the supervisor pleaded. "It's really important that we keep you safe and see you through to the end of this case."

"No, I have to go home," Mubin answered firmly.

The supervisor was struck silent as well.

"What would you do?" Mubin asked him. It wasn't long before he was driven home.

***

The court cases kept coming but now Mubin was ready. In one of the cases the defense attorney tried to besmirch Mubin's reputation by bringing up the cocaine use asking, "We are expected to believe that you just picked yourself up and everything is now okay—that we can trust you to be truthful now?"

"Yes," Mubin proudly answered as he looked over the courtroom. "While all of you were making fun of me, I am proud to say now, in this courtroom, that I have not only been clean for some time, but I have also completed my Master's degree in policing and counter-terrorism."

It was clear that this surprised the attorneys and the community detractors. While they thought Mubin had been spending his time getting high—he had in fact been writing essays by day and hitting the gym at night. He was a very different person now.

As Mubin made his way back into life he began to understand what had happened to him. In May when the RCMP had told him the arrests were going to happen he had lost the new identity he had built since being recruited by CSIS. Nearly overnight he lost touch with the RCMP agents he'd been in near daily contact with and his new career had vanished. And he had nothing to replace it with since his Muslim community also rejected him.

For everyone community and social identity is important, but for a Muslim, Indian immigrant, community had been everything and totally defined who he was—and Mubin had been rejected by a large part of his tribe. And that had been after traveling through a tumultuous adolescence trying to figure out who he wanted to be as he straddled between his Muslim background and his Western education and peer group.

Mubin had emerged from that as a highly disciplined Muslim leader who everyone knew was going places. But he had fallen badly after working undercover and having had the courage to testify about his activities in order to shut down a terrorist ring. He hadn't been ready for the fallout—losing his newfound career, losing esteem in the Muslim community, facing rows of attorneys dedicated to ripping his reputation and motives to shreds. It had all been too much.

Mubin read up on police work and was surprised to find a case study of a CSIS informant who was outed by a journalist. He too suddenly found his identity and career disappear as his job vanished. The only difference was that CSIS sent in psychologists to help him get through it all.

I wish there had been that kind of help for me! Mubin thought ruefully as he read it. Although he also remembered a conversation where the CSIS guys asked him after the fact if he could have used more support. Mubin realized that in pursuing his studies he was finding his own way to enter the same career in a way that was more enduring.

At the end of it all Mubin emerged stronger. Previously his identity had been defined by his role in his Muslim community and how he was perceived. Once that had been turned upside down and his value had gone to zero, or less than zero, and he found his community rallying around and trying to protect those who were plotting terrorism—Mubin finally got free of it all. He saw just how emotional and reactive his community was in their mistrust of government agencies and how that had been directed at him as well. In finally rising above it he became much more of an independent individual—able to judge for himself who he wanted to be and who he wanted to please.

***

After Mubin finished his Master's in Policing and Counter-Terrorism he entered the Department of Psychological Sciences at Liverpool University, studying radicalization and violent extremism in pursuit of his doctoral degree. As Mubin studied, he so often saw himself in the case studies—Western guys from ethnic backgrounds, or converts without a solid base getting confused and drawn into terrorist movements. Angry guys who needed a peg on which to hang all their anger and an ideology that justified acting it out—on someone—anyone really—just as long as they symbolized the original aggressor and the original evildoer. Mubin could totally relate—he'd been there.

Mubin recalled that in the Muslim community—and probably beyond it—when the Soviets occupied Afghanistan most people felt it was wrong and immoral. And those who opposed the Soviets were supported and called "freedom fighters" and many were encouraged to go and fight to throw the Soviets out.

So for many, it was hypocritical to now call those who resisted the United States invasion of Iraq, terrorists—rather than freedom fighters. Mubin himself had wanted to go and fight in Chechnya and Afghanistan because he had felt in the past that Islam was under attack in those countries—so he could see how Fahim especially, being from Afghanistan had fallen into the militant jihad. Although Mubin also understood that an essential difference is that freedom fighters fight with militaries and terrorists attack innocent civilians in order to try to bend political decisions to their favor. And he realized, there is no honor in attacking innocent civilians for any cause—no matter how worthy it may be.

Mubin also read about expert's opinions on the factors involved in radicalization in non-conflict zones and found that having an immigrant background, particularly for Muslims, along with a feeling of marginalization or social alienation were often factors. Mubin could relate to all of those. Other aspects related to radicalization in non-conflict zones also included a quest for significance and life meaning; a willingness to take risks; a desire for adventure; a desire to belong or to impress others—especially among recent converts; motivations posed by female members as challenges to their spouses or would-be-spouses; and the presence of a charismatic leader.[47] Mubin reflected on all he had seen and realized they had all been true with the Toronto 18.

Fahim Ahmad had been cast out of his family when he decided to marry young and became too religious for them. Zakaria Amara's father moved back to Dubai in 2004 after his parents split up. Both young men were vulnerable and drifting through their lives in need of a father figure. They found just that in worshipping with others in their group at the Meadowvale mosque where they fell under the influence of forty-three year old Qayyum Abdul Jamal who warmly nurtured them while espousing views that allegedly fueled the young men's zeal for militant jihad. Qayyum had at times invited the kids home for barbeques and in at least one of his fiery sermons he had spoken about Canadian soldiers raping Muslim women, likely inciting the youth into seeing a need for action.[48]

Fahim Ahmad and Zakaria Amara were also charismatic in their own right. Unlike the other Canadians, Zakaria held a lot of credibility in their group due to his Arabic language skills and self-taught Islamic studies. And Fahim would often persuasively opine on Islamic doctrine, international affairs and the suffering of Muslims worldwide—views informed by the steady diet of militant jihadi videos that he consumed from the so called "university of jihad"[49] found on the Internet. And as Mubin now knew, and Zakaria had discovered over time, Fahim could be very enthusiastic and convincing even when he was just making things up.

Some of the guys were also converts to Islam and had to look to the others for a fuller understanding of their faith which was still new to them. Among extremists elsewhere, Mubin was learning that it is a common pattern to find the converts resonating even more to the extremist views and trying even harder than the rest to prove they were good and serious Muslims. Without a family background in Islam they easily fell prey to teachers—especially those who knew Arabic—who taught them that militant jihad was the correct path to follow.[50] This group was no exception in that regard.

Gulshan, for instance, had burned his mother's Hindu idols at their training camp while mocking her religious beliefs, perhaps trying to impress the guys about what a tough Muslim he had become. Zakaria Amara had also converted to Islam to the dismay of his mother's Greek Orthodox relatives—perhaps to snub them or draw closer to an absent father, or to avoid hell, as his Muslim friends were warning him about. After his parents split Zakaria was encouraged onward into extremism by Fahim, Saad Khalid and others, where he took it to the extreme.

Jahmaal James had also converted from Christianity and went so far as to try to enroll in a Pakistani terrorist training camp. Gulshan was a convert as well and wanted so badly to be a "good" Muslim that his zeal caused Fahim to believe that Gulshan could be convinced to undertake a suicide mission.

These converts would have been much more easily taken in by Fahim's insistence that jihad was an individual duty that each of them was required to carry out on behalf of war torn countries like his native land Afghanistan—where he wanted Western soldiers to leave the Muslims to themselves—than someone who was well-grounded in a moderate Islamic upbringing. Likewise they would also have easily deferred to Zakaria's knowledge of Islamic studies and the Arabic language.

Saad Khalid, one of Toronto 18 members who had taken part in the training camp and who had been ordered by Zakaria to scope out downtown Toronto sites and who ultimately was arrested while unloading what he believed was fertilizer into a warehouse space he had arranged for, had a huge traumatic loss in his background. At age sixteen he returned home to find his mother drowned in the bathtub.[51] In the aftermath of that tragedy Saad had sought out religion and fallen into a militant jihadi interpretation—one that perhaps gave voice to the anger of his traumatic grief over her senseless death and permission to act out his anger for what he came to believe were righteous causes.

Fahim Ahmad had come from Afghanistan at age one and then to Canada from Pakistan at age ten bearing heavy baggage—he more than any of the group knew first hand of actual atrocities that had occurred in his homeland during his early development.[52] For Fahim the suffering ummah included family members and neighbors who hadn't escaped and he became enthralled by the Taliban who emerged after the mujahideen's victory over a world superpower, and by the Chechens who also fought bravely against the Russians. Because his home country was currently at war, with American and Canadian soldiers active there, Fahim more than the others could likely make the suffering of the "ummah" more real and palpable to the others—especially when their own suffering also resonated with it and with the jihadi message.

Ali Dirie, who had smuggled the guns and was imprisoned during much of the Toronto 18's development continued from prison to assist Fahim Ahmad and planned to rejoin them when he got out. Dirie was from war torn Somalia and could, as a result likely resonate with the al Qaeda narrative of Muslims under attack. He, like Fahim Ahmad, opposed Canadian involvement in Afghanistan. He also did not rehabilitate in prison and when he got out he went to join the "jihad" in Syria, reportedly dying there.[53]

The wives, and potential wives, of the group also played a significant part in motivating their spouses to enact terrorism and this too is not an unusual component of radicalization. Women holding themselves out as prizes for men who embrace the militant jihad or who goad their men into action have also been seen before among European jihadi groups as well.[54]

In this group and its affiliate, U.K. actor, Aabid Khan, known as Mr. Fix-It was married to Saima Mohamed, the sister of Mariya, Fahim's wife. Saima was enamored of Khava Baraeva, the first Chechen suicide bomber, a young woman who drove a truck bomb into a Russian checkpoint and said she wanted to take part in a similar "martyrdom" mission.[55] She and her husband communicated by Internet about not expecting to live longer than five years. Saima, along with others was also expected to help arrange appropriate wives for those terrorist plotters who wished to travel to Pakistan for training.

Four of the wives of the Toronto 18 chatted extensively with each other on the extremist Internet forums encouraging their husbands and other potential fanatics forward: Mariya—the wife of Fahim Ahmad; Nada Forooq—the wife of Zakaria Amara; Nada's sister, Rana—wife of suspect Ahmad Ghany; as well as Cheryfa MacAulay Jamal, a Muslim convert from Cape Breton, Nova Scotia—wife of the oldest suspect, forty-three year old Qayyum Abdul Jamal. [56]

The Forooq sisters, Nada and Rana, emigrated with their parents from Karachi, Pakistan and became much more religious than their parents—but unlike their parents—embraced a distorted militant jihadi extremist interpretation of Islam. Nada—the wife of Zakaria Amara was the administrator of an extremist website on which she went by the online name of al-Mujahidah (the Jihadist).

Nada posted in 2004 that she hated Canada and referred to Canada as "this filthy country." She also posted that she demanded of the man she was marrying (Zakaria) to embrace militant jihad—stating, "if he ever refuses a clear opportunity to leave for jihad, then i want the choice of divorce [sic]."[57] Nada also argued, "Those who are sincere in pleasing Allah will go to whatever length to help the true believers," … "Those who fear Allah more than they fear the CSIS. Those are the ones who will succeed in the hereafter."

Nada, like Fahim and Zakaria, was also clearly enamored of the Chechen mujahideen, posting that she wanted to name a future son "Khattab" after the commander of the mujahideen in Chechnya close to Chechen terrorist leader Shamil Basayev. Khattab, the militant she admired is credited with having convinced Basayev to transition the Chechen separatist movement into a militant jihad using "martyrdom" operations that were begun in 2000 beginning with two female suicide bombers. Khattab was "martyred" in 2002 when the Russians assassinated him with a poisoned letter.[58] Nada posted, "And i pray to Allah my sons follow his [Khattab's] footsteps Ameen [Amen]."[59]

Nada's sister, Rana Forooq also appears to be an admirer of female "martyrs" as she frequently posted graphic photos of female militants and suicide bombers.[60]

Fahim met Mariya, his wife on the extremist website *ClearGuidance* which incited hatred of disbelievers and promoted violence against them. At Fahim's trial when Mariya later regretted their actions, she told the judge that she thought the website was misnamed and should be called *Misguidance*.

However, while in the movement Mariya was a fiery participant on it. She posted in response to the targeted assassination of Hamas leader Abdel-Aziz al-Rantissi by missile strike, "May Allah crush these jews, bring them down to their kneees, humuliate them [sic]. Ya Allah make their women widows and their children orphans."[61]

Saima Mohamed, Mariya's sister—who was married to Aabid Khan, was also active on the Internet forums. She first told militant extremist Aabid Khan in a hand written letter and her brother-in-law Fahim in person that she wanted to emulate Khava Baraeva, the first Chechen suicide bomber. Carrying on an online romance with Aabid Khan, Saima chatted in the spring of 2005 telling Khan how "me and faheem were discussing the issue of fidaayee [suicide commando] operations, and i told him what I wanted. Mariya [Saima's older sister] got mad saying if i do something like that, she'll tell dad…she says women dont have to do it… [but] faheem always encourages me [sic]." Khan who ultimately married Saima agreed with Fahim's perspective and added, "i give you permission anyway, so no one can over ride that [sic]."[62]

When Saima wrote in handwritten letters to Aabid Khan about her desire to follow in the footsteps of Khava Baraeva she wrote, "I know what I want to do. And in one way or the other, it has to be related to the imprisoned ikhwan [brothers]. The more I think about my goal in life… let it be a martyrdom operation."[63] Saima was referring mostly to her work on behalf of imprisoned Muslims held at Guantanamo.

Saima ultimately married Aabid Khan, cementing the relationship between Aabid Khan who encouraged her brother-in-law Fahim to move from simply talking about jihad on the Internet forums into seriously organizing an active terror cell, arranging a training camp with the goal of selecting the best participants to train further in Pakistan and ultimately basing terrorist operations in Toronto. It's interesting that in some cases young people are motivated much more deeply into terrorism by falling in love with those who are committed to extremist movements and once married into it, they find it much more difficult to leave. This aspect of getting radicalized via marriage and finding it difficult to leave a terrorist group because it means leaving your family, was also found among the Indonesian group Jemaah Islamiah (JI).

In the case of the Toronto cell, Aabid Khan expected Saima and her network of female friends to help in finding potential "wives" for single males seeking to travel to Pakistan for military training. Khan believed that potential trainees were much more likely to go unnoticed by law enforcement and intelligence agencies if they traveled to Pakistan while married to wives of Pakistani background. In mid-April 2005, Aabid requested Saima to find wives for "two brothers, one masri [Egyptian] one omani. we need sisters from ideally pakistani background, then bangladeshi, indian if no pakistani, and who are ideally here—then over their[sic] in that part of the world—who is over 18 for reasons i.e. able to travel alone without being stopped... so 16/17 min."[64]

Aabid Khan on his side also insulted Saima badly, making her crazed with jealousy, when he expressed a desire to take a second wife for strategic reasons. He explained that the second wife should be one, "who has a non-muslim name in passport if possible and is not arab or asian ethnically." In the face of Saima's jealousy, he wrote, "My intention was i could find someone in america or canada or further down south, kitabiyyah (not muslim), who can be a benefit to us strategically, through having easier access i.e. not having to be caught up in immigration office and that the woman could easily use her name and details as being born and bread [sic] in that country with citizenship which could be advantage for us when the ikhwaan [brothers] need and as a cover to come their [sic] and someone who could have an apartment 'legally' and other things on her name."[65]

Shamil Basayev and other Chechen terrorist leaders also married strategically—taking their multiple wives from clans across Chechnya thereby ensuring themselves safe haven with relatives who would feel obligated by marriage and family ties to protect them and take them in when under search from the authorities.

In Saima's case, she apparently could not reconcile herself to a second "strategic" marriage writing to Aabid, "if you ask me to take a truck full of explosives and run it into a military field, i will do it. aabid, just please please dont ask me for this... please... i will sacrifice my family for you, for the sake of Allaah and even my life. just please sweetheart dont do this please. [sic]"

"Do we have to fight over this when i hope we will not live to see more then five years in the most?" Aabid replied, reminding her of their

joint commitment to "martyrdom." "Please just hold my hand and lets prepare together," he wrote, adding "those who truely wish to fight in Allaah's
path will make preparations like we are doing… if we have a stick, then fight
with it. a stone, fight with it. a gun, what ever we have, what ever resources
we will use them… i cant have the plans ruined, that will be my ruin and
your ruin."[66] Khan ending up in prison ultimately disrupted their marital
"bliss."

Forty-four year old Cheryfa MacAulay Jamal, wife of Qayyum Abdul
Jamal was also a fiery presence in the forums. Using the example of Iraqi
prisoners humiliated at the hands of American soldiers she posted cau-
tions under the title of "Behold your Enemy" warning fellow subscribers to
"Know what you will face one day," … "Let them call you a terrorist, let them
make you look like a savage, but know that THIS is the filth of the earth,
the uncivilised destroyer of humanity." She also warned, "Know from this
day that this is not an Iraqi problem, it is not an Afghan problem, it is not a
Palestinian problem, it is not a Somali problem. IT IS YOUR PROBLEM!!!"

Cheryfa was also an alarmist. "You don't know that the Muslims in
Canada will never be rounded up and put into internment camps like the
Japanese were in WWII!" she wrote in one 2004 post. This is a time when
Muslims "are being systematically cleansed from the earth," she added.

Cheryfa MacAulay Jamal also advised her younger forum members
to reject nearly everything Canadian encouraging them: to boycott federal
elections and reject: banking, membership in the United Nations, support
for women's rights, and secular law. "Voting inherently violates the sover-
eignty of God, making it the most egregious sin against Islam," she wrote.
She also challenged, "Are you accepting a system that separates religion and
state?" … "Are you gonna give your pledge of allegiance to a party that puts
secular laws above the laws of Allah? Are you gonna worship that which they
worship? Are you going to throw away the most important thing that makes
you a Muslim?"

All these women were active supporters of jihad—some voicing the opinion that they themselves would like to be suicide bombers—"martyrs" in their world view—and that they viewed the highest calling for their husbands and children to "martyr" themselves, and some wished to be "martyred" together. They, like many other women who join militant jihadi groups, totally supported self-sacrifice for the cause of militant jihad.[67]

Some of the guys had also married very young and separated from their families making their wives opinions all the more influential in their lives. Fahim and Zakaria both married young—Fahim losing his family as a result, and Zakaria at age eighteen—marrying right after his father divorced his mother and left the country.

Given that nearly all of the guys in the group had failed in some way in their lives and were also bored—they were probably highly excited by the idea of adventures involved in taking part in militant jihad—particularly those that scored them points with the ladies. That they would engage in even violent adventures probably had to do with their underlying anger, concern over legitimate and illegitimate Muslim grievances the world over and their sense of "fictive kin"[68] with other Muslims worldwide (i.e. the ummah), and encouragement and groupthink to justify violent actions that they so easily found in the mosques, Internet forums, friendship circles and study groups they were frequenting.

Zakaria for instance had been an engineering student and had wanted to pursue Islamic studies in Saudi Arabia but failed to get in presumably because in his interview there he condemned the war in Iraq. After dropping out of Canadian university, he worked in the mind-numbing job of gas station attendant where he amused himself making a detonator and dreaming up plans for a homegrown jihad of which he was one of the emirs.

Fahim didn't even work—he was on public assistance. Asad hadn't the money to study at university and was frustrated in achieving his dreams. Dreaming grandiose fantasies of being heroes for the "ummah" likely provided a welcome escape from the dismal realities of their lives which weren't likely to improve much without drastic action on their parts, or help from the outside.

Mubin thought through their various pathways. It was in high school that the group made up of misfits and hurt young men began their first steps onto the terrorist trajectory—transitioning from gangster rap and heavy metal into rap songs with religious themes that later became hardcore jihadi rap. Then they formed a club and blog that endorsed militant jihadi views while also finding mentors that endorsed their violent beliefs. The final boost was likely having Aabid Khan and the two "Atlanta cell" members come to Toronto, with Aabid Khan promising he had the means to get members into paramilitary training and all agreeing they wanted to base an international cell inside Toronto. With that they finally moved to the point where they began actively pursuing training for terrorist activities and materials to carry out terror attacks.

***

As Mubin pursued his higher education in policing and counter-terrorism studies he began to understand his role as an operative with both CSIS and the RCMP and why they distanced so abruptly from him at crucial junctures in the case—making him feel alone in many ways. He also saw clearly the factors that had led to the Toronto 18 members' radicalizations. And he could also see that he too could have just as easily ended up like them had the Shaykh in Syria not intervened to help him understand that his limited militant jihadi view of Islam was all wrong.

Even though he was glad he had been instrumental in stopping terrorists from attacking his homeland, Mubin felt bad for them as they faced the justice system. They were guilty of serious crimes and most would face stiff sentencing, but he still felt pity for their mistaken views and the vulnerabilities that had gotten them to that point along the terrorist trajectory.

Please don't think I'm out to get your family,

Mubin messaged on Facebook to Mariya, Fahim's wife before the adult preliminary hearings. I know you were aware of these things.
You can't be that surprised at what is going on…

Well it's not that I think you are going after
them, she replied, But I think the government is behind
this. I blame the government,not you. You are somewhat of an enigma.

"She knew exactly what he was up to, remember?" Joanne, who was
sitting beside Mubin, remarked. "Remember her Pakistani parents lived in
Dubai. She told me she'd like to return there, but Fahim has 'other' plans!"
Joanne added, recalling talking to Mariya on one of her visits with Fahim to
their home.

To Mubin's chagrin, the defense attorney produced the Facebook
messages, although Mubin explained that he simply felt badly for the families of the accused knowing their spouses and fathers were facing long prison sentences.

In the end the judge in the youth trial wrote, "The evidence is
overwhelming. We have intercepts, audio and corroborated information."
Mubin's testimony was considered credible and charges were brought forward. Yet when the kids came up for trial Mubin was instrumental in getting
some of their charges stayed.

"Isn't it true that in this kind of cultural environment they really had
no choice?" the defense attorney asked Mubin. "That they were in the orbit
of their older influencers and these people were close to their families and
thus even more influential."

"Yes," Mubin answered even though the prosecutor glared at him. He
was supposed to be a witness for the prosecutor—not the defense.

"And isn't it true it would have been dishonorable and disrespectful
to show opposition to them?"

"Yes," Mubin answered.

"Shaikh, you're tanking our case!" The prosecutor fumed at Mubin when there was a break in testimony.

"You know that they weren't all at the same level of involvement and threat," Mubin countered. "I wrote that in my reports way back when."

When it was the prosecutor's turn on redirect he asked, "Isn't it true that you see it as your duty to protect vulnerable youth?"

"I would think that's everyone's duty," Mubin answered after a long hesitation—shocked to now being attacked by his own side.

"And isn't it true that because of that you are lying to protect this young accused?" the prosecutor asked.

"Of course not!" Mubin answered indignantly raising his voice. "I've been telling the truth the whole time and it's supported by the evidence!"

Now the newspapers accused Mubin of lying to protect the youth—versus having entrapped them as they originally accused. Headlines read: If Shaikh is lying Wither the Case? and one journalist wrote, "normally the quickly responding Shaikh was speechless." Again Mubin felt shock. Again he had tried to do the right thing and exonerate those less guilty—the young followers, but everyone turned on him. The presses were full of stories that the whole case was made up—that Mubin was lying about all of it.

But Mubin was not lying. The younger ones had simply been followers and were not highly involved so Mubin did all he could to exonerate them. Finally in the end, Waleed and two other youth had their charges stayed in large part because of testimony provided by Mubin. They had spent seven months in pre-trial custody, some in solitary confinement, and the government decided that was enough. Four adults also had their charges stayed. Mubin later learned that some of them returned right back to their extremist mosque where they had originally been drawn into militant jihadi activities.

The entrapment narratives in which Mubin and Shaher Elsohemy, who joined the case late, were painted as agent provocateurs continued to play out in the press while the adult trials progressed. Sweeping publication bans kept the press in the dark about much of the evidence. Aside from the interview Mubin had given early on, he too was under a gag order and could not publicly dispute these narratives with hard evidence that he had at his fingertips—but was forbidden to discuss. Eventually, however, the judge ruled that the evidence of terrorist plotting prior to Mubin's involvement was overwhelming and that it was *impossible* that the accused had been entrapped. *Finally!* Mubin thought.

"I cannot overlook the fact that Mr. Ahmad must bear considerable responsibility for embroiling other young men in his hateful pursuits." Judge Dawson later wrote in the 2010 Ontario Superior Court sentencing of Fahim Ahmad. "The wiretaps and other intercepts are replete with Mr. Ahmad fostering his views, instilling hatred and justifying terrorist acts in Canada on religious grounds," Judge Dawson wrote adding, "Mr. Ahmad is substantially responsible for virtually ruining the lives of a number of other young men who became involved in terrorist activities and now stand convicted of terrorism offences as a result of Mr. Ahmad's proselytizing."[69] Obviously, Mubin was not in the end held responsible.

In the end, eleven of the plotters who had been trying to procure and actually did procure weapons and explosives were convicted of terrorism charges, with seven pleading guilty to their charges. The cases ultimately revealed eighty-two thousand and two hundred police intercepts.

Zakaria Amara pled guilty in October, 2009 to charges of knowingly participating in the activities of a terrorist group, receiving training, providing training or recruiting, and intent to cause an explosion. In his trial, the court heard how he had plotted together with Fahim Ahmad. The court learned of how together they had organized a terrorist training camp and tried to procure a safe house for their terrorist activities, but that Zakaria became disillusioned when Fahim only managed to produce one handgun after promising delivery of all kinds of weapons. And they heard how after their split, Amara had been planning "The Battle of Toronto" in which he planned to detonate three one-ton fertilizer bombs near the CN Exchange Tower in Toronto, as well as the Toronto office of Canada's intelligence agency, CSIS and at a military base located on highway 401.

Superior Court Justice Bruce Durno wrote in his sentencing of Zakaria Amara on January 18, 2010 that this "was not a spur of the moment plan." The Judge commented that, "Reading through the Agreed Statement, the voice messages, and the bomb manual reveals a plan that was thoroughly researched and meticulously planned to the point that detailed instructions were given to those who did not know all the plans. The plans even included his fleeing the country right after the detonations."

The judge also pinned the responsibility for leadership of the terrorist activities squarely upon Zakaria Amara stating that Amara, "was the directing mind of the bomb plot and one of the directing minds for the camp plot." The judge also wrote that the "meticulous details for the bomb plot were provided by Zakaria Amara. He became knowledgeable about bomb making ingredients and how to avoid detection. In relation to the camp plot, the offender brought a gun to Washago. He was later found in possession of bullets. It is an aggravating factor in relation to the camp plot that firearms were used. He also was seen with deadly hollow point bullets, what he called 'cop killers.'"

The judge also blamed Zakaria Amara for being an active terrorist recruiter "who influenced young men to become involved in a deadly plot. He led some into substantial jail terms." The judge noted how Zakaria had planned at the outset to keep many in the dark in the beginning of the terrorist training camp. He wrote that Zakaria Amara "was involved in recruiting and assessing the candidates for what was to be most serious terrorist conduct. He had photographs and maps of Parliament. He was seeking approval or support from those abroad."

"There is no dispute that what would have occurred was multiple death and injuries," Judge Durno remarked while sentencing Amara to life in prison. "The results would have been catastrophic. What this case revealed was spine-chilling." He went on to conclude, "The potential for loss of life existed on a scale never before seen in Canada." [70]

Zakaria had bragged in his plotting stage that his bombs would be stronger than those used in the London metro bombings. When a blast expert testified, he concluded that Zakaria had "created a bomb equivalent to 768 kilograms of TNT." He also wrote, "That bomb would have caused catastrophic damage to a multi-story glass and steel frame building 35 metres from the bomb site, as well as killing and causing serious injury to people in the path of the blast waves and force."

Judge Durno also wrote, "Had the offender's plan been implemented there would clearly have been injuries and deaths." . . . "On the timetable indicated in the facts with detonation occurring at 9 a.m., the impact would have been magnified as workers arrived for work. With one ton bombs at each location, *the results would have been catastrophic.*" He stated that the results were "unthinkable without the suggestion that metal chips would be put in the bombs [emphasis added]. Had the plan been implemented it would have changed the lives of many, if not all Canadians forever."

The judge continued, "The Exchange Tower has 36 floors, 963 offices occupying over a million square feet of rentable space. It is connected to adjoining buildings by the underground Path system. The CSIS building is also in the downtown area, an area that would be very busy at that time of day. The military base presumably would be occupied by troops and civilian employees, resulting in further injuries and loss of life. This was not an offence that would just impact on those who were injured or killed and their families and friends. This type of offence, even when it is stopped before the plans are implemented, impacts throughout Canada."

He went on to state that Zakaria Amara's arrest and actions also "resulted in embarrassment and anxiety for Muslims" who "were already impacted by the offence. In addition, there would have been massive property damage and to at least some extent an interference with the stock exchange. That it would have impacted the economy cannot be excluded."

"I hope you burn in hell!" Nada, the wife of Zakaria shouted at Mubin as he exited the courtroom after Zakaria received his sentence.

"May Allah forgive you, and your husband," Mubin answered as his protective security detail drew closer around him.

Zakaria Amara appealed but the court dismissed his appeal.

Fahim Ahmad changed his plea to guilty in May 2010 during his jury trial after thirteen days of evidence. He pled guilty to charges of knowingly participating in the activities of a terrorist group—including receiving and providing terrorist training and recruiting; and importing a firearm for the benefit of a terrorist group. He was sentenced to sixteen years in prison in October of 2010.[71]

"It is indisputable that Fahim Ahmad was the original leader of the group," Judge Dawson wrote in the Ontario Superior Court sentencing of Fahim Ahmad. "Zakaria Amara was the second in command and treated Fahim Ahmad as his amir," Judge Dawson concluded stating that Fahim repeatedly expressed the view "that it was religiously permissible to attack targets in Canada because Canada was attacking Muslims in Afghanistan." Judge Dawson also noted that Fahim had told the participants of the Washago camp, nine of which constituted the core group, that they were not yet part of, but held the same beliefs as al Qaeda. He also wrote that Fahim urged his group that they had to enter into a covenant to bring down "Rome"—which symbolized the United States and its allies.[72]

"Mr. Ahmad and Mr. Amara also spoke [picked up on surveillance intercepts] of a promotional video based on the training camp footage that was being produced under Mr. Amara's direction," Judge Dawson wrote. He noted that, "It was to be used for recruiting, to assist in raising money and to impress certain Imams and others who might support their cause. Two such videos were eventually made and one was transmitted to an associate [Aabid Khan] of Mr. Ahmad's in England." Fahim was also cited as "having met with a man called 'Talib' who was engaged in bank and mortgage fraud based on identity theft and the use of fictitious identities" for the purposes of raising money for their terrorist activities.[73]

"The evidence demonstrates that Fahim Ahmad was the driving force behind recruiting and indoctrination," Judge Dawson wrote. "He prepared and distributed collections of fundamentalist Islamic videos advocating violence towards and hatred of non-believers in Islam, and depicting atrocities against Muslims and retaliating violence against Western forces in Iraq and Afghanistan. Some of the material he distributed called for violence in North America." The judge went on to state that "Mr. Ahmad and Mr. Amara were well aware that they were under scrutiny by CSIS and probably the police," and that although they took counter measures they were undeterred by this and even proceeded in their planning after learning that their Atlanta co-conspirators had been arrested.[74]

Judge Dawson did note that Fahim's immigrant status made life difficult for him. He wrote that Fahim's parents were well educated and after fleeing Afghanistan when Fahim was one-year-old had found good jobs in Pakistan—his father was employed as a civil engineer and his mother as a teacher. However when they arrived in Canada "his parents had difficulty having their credentials recognized and both ended up working double shifts in minimum wage jobs to make ends meet."

"In a letter to the court Mr. Ahmad's father has expressed regret that he and his wife were unable to spend more time with their son," Judge Dawson wrote. He also noted that Fahim was a good student and interested in sports but his life went downhill after 9-11 when he felt his friends were treating him differently. He made his primary attachments at the mosques with individuals that taught the al Qaeda narrative that Muslims are under attack by the West.[75]

"Those who the Crown determined to proceed against have now all entered guilty pleas or have already been convicted," Judge Dawson wrote in October 2010 referring to the Toronto 18.[76] Ameen Durrani, the youth known as N.Y. (who we called Gulshan), S.M. (who we called Samir), Z.M., Steven Chand and Ali Dirie were from Scarborough and associated with Fahim Ahmad. Jahmaal James, Asad Ansari, Saad Khalid and Saad Gaya were from Mississauga and ultimately associated themselves with Zakaria Amara.

Saad Khalid who was to deliver one of the bombs, but was not in a leadership role received an equivalent sentence of fourteen years[77] and Saad Gaya, also involved in the bomb plot, but to a slightly lesser degree than Saad Khalid, received an effective sentence of twelve years.[78] Ameen Durrani, who was part of Fahim Ahmad's group, attended both of the training camps and travelled to Opasatika to evaluate the potential safe house was sentenced to one day in jail plus probation after serving almost three years and eight months in pre-trial custody. He received "two for one" credit for pre-trial custody that made his sentence equivalent of almost seven years and six months. Jahmaal James who had gone to Pakistan with the aid of Aabid Khan to enroll in paramilitary training on behalf of the group—but did not do so due to illness—received an almost identical sentence to Ameen Durrani's. Ali Dirie, who smuggled the guns, received an effective sentence of nine years with regard to the effects of pre-trial detention. Asad Ansari, the computer whiz, who was part of Zakaria's group was sentenced to one day in jail to be followed by three years probation which given his pretrial detention was an effective sentence of six years and five months.[79]

Qayyum Abdul Jamal was charged with knowingly participating in the activities of a terrorist group, receiving training and intent to cause an explosion but his charges were stayed in part due to Mubin's testimony. Ahmad Ghany was also charged with knowingly participating in the activities of a terrorist group and receiving training. Charges were subsequently withdrawn or stayed against Jamal, Ghany, Mohamed and Aboud. Three other young persons charged, including Gulshan and Samir, had their charges subsequently withdrawn or stayed.

The two Americans from the "Atlanta" cell whose alleged targets were Washington, D.C. and Atlanta based, but who were coordinating with the Toronto group and also sent their "casing" videos to Aabid Khan and Younes Tsouli (aka Irhabi 007) were also convicted of terrorism charges, but in American courts. Syed Haris Ahmed, a naturalized American citizen who emigrated from Pakistan was convicted on June 9, 2009 of conspiring to provide material support to terrorism in the United States and abroad, and sentenced in 2009 to thirteen years in prison, to be followed by 30 years of supervised release.[80] Ehsanul "Shifa" Sadequee was charged on four terrorism counts, convicted, and sentenced to seventeen years in prison, to be followed by 30 years of supervised release.[81]

Aabid Khan, or "Mr. Fixit" was arrested on June 6, 2006 at Manchester International Airport upon arriving back to the UK from Pakistan. He was in possession of the jihadi tract, *The Clarification Regarding Intentionally Targetting [sic] Women and Children* along with items that implicated him as the administrator of the At-Tibyan Publications website. The items in his possession also made clear that he had been recruiting individuals—like Fahim Ahmad—from the Internet forum *ClearGuidance* and elsewhere to move from just talking about jihad to taking action, including going for paramilitary terrorist training that he would arrange in Pakistan.

Aabid Khan also had on his laptop detailed images, charts, and technical data on the London Underground; the London and Tower Bridges; the Washington D.C. Metro system; the New York City subway system; bridges and tunnels leading into Manhattan; truck routes in boroughs surrounding Manhattan; the New York financial district; the U.S. Capitol building; the White House; the Washington Monument; the World Bank headquarters; Masonic temples in the Washington D.C. area; the D.C. Marine Barracks; and the Golden Gate Bridge in San Francisco. Given his jihadi bent it was hard to believe any of these were for innocent purposes. Likewise he had on his laptop online research regarding the U.S.-Canadian border crossing in Niagara; the purchase of shared passenger railway passes for VIA Rail (Canada) and Amtrak; and options for renting apartments in Toronto, Canada; articles that outlined new government restrictions on the purchase of explosives-grade fertilizer; security techniques in the scanning of airline passengers; and the guidelines used in the inspection of road traffic entering the island of Manhattan.[82]

Aabid Khan was tried in the UK and found guilty of charges that included possessing an article for a purpose connected with the commission, preparation, or instigation of an act of terrorism, and making a record of information likely to be useful in terrorism. He was sentenced to twelve years in prison.[83] Karen Jones, the reviewing lawyer in the case from the U.K. Crown Prosecution Service Counter Terrorism Division wrote, "The evidence showed Khan was a committed and active supporter of Al Qaida ideology. He had extensive amounts of the sort of information that a terrorist would need and use, and the international contacts to pass it on... Aabid Khan was very much the 'Mr. Fix-it' of the group. He preyed on vulnerable young people and turned them into recruits to his cause, using Internet chat to lure them in [and] then incite them to fight. He arranged their passage to Pakistan for terrorism training and talked about a 'worldwide battle.'"[84]

***

Mubin suffered immensely from the court-enforced gag order on information involved in the trials that carried out over a period of three years. The gag effectively allowed the narrative of entrapment, and he as a guilty party, to be bandied about in the press with little he, or others in the know, could say or do in his own defense.

However when all the cases went to trial, it became abundantly clear that Mubin had not entrapped the terrorist plotters and that he had in fact gone out of his way to try to dissuade them as much as he could, given his role. And he had been of invaluable service to both the United States and Canadian governments in protecting the public from potentially horrific attacks. In the youth preliminary trial, Judge Sproat concluded that Mubin was a credible witness and had served his country well. Judge Sproat wrote, "The defence did not seriously challenge Shaikh's credibility. Shaikh exhibited a great number of the hallmarks of a truthful witness. He testified that his involvement came about as a result of a religious conviction that terrorism was contrary to Islamic principles and a corollary sense of civic obligation."

"Shaikh put himself at risk initially without a promise of payment," the judge continued. "From the first meeting, he knew Amara had a handgun and described his hollow point bullets as 'cop killers.' Ahmad and Amara regularly expressed the intention of killing anyone who opposed or might betray them. Shaikh initially expected to be paid $70,000 as a police agent. This increased to $300,000 when the nature and extent of the time commitment far exceeded the original expectations."[85]

"Shaikh's evidence ranged over many individuals and events over a six- month period. There were only a few occasions when counsel pointed out relatively minor inconsistencies in his evidence given at trial and two preliminary inquiries and the facts as recorded in the Source Debriefing Reports.[86] Shaikh is educated and intelligent. In terms of reliability as to precisely what was said and when, Shaikh had the ability to refresh his memory from the Source Debriefing Reports, which were more or less contemporaneous with the events."

The judge also confirmed that the alleged ringleaders invited the youth. "The camp would have been much the same had Shaikh not attended," wrote the judge in his ruling. "The information and indoctrination presented to (the accused) was not influenced or affected by any state action." In all of the cases Mubin was essentially exonerated of any public charges against him of entrapment but it took years to get to that point.

***

It's also interesting to note that both expert witnesses in the cases of Fahim Ahmad and Zakaria Amara did not find them to be mentally ill. Often terrorists are thought to be "crazy" because of their inhumane views and willingness to enact horrific violence on innocent civilians, but in fact researchers find that they are simply people who because of various needs and vulnerabilities in their lives fell under the influence of a group and ideology, took up a narrative, and found like minded individuals to join them and moved slowly or quickly down the terrorist trajectory.

When a judge or anyone else is asked to consider if a terrorist can be rehabilitated, it is not any easy question. In Fahim's case, the expert witness Dr. Gojer, assessed him for his future risk of extremism using an instrument called the Violent Extremism Risk Assessment (VERA).[87] While the VERA is a very good research tool and we do need standardized instruments of this type[88] they can hardly be a replacement for spending a great deal of time getting to know how an individual thinks, how they have acted in the past and what their guiding principles are.

In this case, Dr. Gojer met with Fahim for only two and a half hours and admitted that he hadn't read the intercepts, viewed or read the jihadi materials Fahim had used to recruit others and was not in a position to compare Fahim's answers with the actual evidence produced in the case. The judge therefore did not give much weight to Dr. Gojer's assessment as low, of Fahim's future risk of engaging in terrorism.[89]

As far as predictive models go, it is also interesting that both Fahim and Zakaria had no previous arrest histories. They were what some terrorist experts refer to as "clean skins" because they had no history. Until they did something to catch the attention of security professionals they went undetected.

In this case Fahim Ahmad used his own credit card to rent the car used by the Somali gun smugglers who got caught at the border, he boasted in person and on the Internet and he ran a training camp without a lot of thought to operational security. Without involving himself with Fahim Ahmad, Zakaria Amara may never have taken on the level of extremism that he did. But once he became an extremist, Zakaria was much more careful communicating his intent, especially at the end, when he eschewed telephones and e-mail and resorted to passing messages relayed on memory sticks. Zakaria, if acting without Fahim, might have gone undetected until he committed his crime.

We have Mubin Shaikh, and whoever was working on the U.S. side of things, to thank that neither the Atlanta cell nor the Canadians involved in the Toronto 18 ever achieved their terrorist goals. Mubin paid an extremely high psychosocial price for his work as an undercover jihadi, but in the end emerged stronger and smarter, proud of his work and ready for his next challenges in the world of fighting terrorism.

Epilogue

Mubin Shaikh ultimately was the primary fact witness in the Toronto 18 hearings and was responsible for the conviction of eleven aspiring jihadi terrorists, three who are serving life sentences. Mubin not only finished his Master of Policing, Intelligence and Counter Terrorism (MPICT), he also enrolled in a doctorate in Psychology at the University of Liverpool studying radicalization and violent extremism, which he is currently completing.

Mubin went on to develop a disengagement and deradicalization program that he and his father applied successfully to extremists in Canada.[90] Likewise, when thousands of young militant jihadis started leaving Europe, the U.S. and Canada to join extremist al-Qaeda linked groups in Syria and Iraq, including the Islamic State, Mubin became active on Twitter engaging with many of them. In doing so he sent off Qur'anic Ayaat and Prophetic Ahaadeeth and shamed many into admitting that their militant jihadi beliefs were indeed non-Islamic. Whether any quit as a result still remains to be seen. The important point is that Mubin continues in his work, now as an active ideological fighter against ISIS—engaging directly with ISIS fighters in the battlespace via social media—before and since it proclaimed its false caliphate in "Shaam and Iraq."

Mubin is one of the very few people in the world to have actually gone undercover in a homegrown terror cell. Because of this experience he is considered a primary source for the study of Islamist radicalization and terrorism by academics worldwide and remains an active trainer of military, security and police intelligence on violent Islamist extremists. He goes by the Twitter handle @CaliphateCop and his website is http://www.undercoverjihadi.com.

Please like our book on Amazon!

Readers like to know how other readers liked a book they are considering buying. If you found this a good read, please give us some good words and loads of stars on Amazon, Barnes & Noble or wherever your purchase your books. Thanks for your time in doing so!

Other Books by (or coauthored by) Anne Speckhard, Ph.D.

Talking to Terrorists: Understanding the Psycho-Social Motivations of Militant Jihadi Terrorists, Mass Hostage Takers, Suicide Bombers and "Martyrs", Advances Press, LLC, 2012.

Warrior Princess: A U.S. Navy SEAL's Journey to Coming out Transgender, Kristin Beck & Anne Speckhard, Advances Press, LLC, 2013.

Fetal Abduction: The True Story of Multiple Personalities and Murder, Advances Press, LLC, 2012.

Beyond the Pale: A Story of Love and Friendship from the Minsk Ghetto and Holocaust in Belarus (forthcoming).

Timothy Tottle's Terrific Dream, with Jessica Speckhard, Little Fingerprints Press (an imprint of Advances Press, LLC), 2014.

Author's Note

The events and conversations described in this book rely in part on Mubin Shaikh's memory of them as told to me. When documentation of police intercepts were available—as in court hearings—these references are included in the endnotes to verify that this is in fact what was really said. Likewise we included many journalists' references as well from court proceedings to the events recorded here. For the academic reader we also included in the endnotes many additional readings that pertain to the topics of homegrown radicalization, pathways into and out of terrorism, female contributions to terrorism, deradicalization and disengagement, etc.

We also note that we have used Arabic spelling for the Arabic words used here versus some of the more common English spellings.

We would also like to state emphatically that while we wrote about a specific group of extremist Salafis who endorsed militant jihadi thoughts and actions who influenced Mubin's thinking, that most Salafis are peace-loving and good Muslims and also, more importantly, that many have offered their partnership in fighting terrorism. No one should take from our reference to the few extremist Salafis in this book, that all Salafi Muslims are a problem, advocating violence for achieving religious or political objectives.

Lastly we should note that while the real names of the adult terrorist plotters of the Toronto 18 have been used, the names of those who were minors have been changed.

Acknowledgements

Mubin Shaikh

In the name of Allah, the beneficent and the merciful.

THIS BOOK TELLS A STORY. It is not a fatwa, it is not an action adventure spy story, it is not an academic work and it is not a manifesto either. It is a story based on facts that intends to convey certain important aspects that I learned through this life journey of mine.

Now that I have that out of the way, I begin by thanking YOU, the reader, for getting my book. I hope it accomplished for you what I set out for it to do. Whatever that might lead you into in terms of new thoughts and understanding, just go with it. This is your Jihad: to go through the long, winding journey that life is. It's never neat and tidy—it wasn't meant to be. As for those who made this book possible, a comprehensive list would take many pages but I've decided to break it down into these parts:

Family and friends: My sincerest love and appreciation goes out to my family who not only supported me throughout this whole journey but kept me in check whenever I got out of line—and that was more times than I could honestly admit publicly. To my closest friends from my formative years—including the influential Army Cadet colleagues—who are referenced throughout this book, I have changed names to protect identities (and give you plausible deniability of some of the crazier things we did as teenagers) but you know who you are. To the K&K Café Clan— you are the Inner Circle—I owe you big-time. Thanks to the Music Squad for all the journeys into the abyss and back again, Cheerleaders Against Everything, the warriors at SIAM Muay Thai, Master (Ajahn) Suchart, to the Ninja's who treat my wounds to this day and to the select members of the D-BlockAlleyCats: we have been rambling on for about twenty years—see? We were right all along. All hail to our chief, The Baker. To all those who serve in secret and without the luxury of the limelight, we owe you gratitude for the safety of our family and friends.

Scholars/doers: Wow, the number of erudite minds who have written on the topic of terrorist studies is something to behold. Without you, I could not possibly have achieved what I have and I am indebted to your intellectual greatness and will continue to draw from it in the years ahead. I do have biases for and against some who I have met in person and it is okay to be a Master in aspects of a topic but then also be scholarly enough to go a completely different way in which we may disagree—it is a testament to the diversity of thought related to this topic. The actual list would look like an academic bibliography and perhaps that is why I rendered my list into alphabetical order as follows: The brothers and sisters in the AVE Network (especially the tattooed ones), Mohammad Abbasi, Paul Salahuddin Armstrong, Manwar Ali (been there, done that senior executive), Waleed Aly, Shahed Amanullah, M. Al Azami, Peter Bergen, J. M. Berger (quiet, unassuming and very deadly), Stewart Bell, Alex Beutel (for the Safe Spaces initiative), Jonathan Birdwell, Tore Bjorgo, Mia Bloom (super intelligent), Laila Bokhari, Max Boot, Jarret Brachman, Alison Buchanan (the most helpful research colleague ever), Rabia Chaudry (Muslim woman & counter-terrorism expert), Paul Cruikshank, Jared Cohen and Google Ideas (radicals, I tell you!), Jon Cole (my brilliant, mad scientist Ph.D. supervisor who I drive absolutely "nutters") and the University of Liverpool for supporting my research, Rita Cosby, Mohamed Elibiary (top Muslim CT & CVE expert in my view), Scott Flowers, James Forest (who I did indeed confirm as the Nicest Guy in Terrorism Research), Boaz Ganor, Daveed Gartenstein-Ross (for helping me in the study of radicalization in particular), Rohan Gunaratna, GCTF, HEDAYAH, Chris Heffelfinger (thank you for answering my thousand and one emails), Thomas Hegghammer, Cato Hemmingby (how many researchers can say they were in a building during a major terrorist bombing?!), Bruce Hoffman (another Jedi Master), John Horgan (whose writings influenced me greatly), Ed Husain (for your pioneering experiences), Joe Illardi, Halli Casser-Jayne, Humera Khan (unassuming in size but a giant in real life), Michael King for his help with research related to the Toronto 18, Arie Kruglanski, Robert Lambert, Todd Leventhal (I'm not a liberty to discuss how awesome he is), Charles Lister, Salam Al Marayati, Will McCants, Bruce McFarlane, Ariel Merari, Jacob Michaelson, Sam Mullins (and the rest of the amazingly helpful staff at the George C. Marshall Center), Majid Nawaz (– I may not agree 100% but you're definitely part of the solution), Peter Neumann and the absolutely fantastic work being done by the ICSR, Farhana Qazi, Magnus Ranstorp (for the Swedish jihadi gummy bears), Oliver Roy (one of the best), Marc Sageman (a living legend, seriously), Alex Schmid (Jedi Master of radicalization and terrorism studies) and the top-notch online journal, Perspectives of Terrorism, Neil Shortland, Julie Siddiqi, Stephen Sloan, Ali Soufan and The Soufan Group, Ambassador Daniel Speckhard, START Center, Jessica Stern (easily, one the top women in terrorism studies and wonderful dinner host), Haris Tarin (for the Sheesha!), TSAS research network and the scholars associated with it, Haroon Ullah, VPN Violence Prevention Network, The Wolf (yes, that one), Jeff Weyers (actionable research for police practitioners), Quintan Wiktorowicz, Andrew Zammit, Aaron Zelin.

Government: I would like to thank the agencies such as [redacted], [redacted] and especially, [redacted.] I thank those in your ranks who have helped the Muslim community though they know not. The amount of sleep and sanity you have sacrificed in keeping the public as safe as possible is too much. Also, stop tapping my phone—you're interfering with my crank calling to pizza shops.

Community organizations: A heartfelt shout-out to the Jewish, Christian and Muslim organizations (especially the Shuyukh and Awliyaa) that took the risk of engaging with me notwithstanding the manufactured controversy that came with my work history. The same goes for the other religious groups as well as non-religious groups that all seek a common respect of basic human dignity. Without you, my spiritual growth would have been stunted. Thank you. Many of you I will just not mention so as to preserve your autonomy but you are doing good work in preventing violent extremism (PVE) and countering violent extremism (CVE). Keep on keepin' on!

Even to those related to the Toronto 18 – those still incarcerated and those free – let this chapter in our lives be reflected on and hopefully, move society to a better place. Indeed, all the affairs of this world will eventually return to Allah for Final Judgment.

Last and certainly not least, a very special thanks to our book agent and publicist, Michael Wright of Garson & Wright Publications who never gave up on me and who was always honest in his dealings with me. I could not have done this without your assistance. Thanks also to artist Jessica Speckhard for her design of the book cover, to Rocco Stragapete for his awesome photos, to Jilly Prather and Vanessa Veazie for their careful editing and to Advances Press, LLC for publishing the book. Thanks to Todd Leventhal and Ken Reidy for their review of the final draft and many edits to it. Thanks also to Jessica Stern who wrote the foreword. Of course, I could not sufficiently conclude this acknowledgement without a super kudos to Dr. Anne Speckhard who facilitated my visits to various government departments in the United States, but more importantly, wrote this book, working on it even while she was on vacation. Thank you to your family for putting up with me taking over the dinner table as we recounted these events.

Peace Be Unto You,

Mubin.

About the Authors

Mubin Shaikh comes from the extremely unique background of having been a Muslim extremist throughout his 20's and into his mid-30's after a chance encounter with the Taliban in 1995. The attacks of 9/11 forced him to re-consider his views and he spent the subsequent two years in Syria studying Arabic and Islamic Studies where he gained an almost encyclopedic knowledge of Sunni Islam. Returning in 2004, he began working for the Canadian Security Intelligence Service (CSIS) and was operational and undercover in several (classified) cases until December 2005 when he would traverse to Royal Canadian Mounted Police (RCMP), Integrated National Security Enforcement Team (INSET) in what came to be known as the Toronto 18 terrorism case. His testimony in five legal hearings over four years resulted in the conviction of eleven aspiring militant jihadists. He has since completed a Master of Policing, Intelligence & Counter Terrorism (MPICT, Macquarie) and is now in the Ph.D. program in Psychological Sciences, Tactical Decision Making Research Group, University of Liverpool. He has consulted with U.S. agencies such as the National Counter Terrorism Center, FBI Counterterrorism Division, Department of State (Counter Terrorism branch), civilian law enforcement as well as the Naval Criminal Investigative Service (NCIS), has taught Red Cell courses for Military Intelligence and assists with training (kinetic force) counter terrorism units where requested. Website http://www.undercoverjihadi.com

Anne Speckhard, Ph.D. is an Adjunct Associate Professor of Psychiatry at Georgetown University Medical School and also teaches in the Security Studies Program of the Georgetown University School of Foreign Service. Dr. Speckhard has been working in the field of posttraumatic stress disorder (PTSD) since the 1980's and has extensive experience working in Europe, the Middle East and the former Soviet Union. She was the chair of the *NATO Human Factors & Medicine Research and Technology Experts Group (HFM-140/RTG) on the Psychosocial, Cultural and Organizational Aspects of Terrorism*, served as the co-chair of the *NATO-Russia Human Factors & Medicine Research Task Group on Social Sciences Support to Military Personnel Engaged in Counter-Insurgency and Counter-Terrorism Operations* and served on the *NATO Human Factors & Medicine Research Task Group Moral Dilemmas and Military Mental Health Outcomes*. She is a member of the United Nations Roster of Experts for the Terrorism Prevention Branch Office on Drugs and Crime and was previously awarded a Public Health Service Fellowship in the United States Department of Health & Human Services where she served as a Research Fellow.

She has provided expert consultation to European and Middle Eastern governments as well as U.S. agencies such as the National Counter Terrorism Center, FBI Counterterrorism Division, Department of State (Counter Terrorism Branch) and the U.S. Department of Defense, regarding pathways into terrorism as well as programs for prevention and rehabilitation of individuals committed to political violence and militant jihad. In 2006-2007 she worked with the U.S. Department of Defense to design and pilot test the Detainee Rehabilitation Program in Iraq. In 2002, she interviewed hostages taken in the Moscow Dubrovka Theater about their psychological responses and observations of the suicidal terrorists and did the same in 2005 with surviving hostages from the Beslan school take-over. Since 2002, she has collected more than four hundred research interviews of family members, friends, close associates and hostages of terrorists and militant jihadi extremists in Palestine, Israel, Iraq, Lebanon, Jordan, Morocco, Russia, Chechnya, Belarus, Netherlands, United Kingdom, Belgium and France.

Dr. Speckhard is also the director of the *Holocaust Survivors Oral Histories Project – Belarus,* a project constructing the history of the Minsk Ghetto and Holocaust in Belarus through oral histories and archival research.

She also researched traumatic stress issues in survivors of the Chernobyl disaster and has written about stress responses to toxic disasters. Dr. Speckhard worked with American expatriates after 9-11 (at SHAPE, NATO, the U.S. Embassy to Belgium and Mission to the EU) and conducted research on acute stress responses to terrorism in this population. She also studied psychological resilience to terrorism in various populations including American civilians, military and diplomats serving in Iraq under high threat security conditions.

Dr. Speckhard consults to governments and lectures to security experts worldwide and frequently appears in the national and international media. She is the author of *Talking to Terrorists: Understanding the Psycho-Social Motivations of Militant Jihadi Terrorists; Mass Hostage Takers, Suicide Bombers and "Martyrs"; Fetal Abduction: The True Story of Multiple Personalities and Murder;* **Beyond the Pale: A Story of Love and Friendship from the Minsk Ghetto and Holocaust in Belarus** and *Timothy Tottle's Terrific Dream* and co-author of *Warrior Princess: A U.S. Navy SEALs Journey to Coming out Transgender.* Website: www.AnneSpeckhard.com

Glossary

AllahuAkbar - "Allah is Greater." Can be used in exclamation of anything positive.

Alhamdulillah - "All praise is due to Allah." Used primarily in thanks and gratitude.

Al Qaeda – Normally understood to be the group headed by the late Osama Bin Laden and which declared war on the West. Better illustrated in the statement of Al Suri: It is a system and methodology, not a group per se. AQ has many affiliates under various names.

Caliph - A spiritual leader of Islam, claiming succession from Muhammad.

Caliphate - The rank, jurisdiction, or government of a caliph.

Dar Al Ahd – "The land of covenant" in which Muslims are free to worship and are protected by state police and military systems and otherwise, have treaties with Muslim countries to various degrees. Also known as Dar Al Sulh. Closest designation to what we refer to as "the West." It is prohibited to reside under covenant in such lands and commit acts of violence or insurrection while doing so.

Dar Al Harb – The lands in which non-Muslims reside and which do not have a treaty of non-aggression or peace with the Muslims and otherwise, declare war on Islam and Muslims en masse.

Dar Al Islam – The land where Islam is practiced by the vast majority and where non-Muslims are protected by police and military systems.

Da'wah – "Invitation" (to Islam).

Emir - A title of honor of the descendants of Muhammad, also a commander.

Fard Al Ayn – Individual obligation in Islam, such as the 5 daily prayers.

Fard Al Kifaayah – Communal obligation in Islam, such as funeral prayers where a few, who do so, will absolve the majority to do the same. Jihad has traditionally fallen into this category but modern revisionists among militant ideologues have suggested it is Fard Al Ayn. But traditional scholars state that Jihad is Fard Al Ayn only upon those who are directly impacted by oppression and only if those under attack cannot respond. Only then does the call extend to others in outside areas.

Fatwa – A professional legal opinion in Islamic Law. Issued by, "Mufti" (jurisconsult). An individual Mufti and his (or her) opinion, has never been considered to be binding on the wider Muslim community. In a traditional Islamic context, a Mufti who has state sanction does have binding authority, but that should be considered as in a larger parliamentary-style system where the Qadi (Authorized state judge) has authority to prosecute rulers and Caliphs, regulate and sanction Mufti's and finally, administer policing services. To illustrate the nature of a binding legal opinion in the latter context of modern policing, an Arrest Warrant is akin to a Fatwa.

Fitnah – "Trials and tribulations." Traditionally and historically understood to mean fighting among Muslims. Has also referred more widely, as "corruption on the earth" (kidnapping, hostage-taking, destroying places of worship especially as it relates to killing innocents, Muslim or otherwise, in the name of Islam. Complementary term is, "Fasaad".

Hadith – A traditional account of things said or done by Muhammad or his companions.

Hijab - A traditional scarf worn by Muslim women to cover the hair and neck.

Imam - The title for a Muslim religious leader or chief or anyone who leads prayer.

Iman – Islamic faith, which is based on: Belief in One God, Angels, Revealed Books, human Messengers, the Day of Judgement and destiny, the good and bad from it.

InshaAllah – "If Allah Wills it." Usually said in response to a request or desire. Sometimes cynically described as a polite way of saying, "No."

Islam - The religious faith of Muslims, based on the words and religious system founded by the prophet Muhammad (SalAllahuAlayhiWaSallam) and taught by the Qur'an, the basic principle of which is absolute submission to a unique and personal god, Allah.

ISIS – "Islamic State in Iraq and Syria." A modern day Khawarij group that originated in Iraq, swarmed into Syria in defiance of Al Qaeda's orders, made war upon the Mujaahideen fighting in Syria and retracted back to Iraq to continue their insurgency. Eventually, their leader Abubakr Al Baghdadi unilaterally self-declared himself to be the Caliph of the entire Muslim world. See book by J. Stern & J. M. Berger on ISIS (2015).

Jamaat - An Islamic council or assembly.

Jihad – There are two forms of jihad—the inner struggle every Muslim makes to attempt a life of morality and a second form which involved fighting as a militant for the defense of Muslim lands, people and honor.

Ka'bah – The black cubic structure that marks the direction of Muslim ritual prayer. Associated with Prophet Abraham and Prophet Ishmael who established monotheistic practice in ancient Arabia. Fell into use by polytheistic cults which came to associate multiple gods to the site. Islam claims to have re-established that Abrahamic chain with the Final Semite Prophet, Muhammad (SalAllahuAlayhiWaSallam).

Kuffar – Technically: one who knows the truth but conceals it. Falsely made synonymous with "infidel," a Judeo-Christian concept describing a person unfaithful to God. Complementary terms include, Munafiq and Murtad.

Lota - (In India) a small container for water, usually of brass or copper and round in shape.

Madrasa - A school or college, especially a school attached to a mosque where young men study Islamic theology.

MashaAllah - "What Allah desires is done." Used in exclamation when something is affirmed or achieved.

Militant Jihadi - An Islamic fundamentalist who participates in or supports jihad, especially armed and violent confrontation.

Minaret - A lofty, often slender, tower or turret attached to a mosque, surrounded by or furnished with one or more balconies, from which the muezzin calls the people to prayer.

Muezzin - The person who calls his fellow Muslims to prayer.

Mujahid – One who participates in Jihad. Plural: Mujahideen.

Qur'an – The holy scriptures of Islam.

Radicalization – Very simply, the process by which an individual comes to support non-traditional political views. "Violent radicalization" refers to a process whereby an individual comes to support violent political views. "Violent extremism" refers to a state of being where an individual acts out their violent thoughts in support of particular political extremist groups. Terrorism is thus a type of violent extremism. These terms apply equally to Muslim and non-Muslim extremists and can include ultranationalists, white supremacists and even street gangs.

Salafi – Muslims who claim to follow the beliefs and practices of the Salaf, the earliest of Muslims.

SalAllahuAlayhiWaSallam – The traditional greeting upon the Prophet Muhammad and which literally means, the blessings of Allah be upon him (Muhammad) and blessings furthermore. It is usually abbreviated in closed brackets as "(SAW)" and sometimes anglicized and abbreviated as "PBUH" (Peace Be Upon Him). Other uses include "A.S." (Alayhissalaam – Upon him Be Peace) which is also used as a prefix following the mention of one of the Prophets of God.

Shariah – That which is understood to be the will of Allah in terms of a particular legal position. The effort and mechanism to achieve that is called fiqh which is based on a number of sources: the Qur'an, the Sunnah, Ijma (consensus), Qiyaas (logic), Istihsaan (judicial preference) and other mechanisms that vary with the particular schools of thought (Singular "Madhab" and plural, "Madahib," of which are four main ones: Hanafi, Shaafi, Maaliki and Hanbali).

Shaykh – A respected Muslim scholar, teacher and/or political leader

Shura - a consultative council or assembly

SubhanAllah - "Glory be to Allah." Can be used in exclamation as well as as when receiving negative news

Sufi – a traditional understanding of Islam that focuses in spiritual exercises related to the effacement of ego, ritual repetition of the Names of Allah and others aspects which have been present as a part of Islam since the earliest Islamic period.

Tablighi Jamaat - an Islamic religious movement based on the principle of the

"Work of the Prophets" (Peace be Upon Them) inviting to God in the manner of Muhammad (SalAllahuAlayhiWaSallam).

Taliban – an Islamic fundamentalist political movement in Afghanistan that helped overthrow the Soviet occupation of Afghanistan and then began ruling as the Islamic Emirate of Afghanistan from September 1996 to December 2001.

Takfeer – The act of declaring someone as having violated Islam in such a way so to become a kuffar. It is akin to excommunication. It is considered a grave sin in Islam from which repentance is required. Traditionally understood to be permitted only within the context of state sanction by a Qadi and has never ever been understood to have authority when done by individuals or groups, on their own.

Ummah – "The Muslim Nation." Term used by Prophet SalAllahuAlayhiWaSallam to describe his people and his followers who coexist as a singular entity, whether a spiritual community, a political community, or a mix of the two. The Hadith, "The Ummah is like a body, if one part hurts, the whole body hurts" has frequently been used to suggest a trans-national identity of Muslims in which the suffering of a Muslim in one place, creates a Fard Al Ayn upon another Muslim in some other place, to respond to that suffering. It is widely accepted by radicalized individuals, as a framework in which ideology and moral grievance/outrage narratives are constructed.

Endnotes

1   Sageman, M. (2004). Understanding Terror Networks: University of Pennsylvannia Press.

2   For a complete discussion of the development of al Qaeda and the U.S. war with it see: Bergen, P. (2011). The longest war: The enduring conflict between America and al-Qaeda: Free Press.

3   It should be pointed out that most Salafis are not extremists or violent. They are simply conservative and traditional Muslims who trace their practices and beliefs back to the Prophet and his companions and they do not endorse militant jihad. This passage is not meant any disparagement of Salafis here, as many have been very instrumental in battling against violent ideologies but this particular group was a big proponent of militant jihad. See: Siraat. (November, 2011). Why the Salafis are not a terror problem. In A. Speckhard (Eds.), Psychosocial, organizational and cultural aspects of terrorism Available from http://ftp.rta.nato. int/public//PubFullText/RTO/TR/RTO-TR-HFM-140///TR-HFM-140-09.pdf Likewise for a good discussion of Salafi involvement in fighting terrorism see: Lambert, R. (2012). Countering Al Qaeda in London: Police and Muslims in Partnerships: Hurst.

4   For an excellent and exhaustive discussion of the factors involved in radicalization see Schmid, A. (2013). Radicalisation, de-radicalisation, counter-radicalisation: A conceptual discussion and literature review. Retrieved from http://www. icct.nl/download/file/ICCT-Schmid-Radicalisation-De-Radicalisation-Counter-Radicalisation-March-2013.pdf; See also: Bakker, E. (2006). Jihadi terrorists in Europe: Their characteristics and the circumstances in which they joined Jihad: An exploratory study. The Hague: Netherlands . Institute of International Relations.; Cole, J., & Cole, B. (2009). Martyrdom: Radicalisation and terrorist violence among British Muslims: Pennant Books, Ltd.Silke, A. (December 16, 2008). Holy warriors: Exploring the psychological process of jihadi radicalization. European Journal of Criminology, 5(99), 99-124.; Neumann, P., & Kleinmann, S. (2013). How rigorous is radicalization research? Democracy and Security, 9 (4), 360-382; Post, J. (2006). Social and Psychological Factors in the Genesis of Terrorism. In J. Victoroff (Ed.): IOS Press.; Speckhard, A. (2012). Talking to terrorists: Understanding the psycho-social motivations of militant jihadi terrorists, mass hostage takers, suicide bombers and "martyrs". McLean, VA: Advances Press. and Wiktorowicz, Q. (2005). Radical Islam rising: Muslim extremism in the West: Rowman & Littlefield Publishers.

5   Shaykh Al Arnaut was present in Syria. Mubin also drew inspiration from Saudi scholars whose lectures he could hear online while in Syria): Shaykh Ab-

dulAziz Tarifi, Shaykh Nasser Al Alwan, Shaykh AbdulAziz Fawzan and the Syrian Shaykh Al Tartusi. This group were all plainly against extremism and now speak out against the group, ISIS calling them a Khawarij group referring to an ancient sect of extremists whom the Prophet SalAllahAlayhiWaSallam said would emerge again and again and how they would be cut down whenever they did. The Khawarij were known for the practice of "takfeer"–accusing Muslims of no longer being Muslims and then killing them on flimsy excuses—and represent the most extreme end of Islamic zealots.

6   BBC News. (March 22, 2006). 'Bomb ingredients' kept in depot. Retrieved from http://news.bbc.co.uk/1/hi/uk/4833706.stm; The Canadian Press. (July 3, 2008). Khawaja discussed detonator with plotter, trial hears. CTV News. Retrieved from http://www.ctvnews.ca/khawaja-discussed-detonator-with-plotter-trial-hears-1.306379; Ottawacitizen.com. (October 29, 2008). Khawaja on trial. Retrieved from http://www2.canada.com/ottawacitizen/features/khawajatrial/story.html?id=c47457a8-879e-47f5-847f-a602121c2651

7   BBC News. (March 22, 2006). 'Bomb ingredients' kept in depot. Retrieved from http://news.bbc.co.uk/1/hi/uk/4833706.stm; The Canadian Press. (July 3, 2008). Khawaja discussed detonator with plotter, trial hears. CTV News. Retrieved from http://www.ctvnews.ca/khawaja-discussed-detonator-with-plotter-trial-hears-1.306379; Ottawacitizen.com. (October 29, 2008). Khawaja on trial. Retrieved from http://www2.canada.com/ottawacitizen/features/khawajatrial/story.html?id=c47457a8-879e-47f5-847f-a602121c2651

8   For a full discussion of these doctrines see: Lia, B. (2008). Doctrines for Jihadi Terrorist Training. Terrorism and Political Violence, 20(4), 518-542.

9   BBC News. (March 22, 2006). 'Bomb ingredients' kept in depot. Retrieved from http://news.bbc.co.uk/1/hi/uk/4833706.stm; The Canadian Press. (July 3, 2008). Khawaja discussed detonator with plotter, trial hears. CTV News. Retrieved from http://www.ctvnews.ca/khawaja-discussed-detonator-with-plotter-trial-hears-1.306379; Ottawacitizen.com. (October 29, 2008). Khawaja on trial. Retrieved from http://www2.canada.com/ottawacitizen/features/khawajatrial/story.html?id=c47457a8-879e-47f5-847f-a602121c2651

10   BBC News. (March 22, 2006). 'Bomb ingredients' kept in depot. Retrieved from http://news.bbc.co.uk/1/hi/uk/4833706.stm; The Canadian Press. (July 3, 2008). Khawaja discussed detonator with plotter, trial hears. CTV News. Retrieved from http://www.ctvnews.ca/khawaja-discussed-detonator-with-plotter-trial-hears-1.306379; Ottawacitizen.com. (October 29, 2008). Khawaja on trial. Retrieved from http://www2.canada.com/ottawacitizen/features/khawajatrial/story.html?id=c47457a8-879e-47f5-847f-a602121c2651

11   BBC News. (March 22, 2006). 'Bomb ingredients' kept in depot. Re-

trieved from http://news.bbc.co.uk/1/hi/uk/4833706.stm; The Canadian Press. (July 3, 2008). Khawaja discussed detonator with plotter, trial hears. CTV News. Retrieved from http://www.ctvnews.ca/khawaja-discussed-detonator-with-plotter-trial-hears-1.306379; Ottawacitizen.com. (October 29, 2008). Khawaja on trial. Retrieved from http://www2.canada.com/ottawacitizen/features/khawajatrial/story.html?id=c47457a8-879e-47f5-847f-a602121c2651

12   Mcarthur, G., & Akkad, O. E. (August 22, 2012). Blog offers glimpse of accused. The Globe and Mail. Retrieved from www.theglobeandmail.com/news/national/blog-offers-glimpse-of-accused/article4195934/

13   Akkad, O. E., & Mcarthur, G. (June 29, 2006). Hateful chatter behind the veil. The Globe and Mail. Retrieved from http://www.theglobeandmail.com/news/national/hateful-chatter-behind-the-veil/article1203257/?page=all

14   The lecture to be held was on the plight of Muslim men being held under Canadian 'Security Certificates' which allowed Citizenship and Immigration Canada to detain without charge or trial, suspects deemed to be too dangerous to release based on 'secret information' collected by the Canadian Security Intelligence Service (CSIS). It is of note that these 'Security Certificates' were held to be unconstitutional by the Canadian Supreme Court in 2007. The law was subsequently rewritten to model itself after the UK system and has held up in Canadian courts. See: MacCharles, T. (May 14, 2014). Supreme Court upholds security certificate law in Mohamed Harkat terror case. TheStar.com. Retrieved from http://www.thestar.com/news/canada/2014/05/14/supreme_court_upholds_security_certificate_law_in_mohamed_harkat_terror_case.html

15   For an interesting discussion of UK undercover policing and Salafi Muslim participation in fighting al Qaeda related terrorists see: Lambert, R. (2012). Countering Al Qaeda in London: Police and Muslims in Partnerships: Hurst.

16   Teotonio, I. (2010). Toronto 18. TheStar.com. Retrieved from http://www3.thestar.com/static/toronto18/index.html

17   Teotonio, I. (2010). Toronto 18. TheStar.com. Retrieved from http://www3.thestar.com/static/toronto18/index.html

18   Davison, J., & Thomson, J. (April 16, 2014). Homegrown terrorist: Toronto 18 bomb plotter Saad Khalid recalls his radicalization. Retrieved from http://www.cbc.ca/news/canada/homegrown-terrorist-toronto-18-bomb-plotter-saad-khalid-recalls-his-radicalization-1.2532671

19   See: Teotonio, I. (2010). Toronto 18. TheStar.com. Retrieved from http://www3.thestar.com/static/toronto18/index.html and Struck, D. (June 11, 2006). School ties link alleged plotters. Retrieved from http://www.washingtonpost.com/wp-dyn/content/article/2006/06/10/AR2006061000399.html

20   Teotonio, I. (2010). Toronto 18. TheStar.com. Retrieved from http://www3.thestar.com/static/toronto18/index.html

21   For more details on their trip to Toronto see, U.S. v. Sadequee, (E.D. N.Y.), No. M-06-335, Affidavit of FBI Special Agent Michael Scherck in Support of Arrest Warrant, Filed March 28, 2006.

22   Teotonio, I. (2010). Toronto 18. TheStar.com. Retrieved from http://www3.thestar.com/static/toronto18/index.html

23   They also sent it to Younes Tsouli as well.

24   See: Associated Press. (December 14, 2009). Ehsanul Islam Sadequee gets 17 years in jail for sending video of U.S. landmarks to terror suspects. Retrieved from http://www.nydailynews.com/news/national/ehsanul-islam-sade-quee-17-years-jail-sending-video-u-s-landmarks-terror-suspects-article-1.432868 and Kohlman, E. (January 2008). Irhaby007's American Connections. Target: America and U.S. v. Ahmed, (N.D. GA.), No. 1:06-CR-147-CC, Indictment, Filed July 19, 2006.

25   Aabid Khan also worked with Younes Tsouli who was uploading jihadi videos for al Qaeda in Iraq. They worked together at at-Tibyan Publications. Tsouli was arrested in October 2005 and Aabid Khan took off to Pakistan within some months of that. See: Kohlmann, E. (September, 2008). Anatomy of a modern homegrown terror cell: Aabid Khan et al. Operation Praline. Retrieved from http://acsa2000.net/TW/samples/Kohlman.pdf,pg. 7 and http://internet-haganah.com/harchives/006372.html

26   See: Kohlmann, E. (September, 2008). Anatomy of a modern homegrown terror cell: Aabid Khan et al. Operation Praline. Retrieved from http://acsa2000.net/TW/samples/Kohlman.pdf,pg. 7. and Speckhard, A., & Akhmedova, K. (2006). The New Chechen Jihad: Militant Wahhabism as a Radical Movement and a Source of Suicide Terrorism in Post-War Chechen Society. Democracy and Security, 2(1), 103-155.

27   TheGlobeandMail. (October 25, 2010). Ontario Superior Court of Justice sentencing of Fahim Ahmad. Retrieved from http://www.scribd.com/doc/40098959/Ontario-Superior-Court-of-Justice-sentencing-of-Fahim-Ahmad paragraph 11, pg 6.

28   These events occurred on August 13, 2005 when Mohamed and Dirie entered Canada from the United States at Fort Erie. Both later pleaded guilty to various weapons offences and were sentenced to two years imprisonment. Dirie did not rehabilitate in prison and continued plotting with the Toronto 18. After his release from prison he went to Syria to fight Assad and is believed to have died there. See: Shephard, M. (September 25, 2013). Toronto 18L Ali Mohamed Dirie, convicted in plot, dies in Syria. Retrieved from http://www.thestar.com/news/gta/2013/09/25/

toronto_18_ali_mohamed_dirie_convicted_in_plot_dies_in_syria.html

29   This particular quote is from Teotonio, I. (2010). Toronto 18. TheStar.com. Retrieved from http://www3.thestar.com/static/toronto18/index.html

30   Gillespie, B. (February 26, 2010). Accused in Toronto 18 plot pleads guilty. CBCNews. Retrieved from http://www.cbc.ca/news/canada/toronto/accused-in-toronto-18-plot-pleads-guilty-1.913929

31   See the film here: https://docs.google.com/file/d/0B8Abo3o5NAjuTVFD-VjBwOV9UTFE/edit

32   This training film was not made public in Fahim's case due to the publication ban enacted by the judge in his trial. It was however entered as evidence in Aabid Khan's trial in the UK. Part of the training film can be viewed here: https://docs.google.com/file/d/0B8Abo3o5NAjuTVFDVjBwOV9UTFE/edit

33   Teotonio, I. (2010). Toronto 18. TheStar.com. Retrieved from http://www3.thestar.com/static/toronto18/index.html

34   The content of this section is from nearly verbatim intercepts reported by the judge in the youth trial sentencing documents. See: Ontario Superior Court of Justice - Youth Justice Court - Judge Sproat. (September 25, 2008). Her Majesty the Queen and N.Y.

35   This event in the restaurant is referenced in the youth sentencing report of NY.

36   See the training film here: https://docs.google.com/file/d/0B8Abo3o5NAjuTVFDVjBwOV9UTFE/edit

37   The judge in the youth sentencing trial writes, "An intercept on February 6, 2006 captured Dirie calling Ahmad from Collins Bay Penitentiary. Ahmad inquired about Dirie's 'links for the wives'. It took Dirie a few minutes to recognize that Ahmad was alluding to their earlier discussion, and that 'wives' was code for guns. Dirie said he had the number, referring to a link to obtain guns." See: Ontario Superior Court of Justice - Youth Justice Court - Judge Sproat. (September 25, 2008). Her Majesty the Queen and N.Y.

38   This section is referenced in the youth sentencing report of NY. See: Ontario Superior Court of Justice - Youth Justice Court - Judge Sproat. (September 25, 2008). Her Majesty the Queen and N.Y.

39   This section is referenced in the youth sentencing report of NY See: Ontario Superior Court of Justice - Youth Justice Court - Judge Sproat. (September 25, 2008). Her Majesty the Queen and N.Y. para 144.

40   In the sentencing of Zakaria Amara Judge Durno wrote, "On three occasions over two weeks, Amara went to a public library and conducted computer searches for 'ammonium nitrate in agriculture,' 'nitric acid,' 'rocket fuel,' 'fuel tablets,' 'buy nitric acid,' 'fertilizer,' 'explosives' and 'ways to get ammonium nitrate.'

On one occasion he used the computer to order 'Student Farmer' business cards. He was also seen in the library working with a soldering iron, spools of wire and batteries." See: Ontario Superior Court of Justice - Judge S.B. Durno. (January 18, 2010). Her Majesty the Queen and Zakaria Amara.

41   This message is referenced in the youth sentencing report of NY. See: Ontario Superior Court of Justice - Youth Justice Court - Judge Sproat. (September 25, 2008). Her Majesty the Queen and N.Y.

42   This order was caught in an audio intercept and played in his trial.

43   Indeed in the youth trial ruling the judge writes "In March 2006, Amara in fact ordered three Mobile GSM phone kits ('the MK160 switch') from a company in Texas. The understanding was that these devices could be used to remotely trigger a bomb from a much broader range." Amara later even figured out how to detonate remotely. The judge also cites internet searches by Amara at "Meadowvale Public Library in Mississauga in late March and early April 2006" on the following topics "ammonium nitrate turf fertilizer," "turf fertilizer explosive," "ways of getting ammonium nitrate," "ammonium nitrate in agriculture," "search for fuel tablets," "Al-Qaeda tube bomb plot article link" and "student farmers." See: Ontario Superior Court of Justice - Youth Justice Court - Judge Sproat. (September 25, 2008). Her Majesty the Queen and N.Y.

44   At this point we have taken artistic license as only the second agent was tracking the Mississauga group at this point, but to avoid the awkwardness of introducing the new character too fully, we report this conversation occurring between Mubin and Zakaria.

45   See: Struck, D. (June 11, 2006). School ties link alleged plotters. Retrieved from   http://www.washingtonpost.com/wp-dyn/content/article/2006/06/10/AR2006061000399.html

46   Alfano, S. (June 3, 2006). Canadians nab 17 Terror Suspects. CBS News. Retrieved from http://www.cbsnews.com/news/canadians-nab-17-terror-suspects/

47   See: Mandel, D. R. (November 2011). The role of instigators in radicalization to violent extremism. In A. Speckhard (Eds.), NATO Human Factors & Medicine Research & Technology Organization Research Task Group 140 Final Report on Psychosocial, Organizational and Cultural Aspects of Terrorism Available from http://ftp.rta.nato.int/public//PubFullText/RTO/TR/RTO-TR-HFM-140///TR-HFM-140-02.pdf; Sageman, M. (2004). Understanding Terror Networks: University of Pennsylvannia Press, and Speckhard, A. (2012). Talking to terrorists: Understanding the psycho-social motivations of militant jihadi terrorists, mass hostage takers, suicide bombers and "martyrs". McLean, VA: Advances Press.

48   Teotonio, I. (2010). Toronto 18. TheStar.com. Retrieved from http://www3.

thestar.com/static/toronto18/index.html

49   Paz, R. (2011). Reading their Lips: The Credibility of Militant Jihadi Websites as "Soft Power" in the War of the Minds. In A. C. Speckhard (Eds.), RTO
Technical Report (Vol. Psychosocial, Organizational and Cultural Aspects of Terrorism, Available from http://ftp.rta.nato.int/public//PubFullText/RTO/TR/RTO-
TR-HFM-140///TR-HFM-140-06.pdf

50   For examples of cases like these see: Speckhard, A. (2005). Understanding
Suicide Terrorism: Countering Human Bombs and Their Senders. In J. S. Purcell
& J. D. Weintraub (Eds.), Topics in Terrorism: Toward a Transatlantic Consensus
on the Nature of the Threat. Washington, D.C.: Atlantic Council; Speckhard, A.
(2012). Talking to terrorists: Understanding the psycho-social motivations of militant jihadi terrorists, mass hostage takers, suicide bombers and "martyrs". McLean,
VA: Advances Press.

51   Teotonio, I. (2010). Toronto 18. TheStar.com. Retrieved from http://www3.
thestar.com/static/toronto18/index.html

52   Teotonio, I. (2010). Toronto 18. TheStar.com. Retrieved from http://www3.
thestar.com/static/toronto18/index.html

53   Shephard, M. (September 25, 2013). Toronto 18L Ali Mohamed Dirie,
convicted in plot, dies in Syria. Retrieved from http://www.thestar.com/news/
gta/2013/09/25/toronto_18_ali_mohamed_dirie_convicted_in_plot_dies_in_syr-
ia.htmlk

54   Speckhard, A., & Akhmedova, K. (2006). Black Widows: The Chechen Female Suicide Terrorists. In Y. Schweitzer (Ed.), Female Suicide Terrorists. Tel Aviv:
Jaffe Center Publication.; Speckhard, A., & Akhmedova, K. (2008). Black Widows
and Beyond: Understanding the Motivations and Life Trajectories of Chechen Female Terrorists. In C. Ness (Ed.), Female Terrorism and Militancy: Agency, Utility and Organization: Agency, Utility and Organization Routledge.; Speckhard, A.
(2008). The Emergence of Female Suicide Terrorists. Studies in Conflict and Terrorism 31, 1-29.; Speckhard, A. (2009). Female suicide bombers in Iraq. Democracy and Security, 5(1), 19-50.Speckhard, A. (2012). Talking to terrorists: Understanding the psycho-social motivations of militant jihadi terrorists, mass hostage
takers, suicide bombers and "martyrs". McLean, VA: Advances Press.

55   For information on Saima Mohamed see: Akkad, O. E., & Mcarthur, G.
(June 29, 2006). Hateful chatter behind the veil. The Globe and Mail. Retrieved from
http://www.theglobeandmail.com/news/national/hateful-chatter-behind-the-veil/
article1203257/?page=all; Gillespie, B. (October 22, 2008). Convicted British terrorists had links to accused in Toronto 18 case: UK court documents. CBCNews.
Retrieved from http://www.cbc.ca/news/canada/convicted-british-terrorist-had-
links-to-accused-in-toronto-18-case-u-k-court-documents-1.721495; and Kohl-

mann, E. (September, 2008). Anatomy of a modern homegrown terror cell: Aabid Khan et al. Operation Praline. Retrieved from http://acsa2000.net/TW/samples/ Kohlman.pdfand for Khava Bareava see: Speckhard, A., & Ahkmedova, K. (2006). The Making of a Martyr: Chechen Suicide Terrorism. Journal of Studies in Conflict and Terrorism, 29(5), 429-492. and Speckhard, A., & Akhmedova, K. (2008). Black Widows and Beyond: Understanding the Motivations and Life Trajectories of Chechen Female Terrorists. In C. Ness (Ed.), Female Terrorism and Militancy: Agency, Utility and Organization: Agency, Utility and Organization Routledge.

56   Akkad, O. E., & Mcarthur, G. (June 29, 2006). Hateful chatter behind the veil. The Globe and Mail. Retrieved from http://www.theglobeandmail.com/news/ national/hateful-chatter-behind-the-veil/article1203257/?page=all

57   Akkad, O. E., & Mcarthur, G. (June 29, 2006). Hateful chatter behind the veil. The Globe and Mail. Retrieved from http://www.theglobeandmail.com/news/ national/hateful-chatter-behind-the-veil/article1203257/?page=all

58   Speckhard, A., & Akhmedova, K. (2006). The New Chechen Jihad: Militant Wahhabism as a Radical Movement and a Source of Suicide Terrorism in Post-War Chechen Society. Democracy and Security, 2(1), 103-155.

59   Akkad, O. E., & Mcarthur, G. (June 29, 2006). Hateful chatter behind the veil. The Globe and Mail. Retrieved from http://www.theglobeandmail.com/news/ national/hateful-chatter-behind-the-veil/article1203257/?page=all

60   Akkad, O. E., & Mcarthur, G. (June 29, 2006). Hateful chatter behind the veil. The Globe and Mail. Retrieved from http://www.theglobeandmail.com/news/ national/hateful-chatter-behind-the-veil/article1203257/?page=all

61   Akkad, O. E., & Mcarthur, G. (June 29, 2006). Hateful chatter behind the veil. The Globe and Mail. Retrieved from http://www.theglobeandmail.com/news/ national/hateful-chatter-behind-the-veil/article1203257/?page=all

62   Kohlmann, E. (September, 2008). Anatomy of a modern homegrown terror cell: Aabid Khan et al. Operation Praline. Retrieved from http://acsa2000.net/ TW/samples/Kohlman.pdf, pg. 7..

63   Kohlmann, E. (September, 2008). Anatomy of a modern homegrown terror cell: Aabid Khan et al. Operation Praline. Retrieved from http://acsa2000.net/ TW/samples/Kohlman.pdf,pg. 7.

64   Kohlmann, E. (September, 2008). Anatomy of a modern homegrown terror cell: Aabid Khan et al. Operation Praline. Retrieved from http://acsa2000.net/ TW/samples/Kohlman.pdf pg. 8.

65   Kohlmann, E. (September, 2008). Anatomy of a modern homegrown terror cell: Aabid Khan et al. Operation Praline. Retrieved from http://acsa2000.net/ TW/samples/Kohlman.pdf pg. 8.

66   Kohlmann, E. (September, 2008). Anatomy of a modern homegrown ter-

ror cell: Aabid Khan et al. Operation Praline. Retrieved from http://acsa2000.net/ TW/samples/Kohlman.pdfpg. 9.

67   See: Bloom, M. (2011). Women and terrorism: Bombshell. Philadelphia: University of Pennsylvannia Press. Speckhard, A. (2008). The Emergence of Female Suicide Terrorists. Studies in Conflict and Terrorism 31, 1-29; Speckhard, A. (2009). Female suicide bombers in Iraq. Democracy and Security, 5(1), 19-50.; Speckhard, A., & Akhmedova, K. (2006). Black Widows: The Chechen Female Suicide Terrorists. In Y. Schweitzer (Ed.), Female Suicide Terrorists. Tel Aviv: Jaffe Center Publication.; Speckhard, A., & Akhmedova, K. (2008). Black Widows and Beyond: Understanding the Motivations and Life Trajectories of Chechen Female Terrorists. In C. Ness (Ed.), Female Terrorism and Militancy: Agency, Utility and Organization: Agency, Utility and Organization Routledge,; Schweitzer, Y. (Ed.). (2006). Female Suicide Bombers:Dying for Equality? : The Jaffee Center for Strategic Studies

68   Atran, S. (2003). Genesis of Suicide Terrorism. Science, 299(5612), 1534 - 1539.

69   TheGlobeandMail. (October 25, 2010). Ontario Superior Court of Justice sentencing of Fahim Ahmad. Retrieved from http://www.scribd.com/ doc/40098959/Ontario-Superior-Court-of-Justice-sentencing-of-Fahim-Ahmad- paragraph 56, pg 26.

70   Teotonio, I. (2010). Toronto 18. TheStar.com. Retrieved from http://www3. thestar.com/static/toronto18/index.html

71   TheGlobeandMail. (October 25, 2010). Ontario Superior Court of Justice sentencing of Fahim Ahmad. Retrieved from http://www.scribd.com/ doc/40098959/Ontario-Superior-Court-of-Justice-sentencing-of-Fahim-Ahmad paragraph 21, pg 11.

72   TheGlobeandMail. (October 25, 2010). Ontario Superior Court of Justice sentencing of Fahim Ahmad. Retrieved from http://www.scribd.com/ doc/40098959/Ontario-Superior-Court-of-Justice-sentencing-of-Fahim-Ahmad paragraphs 6-8, pp 2-4.

73   TheGlobeandMail. (October 25, 2010). Ontario Superior Court of Justice sentencing of Fahim Ahmad. Retrieved from http://www.scribd.com/ doc/40098959/Ontario-Superior-Court-of-Justice-sentencing-of-Fahim-Ahmad paragraphs 9, pg 5.

74   TheGlobeandMail. (October 25, 2010). Ontario Superior Court of Justice sentencing of Fahim Ahmad. Retrieved from http://www.scribd.com/ doc/40098959/Ontario-Superior-Court-of-Justice-sentencing-of-Fahim-Ahmad paragraphs 17-19, pg 9-10.

75   TheGlobeandMail. (October 25, 2010). Ontario Superior Court of Justice sentencing of Fahim Ahmad. Retrieved from http://www.scribd.com/

Index

Index

CPSIA information can be obtained at www.ICGtesting.com
Printed in the USA
LVOW12*1914111114

413136LV00013B/1013/P

9 781935 866596